HARVEST SON

A L S O   B Y   D A V I D   M A S   M A S U M O T O

Epitaph for a Peach
Country Voices

H A R V E S T   S O N

Planting Roots in American Soil

D A V I D   M A S   M A S U M O T O

W. W. Norton & Company   New York · London

Copyright © 1998 by David Mas Masumoto

Printed in the United States of America.
First Edition

Parts of this book originally appeared in different form in *Eating Well, Pacific Citizen, Rafu Shimpo, Sunset*, and *Western Folklore*, and in *Silent Strength* (New Currents International, 1985), a collection of short stories by the author.

Illustrations reprinted courtesy of the artist, Tom Uyemaruko.

For information about permission to reproduce selections from this book, write to Permissions, W. W. Norton & Company, Inc., 500 Fifth Avenue, New York, NY 10110.

The text of this book is composed in Granjon with the display set in Lithos Black. Desktop composition by Chelsea Dippel Manufacturing by Courier Companies, Inc. Book design by Chris Welch

Library of Congress Cataloging-in-Publication Data
Masumoto, David Mas.
Harvest son : planting roots in American soil / David Mas Masumoto.
p.   cm.
ISBN 0-393-04673-7
1. Masumoto, David Mas. 2. Farm life—California—Del Rey.
3. Family farms—California—Del Rey. 4. Farmers—California—
Del Rey—Biography. 5. Japanese American farmers—California—
Del Rey—Biography. I. Title.
SB63.M36A3   1998
630'.92—dc21

[B]   98-15702
                                                                                  CIP

W. W. Norton & Company, Inc., 500 Fifth Avenue, New York, NY 10110
http://www.wwnorton.com

W. W. Norton & Company Ltd., 10 Coptic Street, London WC1A 1PU

1 2 3 4 5 6 7 8 9 0

CONTENTS

HARVEST SON

one

PRUNING
GENERATIONS

GRAPEVINES DO NOT HAVE BRILLIANT AUTUMN COLORS, THEY INI-tially turn yellow. With a freeze near Thanksgiving, a white frost dusts the fields and as it melts, the leaves become brown—life has been sucked from them with the cold. The brittle foliage clings to the canes and will not fall off until a good rainstorm pounds them to the ground. That's when I return to farmwork.

Next year's harvest will only emerge from one-year-old wood; the old canes needed to be cut, discarded, and replaced with the new. As a youngster I pruned thousands of vines, yet somehow this year is different. The vines look foreign, shrouded in the damp fog. The moisture stains the canes dark and paints the older bark a glossy black. Each twist of a gnarled trunk casts a deep shadow and creates the illusion of a cavern cut deep into the heart of the stump. Only four or five feet tall, the vines appear hunched over like old men.

Before I start pruning, I remove some of the oddly shaped vines with their contorted features. The worst ones resemble an S shape, decades ago yanked in one direction, pulled back years later, and then bent with yet another season. They're old and the canes grow weaker with each harvest. I open a folding handsaw and grip the wooden handle as I start ripping into the bark with its coarse steel teeth. The brittle wood breaks and peels off in thin strips, scattering onto the green winter weeds and the damp earth. My arms pump back and forth until the teeth finally grab and a familiar "haaack" sound establishes a cadence. The vine topples, and at the stump a white woody membrane is exposed, the living tissue remarkably only a few inches wide, protected by layers and layers of bark. A clear fluid bleeds from the opening, dripping onto the earth and creating a small mud puddle. Later, if there's a morning sun, the beads of moisture catch the light and sparkle.

Most of the time the fog masks landmarks. A hundred feet from our house I'm invisible and alone. I can hear sounds, a door slamming, an engine starting, voices of my mom asking Dad if he'll be in for lunch. I trudge to the farthermost field and start pruning. I can barely see around me—the sky is cast in a glaring gray. The only sounds are my footsteps sliding on the damp earth and fallen leaves and the dripping of dew from saturated vines.

Is this how my *jiichan*/grandpa first saw a grapevine—a strange creature with wild growth dangling from a dark body? The rows of vines look like a silent column of prisoners, their trunks bent and twisted, their arms held upward in surrender. The canes droop like elongated fingers with an occasional leaf clinging as a decorative ring, flapping with a slight shift in the air.

I wonder if Jiichan Masumoto, arriving in America a century ago in 1899 and having never seen a vine before, yet hungry for work, lied to get a job and told the farmer, "Yes, yes, I work," then followed the crew into the vineyard and watched the others while they whispered in Japanese, telling him what to do.

"Give me five canes and two spurs," the farmer may have told my grandfather. Five canes? Spurs? These were words he had never heard before, the language of a new world he had to learn.

Other immigrant groups arrived at a similar time in the San Joaquin Valley of California. They planted their family farm traditions from their homelands—the Germans and Portuguese brought dairies and the Italians their vineyards and wineries. But the Issei came from farming villages where rice and barley were planted each spring, followed by summer weeding and irrigation, and an early autumn harvest. During the winter, the paddies were turned and prepared for another year as they had been for centuries. Pruning vines was not natural for my grandfather.

Did he still think in Japanese? What terms did he use for things he had never seen before? Did he call a vine cane the same word he used for the branches of the wild berries in Japan? What words did he use for "to prune a vine"? It's not the same as a *bonsai* gardener's meticulous pruning and shaping, where a branch is carefully clipped and wired and a stem is trimmed and braced or a stone is roped to a limb, the dangling weight gradually drawing the wood downward, redirecting growth. Did Jiichan think in English? Wasn't learning English part of becoming an American? I grew up sometimes hearing the phrase *Hayaku!* or "Hurry up!" Farmworkers were usually paid by piecework, and the only "art" to pruning was the art of making money by working as fast as you could and racing to the next vine. Good pruners eye the thick wood and quickly hack at the rest, slashing at the mass of canes, yanking the severed limbs and tossing them in between the rows.

Grapevines last for generations; some of ours are eighty years old. The first permanent plantings on this land were in the year my grandmother, Baachan Masumoto, immigrated to America in 1918: according to records, the farmer before us planted 2,640 Thompson seedless vines that year. Jiichan may have pruned our farm's vines as a farmworker. He, along with thousands of immigrant laborers, helped to establish and maintain the lush fields of our valley. Over the decades, little has changed. Farmers still hand-prune each vine, every row needs irrigating and plowing, and the late-summer harvests demand thousands of workers to pick and dry the grapes into raisins. Technology has not replaced the human element. Vineyards still require people to care for them.

I learned to prune by watching my parents and Baachan. They'd take us kids out into the fields, bundle us up to block the winter winds and damp fog. We'd stiffly stand alongside them as they pulled and stripped the clippings from the wire trellis. Mom and Dad tackled two rows at a time, each row twelve feet apart. Most rows were less than a hundred vines long, with a single wire stretching down every column and anchored to end posts. While my older brother and sister helped my parents, I'd play and wrestle with a long branch that sometimes stretched over ten feet, first pretending it to be a snake or whip until it broke into a sword. As I grew older and bored with childish games, I was anxious to learn farmwork. I too wanted to help the family.

By ten, I was given my own pruning shears, an old set with mismatched wooden handles and a well-oiled cutting head. I was allowed to slice the center brush off from the wires, canes from the prior year that were tightly wrapped around the trellis. (Grape bunches grew and hung from these branches.)

One of the few Japanese terms I grew up with was *naka-giri*, meaning "cut the center." *Naka-giri* was a mindless, tedious task, perfectly suited for us three children. We'd slice the wood, making a series of incisions, breaking the cord into smaller sections, then pulling them from the trellis, yanking and snapping the limbs, dragging them to the spaces between the rows. Right behind us worked Mom and Dad, finishing each vine, selecting the right canes for next year.

Baachan Masumoto usually helped me, the youngest and slowest. I'm not sure if she chose to *naka-giri* with the kids or felt too slow and old for the tougher job of finishing a vine. Surely she had mastered the art of pruning after six decades working in the fields. But perhaps she now enjoyed a freedom from responsibility, knowing someone else would complete her work.

Winters in the Central Valley of California are cold but not harsh. Night temperatures drop to freezing but usually warm to the forties by midmorning. Fog dampens spirits with a gray, wet chill. Since vines are spaced only a few feet apart, the whole family could work next to each other, close enough to talk and prune under watchful eyes.

We worked without gloves, and our exposed cheeks and ears turned a rosy blush in the frigid air. Inevitably branches tangled. I'd tug and pull, trying to free the mess, until finally something would crack and a cane would whip loose. Quickly I'd turn and close my eyes, but often too late; a cry would escape my throat as the wood slapped my face: a sharp bite, then a raw sting shooting across my cheek as I grimaced in pain. I'd drop my shears and run my cold fingers across the flesh, feeling for blood. Rarely, though, did my skin break; instead my eyes watered and I gritted my teeth until the stabbing ache gave way to a numbness on the surface. With tears running down, I'd begin again, sniffling and wincing, trying to work despite the throbbing. Through moist eyes, I'd detect a motion and find Dad working the vine ahead of me. He said nothing as his powerful shears chopped the wood into small sections, making it easier to dislodge the old growth.

I can't recall a specific lesson in how to prune. While other boys were learning to catch a ball or cast a line, I watched my father snip and cut, shaping his vines into a work of art. His canes were thick, spread evenly on both sides of the vine, making them easy to lash to the wire without breaking. He snipped and grabbed the end of a branch that wore the telltale gray of frostbite instead of the normal creamy tan. He bent the tip around toward his eyes. The wood crackled and stretched but did not snap. If he found the fiber brittle and dried, he'd chop the limb back until he uncovered the pale green tissue of life.

Grape bunches will emerge from the nodes three or four inches from the trunk but usually not more than four feet away. Stepping back, Dad would scan the entire vine, judging if the remaining canes were too short for a healthy crop, evaluating if skinny ones were worth leaving. On each vine, he also tried to leave three or four "spurs," short stubs from which new canes for next year would sprout, destined to bear another harvest. His eyes darted back and forth, searching and comparing, envisioning the future.

My first attempts to prune made the vines look as though they had passed through a shredder. The canes hung limp and lacked strong structure and definition; they seemed out of balance, as if the branches I had chosen to save did not belong. I sometimes forgot to check for the strangely beautiful but sterile gray hue of frostbite, which meant that later in the year, when sap and water flowed through the rest of the vine, my branches would snap when pulled. They would never again produce grapes. Occasionally I neglected to leave spurs, cleanly snipping off old growth before remembering I should have left a foundation for the future.

Eventually it dawned on me why my early years of pruning resulted in such poor craftsmanship. Some of it had to do with my poor skills, but a lot had to do with a father giving his young son a scraggly old vine to start with. Dad had forced me to learn with the hardest vines. I can hear the collective voice of all sage farmers: why sacrifice a good vine on an inexperienced son?

Now I prune by first selecting the strong and discarding the weak wood. Then I search for the thickest canes evenly spaced around the vine head, leaving spurs in open locations for next year's growth. Over the years I have learned to distinguish wood potentially damaged by frost. I go by color, feel, and sound. A hoary white hue becomes a sign of frostbite. Then, when I snip the end of a stem, healthy tissue will slice but dead wood will snap. Through my shears I can feel and hear the difference if my blade splinters and mangles the dried fibers with a flat "whack" instead of the crisp incision of steel as it severs a limb.

I make over fifty cuts per vine, fifty decisions within a few minutes. Despite the detailed work, I slip into a cadence, a pace that allows time for my thoughts to wander. My arms and hands recall the familiar rhythms; my muscles have retained their memory of farmwork. I yank and the wire stretches and pulls against the metal stakes. The steel creaks and moans. The branches hold fast and I cannot snap the bundled wood. I look for an opening to slip my rounded shear point into and snip the strands into short segments. I then grab and rip the wood free. The entire row shakes with my tug. With brute force I try to snap the remaining branches, but they resist. Older men use more center cuts to free the wood; younger pruners sever the growth by force.

After the first vines I stop struggling. There are too many to fight. I need to play farm games to combat the monotony. I have a friend who, as a child of a poor family, spent hours and hours in the fields. He developed a wild imagination, creating space invaders out of unpruned vines, monsters with tentacles waiting to coil around small boys. In his mind, a young vine next to an old, gnarled one was one of those petrified boys. So he attacked each vine, madly chopping away at the brush in order to defend himself. They'd attack him over and over and he'd chop and clip and slash until he had defeated the vine and only a manageable five canes remained. Then he'd let the branches dangle in defeat. Later the space police would arrive and tie up these prisoners, lashing them to the overhead wires.

I frequently play strategic games of controlling territory, approaching a ten-acre block of vines by attacking each row from the ends and then, over the next few days, advancing toward the middles, pretending to surround my opponent, then asking for unconditional surrender. Working one row at a time becomes overwhelming; I look up and see an entire field unpruned and feel discouraged. Completing the first few vines all along an avenue seems like progress—I can walk home at dusk bolstered with a sense of accomplishment. I think of the Japanese game of *go*—on a grid-patterned gameboard, opponents try to capture territory through a series of encounters, but losing a particular battle does not necessarily mean the loss of the game.

Did my father play games while he pruned? Did Jiichan? I never thought of them engaging in childhood games. I have trouble imagining them as children. As I prune, a loose cane snaps free and grabs my jacket. I whip around and slash at the tentacle, liberating myself with a triumphant "haaa!"

Many of the vines are old and I have trouble finding good canes. I feel like a geriatric nurse searching for good blood vessels in his patients. Yet considering their lengthy time of service and occasional abuse by young pruners, these vines just need to be reshaped. Perhaps I need to ask their forgiveness so that I can just slash away, severing deadwood, amputating arms growing out at odd angles, pruning "hard" to stimulate new, vigorous growth for the coming year.

Occasionally I'll stop at a vine that seems confused. The old growth spreads in all directions, dividing the crown into two or three distinct heads, each with its own scraggly family of canes. I can date most of the wood: the thin gray canes are one or two years old, the thick dark arms come from years past. The shape tells a story of the vine's expansion outward in a constant search for sunlight that results in twisted growth. Farmers try to check that exploration and redirect the vigor.

How did these vines get to be so disordered? Old pruning

errors are evident: a worker left a strong cane branching away from the main trunk, creating a dual-headed vine. I try to correct the growth by pulling it back and braiding the wood together. The vine then responds by growing fat in other places with oddly positioned shoots, resisting my attempt at control.

A vine grows only by gradual accrual, punctuated by the annual rite of pruning. I now add to the living timeline, shaping and cutting, only to return next year and discover new growth with new patterns. I need to be planning on pruning years into the future. I begin to think of these old vines as badly bent, but not broken.

After an initial week of pruning, I'm working as a veteran. My shears glide though a canopy, snipping and clipping, pulling and tugging. My eyes dance from cane to cane, monitoring the growth from old spurs and crowns while identifying strong canes that will bear next year's harvest. The easiest vines grow vigorously, following the patterns established years ago with proper pruning. I pause and talk to myself about where to leave extra spurs, knowing my decisions will effect my work years from now. I also need to trust the lead of those before me, duplicating their efforts to sustain the legacy of a healthy vine.

It takes years to learn how to prune a vine, to grow accustomed to the diverse patterns and changes manifested in a contorted trunk. I can respond to history by leaving healthy wood and strategic spurs—my best pruning works with the past in order to shape the future.

Now I understand why they call these cultural practices. Good pruning is not a science, it's the art of working with a living entity, an annual sojourn to a familiar place with the intention of returning the next year and the year after that. But it goes beyond just the physical structure of a vine. The ghosts of many pruners before me live in my fields—this is a place where generations reside.

two

BROKEN
OLD MEN

I NEVER FELT THE CRUSTY YET GENTLE OLD HANDS OF A GRANDFATHER.
I never knew the history of each scar, the origin of each callus, or
the story behind a flattened fingernail. I never had a *jiichan/*
grandpa.

When I was growing up, our farmhouse porch had no jolly
gray-haired men sitting on hard wooden chairs or benches with
lumpy cushions streaked with black mildew stains and yellowed
from the afternoon sun. I never could climb up onto a big lap and
feel old bony hands tickle my ribs. At family dinners, no one sat

at the head of the table. No deep gentle voices read me bedtime stories.

Both of my grandfathers died before I was born. At our Buddhist altar stood a few snapshots with blurred faces. I cannot see the eyes of the men. Their photographs reek of incense my mom would burn in their honor. But these old black-and-white images are not my grandfathers, they are ghosts that haunt me with questions no one answers.

My family conducts a Buddhist memorial service every few years for our grandfathers. At these services I stare at the photos, and during the chanting I talk with them.

I know one grandfather—Jiichan Sugimoto, my mother's father—solely from a single photograph. His young face is softened by the graininess of the black-and-white image. I can only see his head and shoulders and don't know how tall he stood. I picture him quite short with small hands. His deep-set eyes have an effeminate quality. Unlike most photos of Issei, first-generation Japanese in America, Jiichan Sugimoto wears a slight smile.

A small photo of my other grandfather also stands by the altar. Jiichan Masumoto was a balding old man, slouching with his dark hands dangling to his sides. He wears a baggy suit and a dark tan. He's standing by a row of trees, perhaps on one of the farms where the family labored. Old work boots stick out from under his pants cuffs. He frowns. His facial wrinkles are molded into a glare, not a mean or angry look but a hardened one. The decades of sun and heat are etched deeply.

At every service, a small bell is rung and the sound resonates through the room. The minister begins the chant, a single shrill voice, raspy and biting before we all join together in a single cadence. A chorus of the voices swells to fill our home. The scent of incense seeps into my lungs. I become light-headed and the undulations of the chanting swirl into a mesmerizing rhythm. I ask silent questions. Why does Jiichan Masumoto never seem happy? How old was Jiichan Sugimoto when his photograph was taken? What can I read into their expressions or their eyes? I try to imagine their answers and sometimes make up things to see how they fit into our family history. Neither man was physically big. I picture Jiichan Sugimoto as weak and sickly. I think of Jiichan Masumoto as a hard but slow worker. Both had little formal education, both left Japan carrying the simple immigrant dream of a better life.

My thoughts drift until I try to imagine their lips moving. Then my trance is broken. I have no memory of the spoken voice of either grandfather.

It seems odd that my only memories involve death. Doesn't my family have any other photos of my grandfathers? Don't they have some snapshot taken at Yosemite or a hot spring or at a friend's wedding or during a family picnic? I have no image of my grandfathers proudly standing with a team of mules or in a lush field of vegetables or with vines heavy with grapes just before a raisin harvest. Instead, we have a sparse collection of family photos. In one, Jiichan Masumoto is poised next to his new bride. In another, he stands while his firstborn child is cradled on Baachan's lap. There's one photo with Baachan alone sitting among their five children. Jiichan is no longer seen in the rest of the formal family portraits.

Where are the photographs that tell the saga of the American immigrant, the head of the household with generations of his family spread around him?

Snapshots

I know of one snapshot of Jiichan Sugimoto. It's not exactly a photo of him—he's enclosed in a casket with his family around him. The location is someplace in Phoenix, just north of Gila River Relocation Center. The date is in the summer of 1942, just after all the Japanese Americans were uprooted and relocated to desolate camps scattered across western America.

I remember seeing this photo as a child but always thought it was the funeral of an uncle who had died during the war. On top of the casket sits a picture of a soldier in an army uniform. Later Mom explains that was the photo of Uncle Ted, who was drafted a few months before Pearl Harbor and trapped in the army because the military didn't know what to do with him. One of my uncles interjects, "Goddam army wouldn't even let him come home for his own father's funeral." Later the authorities allowed Uncle Ted to fight in Europe, and there he was wounded by indiscriminate German guns.

Jiichan Sugimoto had stomach cancer and was terribly ill during the long evacuation train ride from Fresno to the Arizona desert. During that journey the train shades were pulled down, questions hovered in the hot August air, rumors drifted between the clicking of metal wheels on the track. Where exactly were they going? Whom could they trust? How long would they have to call this unknown place home?

Jiichan Sugimoto would be dead within a month. He was supposed to be transferred in Southern California to a state hospital in Los Angeles but he screamed and refused to go. He would not be separated from the family. I imagine Baachan/Grandma Sugimoto muffling his cries of pain while her English-speaking sons argued with the authorities. Jiichan remained on the train and they rode into the heat of the Arizona desert. I think he died during that train ride. He kept his heart pumping for a few more weeks, though, allowing the family to settle into the barracks where they would live for four years.

When he passed away, the authorities didn't know what to do. They had no experience at evacuating an entire race. Creating instant housing for 100,000 Japanese Americans was overwhelming. I hope plans to build mortuaries were low on their list. Imagine the thoughts of the arriving Japanese if the first structure they saw was a crematory outside the barbed-wire fences? Eventually the authorities decided to send the body and family to a funeral home in Phoenix. A controversy then arose about whether an armed guard was supposed to accompany them and stay with the dead body.

I have no clear image of Jiichan Sugimoto. Between the infrequent stories I can hear a painful silence when the family talks about him. The confusion of evacuation mutes their stories and muzzles their voices.

I stare at the silent and still faces, expressions frozen in another snapshot dated 1944. The Masumoto family stands to the right of a coffin, Jiichan holds an American flag, Baachan Masumoto lifts a photograph of her dead soldier son. The aunts and uncles gather to the side; they look uncomfortable, cramped next to each other, unsure where to put their hands. It's a memorial service for my Uncle George, who fought in Europe and died for freedom while his family lived behind barbed wire at Gila River Relocation Center.

Jiichan Masumoto stands erect, his chin out, body stiff. He does not press the American flag to his chest. His old hands are loosely folded around the flag. The body of his dead son lies in Europe while the rest of the family is exiled to the Arizona desert. Baachan Masumoto clutches the photograph of her dead son. She stands next to Jiichan with their children on the other side. She lifts the gold-framed picture, her dark hands curled around the edges as she elevates it slightly, trying to hold it steady between herself and husband.

Two other families share the snapshot. They too lost a son, a brother, a soldier to the war. One family stands to one side, the children bow their heads. A brother of the deceased drops his eyes to the ground as he holds the photograph upright. Their flag is rolled instead of tightly wrapped. Only the Issei mother peers bravely at the camera, and she holds the flag to her heart.

The other family stands at attention in the center. One son holds the picture of the slain soldier with both hands and perfectly straight. He stands erect in his army uniform, tall compared to everyone else in the photograph. Is he a brother of the deceased and will he too die in battle? Their mother wears a grieving face, with closed eyes, and her head slightly tilted. She seems oblivious to the camera. She cradles the flag and holds it like an infant. She has a lost look on her face.

Jiichan seems confused. The American flag droops in his hands. He is the only old man in the picture. What happened to the other fathers? Why did Jiichan Masumoto survive? My dad says Jiichan once said that it wasn't right for a father to bury his son.

Three families, three different expressions captured for an instant at a common burial. I do not and cannot know what my family felt. I was born ten years later in a different time and place. But a silence penetrates such gaps, linking me with the past—a silence felt by my family and carried throughout the generations.

MY GRANDFATHERS LEFT little behind. They never could own a farm; the Alien Land Laws prevented "Orientals" from land purchases, singling out immigrants from Asia and condemning a generation to life as farm laborers. But they stayed, working the land for strangers. Some saved and purchased land by forming an American company or waiting until they had children and buying the land in the name of the second generation, the Nisei— Americans by birth. Most, though, waited until their Nisei children were grown and working so they could all save money, pool their labor, and buy a place together as family. A generation sacrificed so the next could have opportunity.

There is no Jiichan Masumoto homestead or old farmhouse. I cannot walk through the old red barn where the harnesses my grandfather used hang on the wall. The farm equipment on our farm comes from other families and their grandfathers. I cannot picture Jiichan riding on the old dump rake or vineyard wagon. I will never find his record of a raisin crop, a scribbled notepad buried beneath generations of barn dust, a collection of numbers and figures as a farmer calculated his harvest.

I know of no trunk full of old heirlooms, no felt hats or army uniforms. There are no tarnished medals or gold watches. I've stopped dreaming of discovering the old shoe box filled with the history of our family, the documents and letters that recorded our family's arrival and the historical milestones as my grandfathers left their mark on a place. There is no journal or diary. I do not know if they knew how to read or write.

I could easily dismiss their existence. Their lives seem empty and still, void of emotion. I cannot tell if they wear scars. I only know of my grandfathers as broken old men.

three

CHANGING
SEASONS

OUR FARM RESTS IN A GREAT VALLEY FOUR HUNDRED MILES LONG AND
fifty miles wide. We work an ancient lake bed thousands of years
in the making. As the water drained and evaporated, a long, flat
corridor of mostly fine silt was left behind, deep and rich in nutrients. While other regions of the nation have their own rocks—the
hard limestone of the Midwest or the granite stones of New Eng-
land—we battle hardpan, a mineralized layer of clay compressed
over the centuries. Vines and orchards do not grow well in the
company of these rocks, and every season, no matter how often

we try to remove them, our disk blades encounter new chunks that must be hauled out of the fields. A generation of farmers have tried to clear our lands, yet more stones hide beneath the surface awaiting the next pair of hands and gloves.

The Sierra Nevadas stand majestically to the east, their snow-capped ridges visible even on scorching hundred-degree summer days. The mountains rapidly ascend forty miles from our fields and thrust upward over ten thousand feet. I begin my day with a morning shadow across my fields that shrinks with each passing minute of a sunrise. Driving a tractor in the chilly half-light of early day, I tightly grip the steering wheel, grit my teeth, and clench my arms close to my body, trying to retain heat. Then as I drive into sunlight peaking over the mountaintops, I relax and stretch, exhale with a low, deep sigh, allowing the warmth to penetrate. To the west lie the Coast Ranges, a lower mountain chain that completes the circle around our valley. Days end with a brilliant lavender hue on their horizon, layers of orange dancing around the setting sun. I often stop my work and wonder about life on the other side of our mountains, yet to many of us farm kids, the center of the world lies here with our families working the land.

Along one border of our farm, a large ditch over twenty feet across carries water from the Sierra snowmelt. During the long, hot summers, our eighty acres of vines and orchards are irrigated from this man-made canal. The ditch gives life to what otherwise would be arid and parched desolation. Along the bank, clumps of a weed called horsetail grow in uneven clusters. The bright green stalks look like a bamboo with segmented sections and random heights. They out-compete the intrusion of johnsongrass and Bermuda, nonnative weeds that voraciously spread in the damp earth and monopolize territory.

Beyond the canal, our neighbor has planted grapes on the flat, level portions of his land. A knoll gently rises in the center of his place, ten acres of high ground that, until a few years ago, remained untilled and filled with wild Italian ryegrass and chick-weed in the wet springs and a hardy filaree during the arid sum-mers. Occasionally, a horse grazed on the sparse turf, lowering his neck and shaking his mane. His massive black frame was silhou-etted against the rolling rise, a symbol of a past when all farms had work animals.

Only in my lifetime, with churning Caterpillar tractors and land-leveling equipment burning diesel and grunting smoke, were these elevated rises conquered. Now rows and rows of grapes march up "the hill" and over the crest. Kept free of weeds by herbicides and irrigated with sleek black plastic drip lines, the dark stumps of the vines stand alone. The only green allowed to survive emerges from the vine canes while the earth turns a pale brown.

I think of pioneers when they first migrated into this valley. Men and animals labored in tandem to turn the virgin flatlands into lush fields. My grandfathers worked behind mules and horses, opening the earth for the first time with plow and scraper, claiming the land from the wild, not as explorers but settlers who came to stay and live.

My parents lugged all three of us kids out into the fields while we were growing up. They say as an infant, I spent many hours under a grapevine or in the shade of a fruit tree for my morning and afternoon naps. I claim that's why I have an affinity with raisins and peaches.

As soon as we could, each child began farm chores. Being the youngest, I was able to watch and learn as my older brother and sister struggled with a pitchfork, tried to pile the pruned brush from trees and to work a shovel while attacking a clump of weeds. Eventually I too started pulling grape clippings away from the vines and dragging them to the center of the row, where they would be shredded. We grew up expecting *and* wanting to help—this was a family farm.

The busiest days started early with Dad leaving at dawn,

before we woke. We joined him an hour or two later, and I think Mom enjoyed the extra time at home and expressed her thanks with thick pancakes and lots of syrup on our breakfast plates. Once out in the fields we initially attacked our work with high spirits. The air was crisp and dew sparkled on the leaves. We worked silently, accompanied with a clipping of a pruning shear and the occasional rustling of leaves. In order to pass the time, the kids silently repeated rock and roll tunes over and over in our minds. Sometimes I played a game of suddenly stopping and shouting out a song name to my brother and sister. "All Shook Up." "You've Lost That Lovin' Feeling." "Surf City." "Twist and Shout." "Light My Fire." I wanted to believe that the three of us siblings shared some mystical power—that we would be thinking the same thing at the same time. Rarely was I right, except that once a song was named, we often couldn't get it out of our minds. Later, we found ourselves singing a chorus together very much out of key.

As the sun rose in the sky, our youthful work ethic dissolved. By midday we regressed to playing more than working. I had sword fights with my brother and made modern art sculptures out of the vine canes by sticking them in the dirt and wrapping them around each other. Most of the time we marched home for lunch and had to be dragged out for the afternoon shift, complaining until Dad gave up and went out on his own. Once in a while we ate lunch out in the fields as a grand summer picnic. Afterward we protested going back to work, pleading that we needed to digest our food. My folks usually gave in. Soon, though, I was back to my swashbuckling adventures, conquering new vines or exploring the far corners of the orchard.

With the afternoon sun casting shadows, I grew bored and learned to take quick naps, dozing while leaning against a trunk. My head nodded into contorted positions and my mouth fell open, as if locked in a prolonged sigh. Sometimes in the soft earth I carved out a smooth hollow and lined my sleeping station with leaves before curling up with my dreams. I'd often awake to radiant clouds sitting still against the distant mountains. I then trudged back to the house with my siblings and we waited for our parents to return with the chill of the evening air. In the course of a simple workday I lived through four seasons and felt the passing rhythms of life.

Baachan's Bridge

For a few weeks during each summer of my childhood, we'd work at my uncle's farm a few miles away. In the early morning, Mom herded us into the car and we'd sleep a few extra minutes as she hurried down bumpy country roads to the waiting lugs of peaches, plums, and nectarines that needed to be sorted. Baachan Masumoto, family friend Yuri Kanagawa, and Mom packed the fruit into wooden boxes for shipment. We stacked empty boxes and culled the fat, soft overripe fruits, tossing them into a wagon with a splat. By midmorning we grew tired and bored, looking at the clock hands moving as slow as ours, complaining louder and louder until a few sharp words snapped from my uncle's mouth and Mom whipped around her face and delivered a hardened stare at us. We then tugged at Baachan Masumoto's crusty hands, begging her to take us for a long farm walk. She hesitated, not wanting to leave the stacks of unpacked fruit, but during a break she led us out into the bright sunshine.

The dust from the earthen avenue kicked up with each step. I dragged my feet, creating a cloud that enveloped my shoes and ankles, and insisted my older brother and sister notice the talents of their seven-year-old sibling. Baachan marched ahead of us, her hands clasped behind her back, leaning forward with deliberate strides. She never looked back to see how far we had strayed. By the time we reached the orchard with the blushing peaches and the voices of workers, Baachan popped out from the trees. She had already checked on their progress and probably counted the number of lugs for the afternoon's shed work, calculating how long our lunch break would be.

We immediately turned and raced back toward the shed, trying to beat Baachan. Sweat began beading on my forehead with drops slithering down my temples. My stride conceded to the heat and was cut in half. Baachan easily caught up and reduced her tempo to walk with me. We stopped to rest in the shade of an old walnut tree next to what we called "the river."

The twelve-foot-wide irrigation ditch cut through the center of my uncle's land. The cold water from the Sierra snowmelt was channeled through canals and small ditches to serve individual farmers. For most of the summer, water filled the grassy banks and passed with a brisk pace. I threw in a stick and watched it drift, slowly at first until it gained momentum, darting past small whirlpools and racing toward the next farmer and his thirsty fields.

The wooden bridge that we had taken on our way out to the fields stood a half mile away. A short cut lay in front of us, a narrow wooden plank about six inches wide. The footbridge sagged low in the center, badly warped from years in the sun and daily traffic back and forth.

All of us kids were terrified by this crossing. Encouraging us by example, Baachan demonstrated her technique and took small steps in rhythm with the plank as it bounced with each stride. Her normally rough movements suddenly melted into an effortless glide with grace. Her tiny legs shifted back and forth quickly, the wood swayed in an even rhythm. Her upper body remained motionless, the current danced beneath her. She floated over the water with a strand of gray hair licking her cheek in the gentle breeze.

Once on the other side, she cajoled my older brother to try. He hesitated. She drifted back and took his hand and they dashed across. Then my sister advanced forward, yelled for Baachan, and together they marched over the water. Both kept the same tempo as my sister followed in Baachan's footsteps, holding on to her waist as they crossed the narrow path. I grew terrified as the water seemed to churn more threateningly with each minute.

I was paralyzed and would not cross. Baachan grinned and said something in Japanese I could not understand. Finally she squatted in front of me and I slipped onto her back. She rose and steadied her feet, surprised by my weight. I hugged her tightly, clinging to her leathery skin. She stepped onto the plank, it began to bounce, and I dug my fingers deep into her muscles. At the lowest point the bucking reached a crescendo and I looked down at the blue currents racing below us. The wood dipped lower and water splashed onto the board, staining it a dark brown, shiny with moisture. Baachan's faded blue denim pants were wet and clung to her ankles.

My muscles tensed and I wrapped my arms around her neck and chest, clutching to her tiny four-and-a-half-foot frame. I shrieked "Baaaaachan" and felt us swing to one side and then the other. She pushed forward despite my erratic movements. As we neared the other side, the rocking lessened but my heart kept racing. Next I found myself sitting in the ditch-bank grass. Baachan held her hands up to her face, cupping them over her eyes to block the glare as she peered over the vineyards and orchards.

I remembered this bridge and the many times Baachan carried me. I never grew accustomed to it and was always fearful. Then one spring, after a long winter, I walked out alone into the fields and discovered that the ditch was gone. My uncle had found a way to pipe the water and had covered the trench with dirt, reclaiming a few more acres for trees and vines. The land could now be farmed and he no longer needed to depend on bridges for passage. Cast to the side was our old, sagging wooden plank, looking odd lying on its side in the dirt. I no longer needed Baachan to carry me.

Few Old Men

During my childhood, only a few old men worked the neighboring farms. Much of this land was still being settled by young farmers. Rarely did I see frail bodies hunched over shovels; only occasionally did old legs wobble down the dirt paths and shuffle through the fields. Many of the original pioneer men had died and left behind widows often years younger. Even Baachan Masumoto, who was sixty-one when I was born and twenty years younger than Jiichan, seemed too strong to be considered elderly. She walked through the fields carrying a shovel for Bermuda grass and johnsongrass, weeds she called *abunai,* dangerous. Unchecked, these pests strangled a vine or stunted the growth of a peach tree. "*Abunai!*" she told us kids while attacking clumps. Through her faded work shirt, I saw bulging biceps that looked like stone eggs. Her taut skin defied the wrinkles of age except around her eyes, which had withdrawn with the years. I didn't think of her as old—she worked too damn hard.

But there were exceptions. I sometimes caught glimpses of a few old Issei men who seemed to hide inside their farmhouses, waiting to pass away. They could no longer work the fields and age seemed to have played an evil trick on them. With little to show for a lifetime of work, they quickly slipped into back rooms when I visited my friends or they sat alone in the sun at our community picnics.

When I saw photographs of other non-Japanese grandfathers, I concluded elderly men were supposed to spend hours strolling through elaborate gardens or resting on verandas, surveying family estates like emperors, elegantly enjoying their final years. My aunts said that some Issei had once constructed magnificent Japanese gardens and ponds with granite stones from the Sierras carried down into the valley. Many of their gardens did not survive the war and evacuation. After they returned, these Issei had to replant pines that would require years to shape. I wonder if they hesitated restocking *koi*/carp ponds. These fish grew slowly and only after many years would their colors grow brilliant and radiant.

For Jiichan Masumoto, the very early 1940s once showed promise. The Great Depression was ending, work was available for those willing, and four sons were hungry to prove themselves and establish a family estate. My oldest uncle had purchased a new car, a '40 Chevy roadster, black with whitewalls. It was the first step in the Masumotos' "getting back on their feet," as Dad explained. Then came Pearl Harbor and the confusion of evacuation and the years of exile to the Arizona desert. Dad bought our farm in 1948 from an Italian who had the property during the war and decided to move on to another farm he owned. The Italian had purchased the land from the Kawamoto family during the frantic weeks prior to evacuation. When we moved here, the land already had Japanese ghosts working the soil.

Without an old farmer around, Dad could not talk with someone who had worked this earth before him, who knew the lay of this land. I never overheard a conversation about the history of a field—why one row of vines was planted closer together than any other row or why our irrigation well was only fifty feet deep and whether the water table had changed over the decades. I heard no tales about the rainstorm at the turn of the century or the Depression years or the hail just before World War II. Until we had a devastating freeze, no one told us about the lowland area where the killing cold air could gather, freezing the delicate new shoots of spring. All the farm stories I heard were new.

My parents tended our vineyards and orchards by themselves. They lacked an extra set of experienced hands that could become invaluable during a threatening rainstorm while the raisins were drying or during the blistering heat in the middle of a peach harvest. Mom and Dad worked hard. I watched both trudge home after a full day of rolling raisin trays, spending hours in the fields crawling on their knees, folding the paper that held the grapes that dried into dark morsels. They had strong backs, but I could see the physical labor come near to breaking them. I began to realize why so few old farmers were alive—they must have worked themselves to an early death.

Once in elementary school, I visited a friend and an old man charged out of the shadows and surprised me. I wondered how long he sat camouflaged, squatting under a tree in a worn brown work shirt, watching cars and tractors drive past. I was scared by his scraggy weather-beaten face, dark from years in the sun and hardened with wrinkles etched into the skin. Half of a cigarette dangled from the corner of a mouth, most of the ashes somehow hanging intact, a slow-burning timeline that captured the last hour of inactivity. The old-timer spoke with a heavy Armenian accent, waving a walking cane as he advanced toward me. Then someone came running out of the farmhouse, yelling, "Papa, come back in," and an argument ensued. At first I mistook the loud voices as expressions of anger until later I learned these families always spoke in booming volumes; they saw it as a sign of love.

I did not understand this, because my grandmother never yelled. She was quiet, reserved, and I didn't understand her Japanese. Our exchanges were very brief. For the first twenty years of my life, I spoke fewer than fifty words to her. She knew little English and I could only repeat a few Japanese phrases over and over. "Baachan, *ohaiyo*"—good morning. "*Mizu?*"—water? "*Shoyuu?*"—soy sauce? "More *gohan!*"—rice. "*Oyasuminasai*"— sweet dreams.

Dad says that Jiichan didn't know much English either. If he were alive, our conversations would have also been limited. We would have had to find other ways to talk.

IN CALIFORNIA, FAMILY traditions usually do not interfere with our farming. With few elderly farmers around, it's rare that feelings get hurt when we work a piece of land differently. Few seem to mind when a vineyard is bulldozed over or an orchard toppled, making way for a new variety of grapes or peaches. Scrapers filling in low spots or leveling high ground draw little attention. A distant farm hill or mound can disappear in a few days. We often don't have emotional attachments to land worked for only a few years. I imagine it's different in other parts of the country where the old apple orchard or the hay field have become landmarks. "That pasture" may serve as a guidepost. While traveling, I've received directions based on a local perspective: "You take Pioneer Road past the Kutz place and next to their hay field, turn left." In those cases, changes to the lay of the land can disorient an entire community.

Many worm sprays were first introduced to our valley when I was a child. At first, farmers grumbled about the changes because it meant more work, since few owned sprayers and most were not trained to use chemicals on the farm. Then field men for chemical companies dropped by the farms and persuaded farmers of the effectiveness of the new technology. The best promotion came in a "wormy year" when a neighbor's fields were free of damage because of his spray program, and his peaches and nectarines were in demand for good prices. Farmers then commented, "What's the matter with the old ways? In one word I'll tell you—worms." We too experimented with pesticides like DDT that killed every sort of insect, promising an end to our worries.

Dad was slow to adopt the innovation. He talked with my uncles, attended informational meetings, read a few articles and editorials in the trade magazines, which urged American farmers to be progressive and change. Dad experimented and tested a few sprays, never completely believing the field men nor their recommended levels of pesticides. "They're really just salesmen," he explained.

But it seemed easy to bastardize old, traditional ways without a chiding, grating voice responding to each decision and experiment. Dad didn't need to keep looking over his shoulder, wary of each action, wondering if it would meet with approval, apprehensive that visible results would be delayed, allowing an opportunity for criticism. (Of course, one of the hallmarks of our new methods was that results were often immediate—worms dropped from trees in minutes, weeds withered in hours. We witnessed the changes and convinced ourselves this was good.) Every year, technology seemed to offer us a better way to farm. The acceptance of modern farming met little resistance.

Once when we were teenagers, my cousin Ralph came by for a visit and we retreated to my room to study the annual *Yearbook of Agriculture*, produced by the United States Department of Agriculture. Bigger and faster equipment was glorified in glossy photographs, and more and more science was touted to solve all our problems. "When I go to college," Ralph proclaimed, "I'm going to become a scientist. It's the best way to help Dad on the farm."

The yearbook also had some charts and graphs, showing facets of agribusiness on the rise. I was proud that California led the nation, producing more fruits and vegetables than any other state. We were the model for the industrial world, our soils were young and rich, our Central Valley had become the nation's cornucopia. The land had made many of the large farmers very rich. The wealth contributed to a type of historical amnesia. We all wanted to forget the hard work of the past and move on. This was a valley for young farmers.

California was the last stage of America's westward expansion. Historically, those restless for something new could always forge into new territory, staking fresh claims. Settlers came here from other places because they sought the freedom to be different. The land offered seemingly endless opportunity, and our histories were not bound by tradition. Here, most of the old ways never arrived.

A few traditions from other cultures, though, have become established. When I was ten or eleven, an Armenian friend and his family took me to their community's annual Blessing of the Grapes. Mounds of green and red grape bunches were piled high on a large table. A priest walked by and swept his hand over them while making the sign of the cross. He prayed aloud in Armenian. My friend's mother explained, "He prays for good weather and the strength to see us through the harvest." She was not exactly sure of the words, as the prayer was spoken in a formal Armenian. "It's not what we speak at home," she added. The farmers in the audience took this ritual very seriously, believing a good harvest counted on the success of this ceremony. Their eyes dropped to the ground, heads bowed before the juicy clusters. Afterward we all received a bunch of grapes. I munched the berries and I felt as if I had received communion.

When I came home, I asked Dad if Japanese practiced such a ritual. "I don't think grapes were grown very much in Japan," he said.

"I guess we need to rely on the Armenians to help bless our raisins," I concluded.

"But Japanese did grow peaches," my mother added. She told me the story of Momotaro, Peach Boy. Once an old farm couple longed for a child. They worked very hard, and one day they found a giant peach and inside was a boy who became their son. They named him Momotaro, Peach Boy, and for years they were very happy. Later, Momotaro journeyed to fight evil creatures and allied himself with a dog, a monkey, and a bird. Together they were victorious, and he returned to his family with riches. Good conquered evil, a son came home with a harvest of wealth, family was renewed.

But I didn't believe in Momotaro. I spent my summers learning about new machines and chemicals and not folk tales.

Our family broke tradition when my mom took a city job. She felt bad about leaving the kids at home, especially "her baby" as I

finished elementary school. Not many farm wives worked in the
city, and I became concerned because most farm jobs involved two
people laboring as a team. Who would drive the tractor while
Dad picked up the raisin trays? Who could manage the packing
shed as we filled boxes of peaches for market? Would the workers' checks be written in time and our accounting books be kept
up to date? I worried about Dad because he would be alone on the
farm.

But my brother desperately wanted to go to college, and the
farm needed the stability of off-farm income. My parents wore
long faces when they softly talked about money. Peach prices
seemed to hover for years at two or three dollars for a twenty-
three-pound box. Raisins sold for $260 a ton in 1950 (and that
was a great year), and in 1970, despite our costs steadily creeping
upward, our prices averaged about $200 a ton. Dad and Mom
had cut costs as much as possible. The traditional answer, "We'll
just have to work harder," no longer worked. My folks joked that
with Mom working, in lean years, she would become the banker
who would finance the farm. They rationalized that at least
Mom's job with the U.S. Department of Agriculture still involved
farming. Somehow that lessened their uneasiness. Also, working
in an office could add years to Mom's life. The demanding physical labor coupled with lousy prices broke the strongest of bodies
and spirits. I began to hear talk about "getting out of the fields"
as my brother started college, as if that were our new goal.

four

AMERICAN
EDUCATION

At Del Rey, my small elementary school, the majority of kids were Mexican. I saw them throughout the summer, though, when their families came to pick our peaches. Then during raisin harvest in late August their extended families arrived and picked our grapes, laying them on paper trays to dry in the sun into raisins. I learned who were brothers and sisters and cousins, if the Ramirez clan had more boys coming along the way to star on our flag football teams. We joked about renaming our school Del

Reyna Elementary after the huge Reyna family with their dozen children and nieces and nephews.

Normally, we started school right after Labor Day. (For years I believed the Labor Day holiday was in honor of farm families, a final weekend of work in the fields that marked the end of summer.) But farming could take precedence over our education—we postponed the start of school if the grapes sugared later than usual and harvest was delayed.

Though the Japanese and Armenian kids were children of farmers and most of the Mexicans were from farmworker families, I wanted to believe we all belonged to the same large farm family community, owners and workers laboring side by side. Since José and Catalina could outrun me on the playground, it felt proper to be their "water boy" during harvests and take them sodas during breaks and make sure the water jug was filled with ice. But as I grew older and entered the sixth grade, I noticed the sons and daughters of the farmers never missed the first day of school while the kids from farmworker families were absent, sometimes starting weeks behind us. During one year when the grapes produced a bumper crop with thousands of extra tons to be picked, the harvest lasted into October with steady work seven days a week. I saw Lalo one afternoon after getting dropped off the bus and asked when he'd come back to school. We missed his long arms catching football passes for our team. He said his family were making such good money they'd leave for Mexico right away. "I won't even have to go to Del Rey!" He grinned.

I was shocked because my parents told me to study hard—education was the one way our family could become something. What was the matter with Lalo? Later that year I was stunned when other kids teased me about being Japanese. They pulled up the corners of their eyes and taunted, "Chinese, Japanese," then slapped their laps and shouted, "American knees." When I stared into a mirror, I couldn't understand how they knew I was different. Then I blamed my grandparents for immigrating from the wrong country. At least if they came from Mexico, I'd be like the majority of other kids.

Living in the Central Valley of California feels like stepping back into feudalism. The scattered towns stand in the valley like walled cities. In the distance I can see their lights glow at night. The farmers are the peasants, working the surrounding lands, shipping food off to urban centers. We live docile lives in the shadows of the nearby castles. A few times a year we venture into the big city but quickly return to the safety of our farmlands. People here are born laborers and will die as laborers. Our lords and leaders live far away, and though some may complain, no one protests or demands change. We are loyal. Most of my neighbors seem content and serene. Everyone is strangely comfortable. As a teenager, I longed for excitement.

In the 1970s, we heard stories of revolutions. The protests of the sixties finally arrived in the valley a decade late with a rural flavor. When an advocate for farmworker rights spoke to a large crowd at Fresno State, the small band of supporters huddled near the podium. Around them gathered hundreds of "aggies" with their cowboy hats or baseball caps imprinted with "Ford" in bright blue lettering or "John Deere" with the traditional green. By studying the various emblems on their caps I could distinguish sons of grape growers—who wore "Kryocide" lavender, a pesticide used in grapes—from those of row-crop farmers in their "NK" green, a national seed company. They jeered and booed, disrupting the speech. At one point no one could hear the speaker.

At my high school, we formed the Environmental Club, inspired by the student body president from a Fresno city high school. During the school week, we farm kids recycled cans and newspapers, and on weekends we helped our parents spray pesticides. One raisin farmer's son named Greg Minasian proposed that the chemical companies should start packaging their herbicides in aluminum cans so we could recycle them too.

A<small>N ANNUAL</small> Y<small>OUNG</small> Buddhist Association conference was held every fall in Fresno. Teenage Sansei—third-generation Japanese Americans—gathered in Fresno for a day, to hear a minister lecture, to talk about Buddhist teachings, but most important to dance at night. This was where the *right* boys met the *right* girls—in other words, kids who were both Japanese and Buddhist—and if they were also children from farm families, even better. We tried to follow in our parents' footsteps.

During my senior year in high school, the fall conference was organized by a woman who had left the countryside for college in San Francisco. She returned with many of her friends to help with the program. Their presence stirred controversy. They had long hair, wore patches on their jeans, and talked about being Asian-American. Nisei parents huddled in the back of the church hall, uneasy about these outsiders and their appearance. I was energized by their stories, curious to know more about politics and being "Asian." But for most, the evening dance eclipsed all revolutionary idealism.

Weeks later, dozens of parents attended a heated meeting at the Buddhist church and demanded changes. Otherwise, they threatened, they would not allow their kids to participate in the next conference. The adults would not tolerate the long hair, even though they couldn't force such strict standards even on their own children. Others complained about the radicals' scraggly facial hair—that had more to do with the fact that most Japanese-American boys had trouble growing a decent mustache or beard. Finally, the parents focused their protest on the torn pants, embroidered work shirts, patches, and sandals. Banning jeans and denim shirts and insisting shoes and socks be worn would keep the radicals out of our valley and the children safe.

By the summer, though, most farmers and their families had forgotten about the jeans and long hair. The valley exploded with the movement to unionize farmworkers. The debate divided us into two camps, "they"—the poor, Chicano, radical troublemakers—and "us"—wealthy, oppressive, conservative land barons. I watched stories on the national evening news broadcast from Delano, a farm town a few miles south down Highway 99, and I saw people I recognized marching with Hollywood stars, and occasionally a local farmer mumbled to a reporter about not understanding what all the fuss was about and shook his head. His face remained half hidden in the shadows created by a silly-looking beat-up baseball cap. Farmers and farmworkers had become celebrities.

As a member of the Nisei Farmers League, Dad joined a bus-load of other farmers who wanted to demonstrate their unity and strength by trying to harvest grapes on a forty-acre farm that was being picketed. I heard the term "solidarity" for the first time and applied it to my dad. The farmers left hours before dawn, and at the vineyard they were met by protesters and their signs and red United Farm Workers flags. As they drove onto the dirt avenue of the vineyard, the union sympathizers pounded on the side of the bus and tried to rock it back and forth. Obscenities were yelled, "Fucking farmers, get out of here!" "Damned Japs, go home!" *"Viva la huelga! Viva la huelga!"*

Dad said, "I thought I was just going to help a farmer get his crop harvested."

As the farmers got off the bus in the middle of the vineyard, the protesters hurled dirt clods as far as they could. The earthen bombs sailed through the air and crashed through the grape-leaf canopies or exploded against the side of the bus. The scene looked like a medieval battle where territory was claimed according to the distance a spear could be tossed or a catapult could fling rocks and boulders. The farmers moved inward a few rows and the clods fell harmlessly to the earth. As arms tired, the barrage became less intimidating and finally stopped.

By midmorning, with the moral support of a hundred farmers and shielded from the hundred union supporters, work crews were able to pick grapes. During a work break, the farmers reconvened for coffee and doughnuts served on a vineyard wagon. The sound of a gunshot rang out, and farmers and workers ducked their heads and dropped to their knees, hiding behind tractors and wagons. A silence suddenly filled the vineyard, a stillness gripped the men and women. Only a lone tractor grunted unevenly in the distance.

"Just an engine backfiring," someone yelled. The farmers picked themselves up and began patting themselves, knocking the dirt from their clothes—chest and arms, then legs and thighs. A haze filled the gathering area, and as the farmers looked up, they saw the protesters doing the same. A few feet above them, their dust clouds met and merged.

Near the end of summer, we harvested our final block of nectarines with a small crew of field workers. The trees bordered the road, and as the crew advanced toward asphalt, they were spotted by someone in a small car that abruptly turned and sped away. A few minutes later, a caravan of cars stopped along our roadside. People honked their car horns and yelled and waved red UFW flags as they got out of their vehicles and set up a spontaneous picket line along our field. Media people followed in a small car and jumped out to snap photographs.

We instructed our workers to stop and move away from the disturbance into the interiors of our fields. One of the organizers screamed into a bullhorn in Spanish, telling our workers to join *la raza* and stand up to the farmers. A union representative demanded access into our fields, and we had no choice but to grant it. He then began rapidly talking and waving his hands. He pointed to my dad and spat on the ground.

I then recognized my friend Jessie on the other side of the line. We had gone to school together for over thirteen years, ever since kindergarten. We saw each other almost every day except during December and January, when his family left for Mexico, or in the summers when we worked in separate fields. We made eye contact, and he dipped his head to the left, motioning to meet to one side, away from the crowd.

"Hey, man, how you doing?" he said as we shook hands. I

asked him about his family and then we talked about his brother's '56 Chevy.

Our conversation abruptly ended when a bullhorn blared and both sides started to pile into their cars and pickups. The protest then headed down the street toward the next farm. Jessie didn't say goodbye. He turned and his smile slipped away. Someone came up to him, glared at me, then leaned into his face to yell something. Jessie whipped his arm and shoulder up, shrugged off the advice, and marched on. In less than a minute, they were all gone, their dust wandering into our orchard and settling back onto the earth.

The rest of that summer, everything seemed turned upside down. People were filled with emotion. Lively discussions erupted over dinner tables. For one season, I saw a different world. A passion filled our valley, an engaging energy fueled by the tension not normally found there. I questioned how long the fervor would last, because my family, the neighbors, and our farmworkers wanted to settle this issue and go back to working. But I still longed for something not found in the valley.

I devised a perfect plan. I would exploit my good grades and use higher education as my ticket out of the valley. I had applied to lots of colleges and was accepted into a few. Some I knew our family couldn't afford. I was interviewed for a University of California scholarship, and during the conversation I was asked about summer work. I told the panel the story about our home packing shed operation—where the whole family, including my "city cousins," came to spend the summer working on the farm as we picked, packed, and shipped our peaches to market. They liked the story, and I felt relieved.

Then a middle-aged man with a stiff white shirt and dark blue blazer asked, "When you say 'city' cousins, who do you mean? Where are your cousins from, Los Angeles or San Francisco?"

Without hesitation I said, "Fresno."

Having never thought of Fresno as a major urban area, they

all chuckled. I feared I had just lost my scholarship. I was then even more determined to leave and live on the other side of the mountains that ringed our valley.

Textbook Grandfathers

At the University of California in Berkeley, lively debates filled my classes and discussion groups as students challenged each other and the professors. The energy of college tingled like mild electrical shocks. But did farmers belong in the coming rebellion? My radical friends did not talk about good-tasting peaches when they spoke about workers uniting. Sweet raisins didn't fit in their vision of a new world of change and progressive thinking. The produce from our farm might or might not have political or economic value. Farmers were not necessarily oppressive capitalists, nor were we revolutionaries.

The protest began along Telegraph and Bancroft avenues. Students naturally gathered there at the main entrance of the Berkeley campus by the student union, where impromptu speeches were screamed by political zealots or born-again Christians. I stood next to the orange juice wagon vendor and enjoyed the odor of the vegetarian falafel cooking nearby.

I was holding a sign, a poster of a leader with a new vision for a nation. A few years ago, back in the valley, it might have been a picture of Nixon that I'd received from the Committee to Reelect the President. Now I held a poster of the leader and teacher Chairman Mao. Both men seemed to share the stately appearance of a leader, someone you could trust. But now I believed Mao more than Nixon.

I had read Mao's little red book filled with passionate parables about politics. I imagined hearing his deep voice telling us wise stories about power and society. I joined study groups and we discussed Maoist social thought. These were ideas I'd never heard before, concepts that swelled and swirled in my mind. Yes, we had become alienated from our government, our economy, our own labor and the true means of production. Yes, correct ideas came from social practice. Yes, the workers of the world had nothing to lose but their shackles. Yes, power did come from the end of a gun.

"But what about farmers?" I had asked.

Yoko, one of the leaders of our study group, had said, "Everyone has their place in society, even the agrarian population." She hesitated, then added, "But that's an excellent question for our next session." Yoko and I chatted. She was from the city, a transfer from San Francisco State, and had grown up in a working-class family. She used little or no makeup, was slender, with dark eyes and high cheekbones, and dressed in black with a dark blue Mao jacket. She wore a hardness in her expressions. I found her scowl strangely attractive.

At our next meeting she had discussed how farmers were not the enemy. True, they owned land and exploited their workers, but they were mere pawns of the capitalists. "Farmers are petty bourgeois," she proclaimed. I was relieved. She liked me.

"The time has come to march, to march for our rights!" the voice screamed. The people cheered, I waved my poster up and down. We surged onto campus and managed to pull in a few curious supporters from those who had just finished a falafel lunch. The campus police were parked down the road, watching. I held my poster as high as I could, jabbing it into the breeze, spinning and rocking the Chairman in cadence with our chants.

We paraded past the library, and students peered through the windows and came strolling out the doors, taking a study break. We stopped at Haviland Hall and marched around the gray structure. A few pale-faced scholarly types stumbled out of the door. They looked haggard and confused. I thought of them as prisoners of war we had freed. As the building emptied, we invaded. That was when the campus police and Berkeley city cops descended. They marched in with their riot gear, shields in hand. They had done this before. Their strategy was to cut off large numbers of students from entering the building. With the structure surrounded, they allowed the majority of us protesters to march around outside until nightfall or we grew hungry for dinner. Our ranks were divided.

Yoko jumped into the doorway. She turned and yelled, "People, let's go! What are you waiting for?" She glanced at me and beckoned.

I froze. A large policeman stepped in between us with his nightstick drawn. The door was slammed shut.

We marched outside and yelled to those inside, "So-li-dar-ity! So-li-dar-ity!" The insiders opened upstairs windows and cheered with clenched fists. I spied Yoko in one of the windows, I believed she saw me and I waved my poster. She abruptly looked the other way. The Chairman and I stopped celebrating. Dusk arrived, our numbers dwindled, my arms tired. I let Mao take a break.

I leaned against one of the large, dramatic pine trees planted decades ago. Mao was at my side. I asked him if I was a failure. His eyes looked rather gentle, not the gaze of the spirited radical. I asked him again if farmers belonged in this revolution for equality. I argued that my family was just as exploited as anyone else. They still were connected with the land, and not alienated from their work. I had spent time in the fields, I knew my work, I touched and smelled the fruits of my labor. Where was that in your red book? He looked gentle, and his round, chubby face was not so intimidating. The answer for me was not political.

The airbrush strokes softened Mao's features. Maybe we had more in common than I'd thought. We were both struggling to scratch out a living from the earth. I shared the Asian features of this pudgy old man—a face that marked me as different in America. But I was not Chinese. My grandfathers once called Japan their home. Perhaps my journey was to begin with family on a farm across an ocean and thousands of miles away from America.

Instead of Chairman I secretly thought of Grandpa Mao. I smiled and closed my eyes. I felt forgiven and could now go home.

Burden to Return

When Mom had explained my plans to study in Japan, Baachan's eyes grew wide in surprise and an "Oooh?" escaped her throat. We were weeding the yard, our shovels scraping the earth, severing weeds from their spring homes. We worked in unison, a slow-moving line progressing across the yard toward the barn. As we neared the workshop, we stopped and took a break.

Baachan knelt into her familiar squatting position. Her feet were flat against the ground and her knees poked upward with her bottom almost touching the dirt. She rested her elbows on her thighs and clasped her hands in front of her face. A calm, soothing gaze swept over her as she rested in a tranquil, meditative position. She could sit like that for hours. I'd mimic her but quickly found my knees aching and leg muscles tightening. I lacked her flexibility and limber joints.

Mom explained that while in Japan, I wanted to visit Baachan's native village. During the 1910s, in a small village just outside of Kumamoto, Baachan's household had faced crisis after crisis. Her father had died, and the family struggled through a series of disastrous rice crops. She and her only brother were teenagers. A marriage was then hastily arranged for Baachan and she departed for California. She never again saw her brother.

Baachan tilted her head and stared off into the nearby vineyards before answering, "*Heeeiii* . . ." As we rested without talking, Baachan began to gently rock back and forth ever so slightly. Then she said that I would be the first of the American family to return to Japan. We listened to the occasional popping sound of the metal expanding as the midday sun heated the tin shed roof. My legs grew cramped, so I stood. Baachan thought it was a signal to begin work again.

We continued our shoveling and said no more. In a few months, the weed seeds would resprout and we'd repeat the process. But after many years of weeding and turning the plants back into the ground, we had gradually increased the organic matter of the soil, softening the earth so we could slip our shovel blades into her surface with ease. The metal made a "shhhing" sound as it scratched the dirt, leaving a pattern of small divots of grass behind to dry in the sun.

TWO DAYS BEFORE I left for Japan, my uncles, aunts, and most of my cousins came to the farm for a farewell visit. As they arrived, Mom or Baachan stepped out to greet them, graciously accepting *omiyage*—small presents of pastries, ice cream, and homemade *manju*, Japanese pastry.

"You didn't need to bring anything," Mom said.

"It's nothing," my aunts answered. "We'd feel funny coming empty-handed."

Everyone gently smiled as the welcoming ritual between host and guest was completed, a cordial but simple act of giving and receiving gifts.

We usually met for weddings, funerals, or memorial services and once-in-a-lifetime events like a birth or special anniversary. I was surprised my trip ranked high enough for a family gathering, but there were some half-serious questions by two aunts about whether or not I was coming back. My uncle Herky helped me with an answer: "He'll be back with a good Nihon wife—a Japanese bride!" That sent two aunts scurrying off, contemplating new family arrangements.

Most of my cousins arrived late and didn't stay long. They had to park out near the vineyard, and we chatted as they hosed off the field dust from their sandals. Whenever they returned to the farm, we reminisced about working in the barn, packing fruit during our childhood summer months. Nostalgia was mixed with the reality that the work was hard and dirty. Yet the orange setting sun and the hues of red and purple reminded us of the long hours of dusk when a coolness broke the heat and cousins played outside for hours.

Inside the farmhouse, voices ebbed and flowed with multiple conversations broken by roars of laughter and surprise. The old folks gathered around the kitchen dining table, pulling together a mixed assortment of chairs, bumping knees and rubbing elbows as they scooted seats. The kids retreated to the living room, drawn to a baseball game on television, splitting allegiance between the Dodgers and Giants, filling the gaps between innings with snippets of conversations. Sounds easily penetrated the two rooms and the chatter swelled in competing crescendos.

Eventually Baachan wandered near us and stood in the doorway. Heads turned and we greeted her with a smile, then asked in English, "Baachan, how are you?" She didn't understand, and some of us repeated the question slower and louder. She smiled and nodded her head. We were caught in an uncomfortable moment as we stared at each other. None of us knew enough Japanese to invite her to sit.

Later, she relocated to a corner of the dining room where our piano sat unused and obscure. There she hummed to herself, not quite loud enough for others to hear. I watched her hands pat out a wandering rhythm on her thighs. The cadence increased and eventually she began to swing her legs and knock her shoes together with each beat. As her song continued, farm dirt, a fine, powdery earth, fell from her shoes, collecting in a pile that grew with the pace of her songs.

I strayed from the conversations and slipped down the hall to the bedrooms. Two of my youngest cousins, girls four and six years old, were playing with dolls that had once belonged to my sister. I scared them when I walked in; their expressions froze for a second, with open mouths and wide eyes. I laughed and they did too. "Don't do that!" the older one yelled and playfully slapped my thigh.

I hugged them and recalled a conversation with their mom.

She had tried to explain to the children that I would soon be leaving for Japan.

"How long?" they asked.

"A year. Maybe two," I answered.

"Oh, that long?" one said. The other followed with, "Well . . . okay. You can go!" Both sisters began giggling.

Later, they whispered to their mom, "Where's Japan?"

I WATCHED BAACHAN rise, shaking her head, tugging at loose strands of gray hair, talking to herself. She withdrew into the laundry room, finding company among farm clothes and work boots. We called that place the mud room, where we changed from dirty to clean clothes. Seasons were identified by the row of work shoes and the dirt and leaves tramped in. Mud-caked boots meant winter rain. Damp sand usually followed a spring storm. The hoary, powdery dirt of the long dry summer was the most common. In the autumn, crushed and yellowed leaves and fine silt collected in the cracks of our soles.

She sat on an old wooden chair between the bathroom and a pile of Dad's farm and shop magazines. We kids called that area Dad's office, since it was where he made farm plans and decisions. I often discovered scribbled figures on the backs of envelopes and notes written on dog-eared pages. One box was stuffed with scraps of brown tray paper from raisin harvests. The annual tray count had been scribbled on the pages. Secluded between cardboard boxes marked "taxes and expenses" and a pair of patched, faded blue coveralls, Baachan tried to hide.

After a few minutes, we searched for her and located her. My aunts asked, "What's the matter?"

Baachan worried about how much trouble she created, about always "getting in the way."

We comforted her. "No, that's not true."

She shook her head, though, certain of her convictions. She

then talked of death, wanting to free everyone of the "burden" of caring for an old person. Her face quivered, her voice began to shriek—"Ahh. Ahhh. Ahhhh." She pounded her fists in the air and stomped her feet. Then a low, guttural cry escaped from her throat, a raspy, bitter scream that frightened me. Her legs pumped up and down and her shoes beat against the cement floor. A faint cloud of dust engulfed her corner. Finally, a piercing wail— "Yaaaaa . . ."—shook the room as we stood in shock.

I understood only a few of her phrases—"I'm old and a burden. I just want to go away."

As she calmed and slowed, two aunts quickly reached for her hands and gently held them. Both parties gradually tightened their grips. They huddled in the corner, squeezed between the work clothes and boots. I could see the women's chests rising up and down in short gasps of air before settling into a controlled yet rapid cadence.

The relatives began to line up near the back door. The uncles waited while the aunts made a final effort to clear the table, offering to help clean up, asking where to put the cream and sugar. Mom responded, "Oh, leave it and don't worry," as she pointed to the cabinet shelf where it was stored.

"Good luck in Japan," an uncle said and shook my hand. He then whispered to his wife, "Your purse, don't forget your purse." She was confused, because her purse hung on her arm. He looked at her and repeated, "Don't forget your purse."

"Oh? Oh yes!" she said and reached into her bag and produced a white envelope with money inside. "Something for your trip," she said. "We want you to enjoy yourself."

I recalled accepting the envelope and stammering, "You don't have to give me anything . . . but, thanks." Everyone laughed with my "thanks" as if I placed too much of an emphasis on it. The scene was then repeated with each set of relatives.

One aunt handed me a bag filled with boxes of raisins. "*Omiyage*—gifts for the family," she explained. "They only know us as farmers, so you should give them something from our farms!" She then handed me a slip of paper. "It's an address from Japan," she whispered. "I'm sorry! Don't have your mother's family from Hiroshima, darn it! But this is one from one of Baachan's letters." No one knew if the address was current; Baachan rarely received mail from Japan. "Try and see them if you can," the aunt said. "We never met the Japan family!" The farewells abruptly ended with final handshakes and an embarrassing silence as we stood opposite each other.

I was not sure when she returned inside or how she slipped past without someone saying something. Baachan appeared at my side, her black pants streaked with dust from the laundry room. I was surprised by her change in mood.

Suddenly two arms were wrapped around me. I stepped back, but the arms and body followed, clinging to my waist. Baachan was hugging me. She had never done this before; in fact, I had never seen her hug anyone. She always bowed. But her arms grabbed fast like a clamp and her hands rubbed my back, moving in quick, uneven rhythms. I felt her bony fingers press into my skin, revealing a hidden strength within her aging joints.

I looked up, and everyone was staring. Mom and Dad stood to the side and weakly smiled. I gently pushed, but the arms pulled tighter. I was confused, emotionally charged yet embarrassed by this show of emotion. Around me I felt the presence of the silent faces.

Baachan said something in Japanese. I looked to Dad for translation. "Baachan said she's happy you're going to Japan."

I tried to answer her with my limited Japanese, "Baachan, *iki-mashoo* —let's go together!"

She mumbled something. I looked again to Dad for help. "She says she's too old. She says you go for her."

five

(G R A N D) F A T H E R
L A N D

WHEN MY GRANDFATHERS FIRST ARRIVED IN AMERICA, I HEARD STO-
ries of their ship docking and groups of men disembarking onto
American soil. During their two- or three-week voyage, many
had befriended those who spoke the same dialect and were from
the same region of Japan. When the new friends stepped onto
land, they were met by other fellow countrymen who directed
them to board a train bound for Fresno, where plenty of work
was to be had and expatriates from Kumamoto and Hiroshima
prefectures had settled.

As I stepped onto Japanese soil, I gazed at the mass of strange faces surging in all directions, the airport churning with motion and noise. I looked for, but did not find, a guide waiting for me. Did my grandfathers feel as lost as I suddenly felt? For weeks I attended an intensive Japanese language class that met six days a week, eight hours a day, with homework. We concluded each day with *kanji* practice. Around me I could hear the tapping of pencils and the dragging of lead across the paper as the black lines, dashes, and dots combined into symbols with meaning. I steadily fell farther and farther behind, buried by my homework in a small dorm room in the heart of Tokyo. Weekly we were tested according to the number of characters we could read, and I was the at the bottom. I was illiterate.

I was not sure if my grandfathers were also illiterate. I knew neither *jiichan* could read English, but Japanese? Baachan Masumoto could not read—she had received only a few years of formal education before immigrating to America. I remembered her visiting friends a few farms away and asking them to translate her letters from Japan. Afterward, she carefully stored the precious documents, bundling the handful of envelopes in a white muslin cloth, wrapping them with string and placing them in the back of her dresser drawer. They were important, but without translation they were only black scratches on pieces of paper. She never pulled them out to look at them. Were any letters addressed to my grandfather? I had no way of knowing. I could not even read his name in Japanese.

I asked my language *sensei* if there was a book of Japanese names. He directed me to the library, where official *kanji* and family names were catalogued in a reference volume. The librarian spoke English. " Masu-moto?" she asked. "Not Matsu-moto?"

I shook my head, "No. Ma-su-mo-to."

She nodded, and as we walked to a stack, she said, "Not a popular name. Do you know the *kanji*?" I scribbled the character that I had learned from Baachan.

She stopped to study it and gently whispered *"Chotto . . .
okashi. . . .* This looks a little . . . odd." She tried to locate a matching character, but nothing was close to my rendering. "I'm sorry,"
she politely concluded, not wanting to offend.

Our classes started at seven in the morning and ended at three.
For weeks we drilled and read and were assigned ten new characters a day. Every evening I studied new vocabulary and expressions and wrote each character dozens of times. There was no way
to learn *kanji* other than repetition and rote memorization. One
character had eight strokes written in a certain pattern, another
five strokes, another twelve strokes. Though based on ancient pic-
tographs, they resembled little that I could recognize.

In the third week, my new *sensei* called me into his office. I was
failing *kanji* miserably. Many of my characters looked rough, not
quite wrong but not correct. We reviewed my worksheet. Almost
every one had a minor error, a stroke too long, another line too flat
or thick; some seemed to end abruptly, others looked uneven. He
asked me to write a few characters and immediately discovered
the problem. "You're left-handed!" he said, almost a glee in his
voice. "No wonder everything looked backward. Masumoto-san,
you have to practice extra hard, because *kanji* is written for right
hand. Each push or pull works for right hand, not the left." He
ended our meeting with a simple solution: "You just need to work
twice as hard as everyone else."

The next day, I dropped down to the lowest level of language
classes, accepting my place in the beginning course, which empha-
sized verbal more than written skills. The class was filled with
exchange students from the United States visiting for a summer, a
couple from Switzerland exploring a new land, a group of Chinese men wanting to learn another Asian language, a young businessman from New Zealand expanding his skills, and other
Americans who shared my outlook—we had quickly concluded
that none of us would become interpreters or translators. So
instead of daylong classes, we met for half days, then explored

the massive city and complex culture around us. Daily we made fools of ourselves out in the streets with our pathetic conversational Japanese. We learned what a friend called "guerrilla *kanji*"—we wandered into situations such as trying to differentiate men's and women's toilet signs and quickly learned to decipher the correct meaning of the characters.

IWAMURA *SENSEI* CHASTISED my pronunciation. "*Mo, ichidoo*—one more time," he grunted. I repeated the expression and then added an extra line of conversation. *Sensei* nodded and eyed the next student, a middle-aged Australian man with a rough complexion and leatherlike skin. The foreigner stumbled through a basic phrase with Japanese words contorted by his heavy accent. Listening to him made some of us cringe; we hated to follow him, because it was hard to get his voice out of our minds as we tried to return to the naturally soft rhythms of Japanese. But Iwamura *sensei* listened and commended the Australian, "Much better. You are now learning our language!"

I clenched my teeth. I could not believe *sensei* criticized my accent and allowed another to go uncorrected. After class, I met with my teacher privately. At first we tried to converse using only Japanese. I explained my problem, and because of my limited vocabulary, I ended up asking him, "Why don't you like me?" He raised his eyebrows at the bluntness of my question and we switched to English.

"Your Japanese needs more work, Masumoto-san," he concluded.

"Yes, and I am working hard, *sensei*." I bowed my head with my apology and realized I was acting Japanese. "But..." I looked up, and our eyes met. "But why are you so critical of my accent?"

Sensei raised his eyebrows. I could tell he had not thought of this before. He paused, recalling my voice from the last few months of classes. Suddenly a grin appeared on his face.

"Masumoto-san," he said, "I cannot help it. When I see your face, I *expect* to hear proper Japanese."

I was unsure if I should be honored by such a double standard. *Sensei* subtly nodded his head with a slight dropping of his chin and a quick blink. I saw this gesture, bowed to him and said, "*Hai*," then left his office.

For a break between semesters, all the exchange students took an excursion just outside of Tokyo. We visited temples and shrines, which began to look the same. At one site, a registry welcomed visitors, and some of us stopped to sign the book. I signed the Masumoto name using the *kanji* I had learned from my dad and Baachan. It didn't look right next to the other Japanese names.

Our tour guide was a fat, insolent middle-aged man who constantly corrected everyone's Japanese and chided us for deviating to examine some artifacts that he had not deemed worthy of attention. I became concerned when he left his position at the front of the group and lined up behind me.

"Haaa . . . Masumoto-san, what is this?" he sneered and pointed.

"My name," I answered.

He began laughing, his fat cheeks bouncing with each chuckle. Through his shirt I saw the loose flesh of his arms and chest wiggle with his short gasps of air in between the snickering.

"This is not a name. This is not Japanese," he bellowed. "Where did you learn this?"

I was too embarrassed to answer.

"Let me show you the correct way." He then skillfully stroked a beautiful *kanji* with long flowing lines. He made light, quick movements as his brush danced on the page. His *kanji* was beautiful. He announced, "Masumoto-san, this is Masumoto." A smirk at his own cleverness spread over his plump face.

Becoming Japanese

Tanaka-san, one of my Japanese roommates, who came from the rural island of Shikoku, borrowed a music tape from my soul music collection. He had a slight *inaka*/country dialect, and once I witnessed his embarrassment at a large downtown Tokyo *depaato*/department store when behind a fragrance counter, two young women with bright red lipstick and pale white faces giggled when he asked them a question about some perfume for his mother.

"Why are they laughing?" I whispered to Tanaka-san.

"My Japanese," he answered. He weakly grinned, and as we turned away he said, "*Saaa*, I have to study too, Masumoto-san."

As he looked through my tapes and studied the few with photographs of the bands, he asked, "Why do you have so much music from black people?"

I had no good answer but tried to explain that many Asian-Americans felt soul music captured their emotions. "We identify with blacks," I added, and watched his face contort in a confused look. "And because we want to be cool."

"*Samui?*"—Cold?—he asked.

He selected a tape from the Stylistics, then returned for my entire collection of their music and transcribed all their songs. He was disappointed because I had no photograph of them. Later, he asked if I would listen to his speech for his English language class as he described his intimate emotions aroused by this American singing group. I nodded my head and was impressed with his openness. Japanese did not usually want to express themselves, especially Japanese males. He smiled and read, "The Sty-lis-tics voices, very soft and calming. The high-pitched songs from the women's voices have helped me concentrate on English words and their true meanings. I have begun to understand the America feeling of a love relationship."

I blinked and said, "Eh? Tanaka-san, *chotto* . . . *chotto*"—
wait . . . wait. I tried to look up a word in my English-to-Japan-
ese dictionary but had to rely on trying to explain "falsetto" with
my limited Japanese. Finally I said, "Tanaka-san, it's good to feel
any way you want to . . . but did you know that the Sty-lis-tics
are all men?"

Tanaka's face drained of blood and he crumpled his English
report. Our other roommates snickered, but were kind. The
evening grew quiet except for the cicada singing outside our dorm
windows.

I was warned about rush hour in Tokyo. I recalled a photograph of policemen who helped literally stuff people into trains.
The commuter train cars were packed with people shoulder to
shoulder, and white-gloved officers were pushing against the final
passengers jutting out of the entry doors in order to cram them
in tighter, like someone sitting on a stuffed suitcase in order to
engage the latches.

Intrigued, I initially didn't mind the crush of travelers despite
getting caught at a major junction where subway and train lines
crossed. The wave of commuters arrived with one train and
rushed to stairways in order to transfer to another line. No one
ran, but the pace was swift and churned with an energy intensi-
fied by the hundreds of bodies marching together. I was swept
into one of these currents—it was impossible to stop or deviate.
This must be how swarms of insects moved; the ones squeezed
inside could not alter their direction, and those on the outside kept
circling and pushing back toward the center in order to become
part of the group. We all moved as a single mass, departing one
train, rushing up a set of stairs, through a tunnel, and down
another flight of steps toward the connecting train.

At the bottom of one flight I managed to maneuver to the edge
and turned to look behind me. Thousands of faces peered
down—their bodies seemed to float down toward me. Their
heads bobbed in unison, their black hair and dark jackets or

school uniforms blurred together in a ceaseless procession. A train rumbled behind me, another screeched to a halt above us. The drone of shoes shuffling on cement station platforms and clattering up and down the maze of stairs contributed to a pulsating frenzy of humanity. We formed a seemingly endless column ten bodies wide, and every face looked like mine.

From the time I arrived in Japan, I felt the most comfortable during meals. I grew up with Japanese food—we had rice at every lunch and dinner, sometimes even for breakfast, and holidays were filled with *sushi, teriyaki, sashimi,* and *manju.* In Japan, eating was a favorite time of the day. I heard familiar words and saw comforting images. I knew these smells and fragrances. Even the rhythms of a small restaurant reminded me of a family kitchen. When sitting before food, I considered my Japanese-American upbringing to be an asset.

However, in Japan, the flavors were different, familiar but not what I anticipated. Most of the *sushi* had a tarter flavor, the *yakitori* and other noodle dishes seemed to use stronger seasoning, a bit more *karai*/salty, and the *teriyaki* sauce on chicken did not taste as sweet. When I first noticed the difference, I thought each restaurant had a regional flavor; perhaps I could not read the door sign or menu promoting a "southern-style" or "east coast" cuisine. Maybe Tokyo had its own style of stir-frying vegetables or making *dashi*/soup stock. Japanese food had subtle tastes and flavors that did not match my childhood memories.

What I really longed for was too expensive—fresh peaches and grapes. I wandered through marketplaces and saw wonderful-looking large and succulent peaches. They were brushed with a red blush, a rouge that was darker on the sunny side of the fruit, giving way to a lighter rose color on the opposite side. Each peach had a gentle cleavage on one side, the round cheeks of the suture gently folded around each other. The aroma of peach lingered above the cases, an enchanting invitation to share in the bounty of nature. They were individually wrapped in tissue and displayed in decorative boxes, and one *omiyage*/gift set of three pristine fruits cost over twenty-five dollars.

Another box with a plastic window held a gorgeous collection of huge green grapes. Each cluster looked as if it were artistically arranged, grown so that the individual shoulders of a bunch hung loose and open, each grape just brushing the other and never crowding a neighbor. The shape of the bunch was balanced, a natural symmetry like the low hills of a rolling countryside. This box was marked with a red sign as if it were a specialty item declaring the same twenty-five-dollar price as the peaches.

Once I visited the home of a businessman and the hostess carefully cut a peach for me and laid each slice on its side in a pattern on a small plate. I was handed a dainty fork to slowly savor each bite. The juicy peach flesh melted on my tongue. I almost did not have to chew; the meat seemed to liquefy into a dazzling nectar. Then they served grapes. The host had peeled and sliced each berry. I ate my dessert as if it were a part of a sacred ritual. The Japanese treated their produce as a luxury, and peaches and grapes were honored. I thought of Japanese farmers as artists creating gifts.

AFTER MONTHS IN Tokyo with its tightly compacted houses stretching as far as I could see and crowded gray structures at each station intersection packed with people at all hours of the day, I ventured for a weekend trip far outside the city boundaries. I dozed while the train journeyed for hours and awakened in a new world, on the Kanto Plain. Rice fields spread for miles and miles, with mountains on the horizon. Farmers were working their land with small equipment, a self-propelled mower in one field, a large rototiller in another. On a few farms, the rice had grown high and swayed with the midsummer breezes. An occasional gust sent a wave rolling across the green ocean as if a hand gently stroked the lush prairie.

We stopped on a side track in order to allow an express train to pass. I watched the men and women working outside, stooping and lumbering down a row, their hands slashing with a hoe and pulling weeds, flinging them to the side. Four workers quickly marched through the patch. At the end they stood and stretched. Hands rubbed and massaged tired back muscles. A few arched their torsos toward the horizon and rolled their shoulders as they inhaled a chestful of air.

I could imagine a deep but quiet sigh escaping from their lips—"ahhhh." They closed their eyes and allowed the late-afternoon sun to warm their faces, giving themselves permission to pause for a moment. They peered over the countryside and the panorama of their lands, their farms, their livelihoods. I too stared at the open fields and longed for the physical nature of farmwork.

Later, walking through the train, I glanced at a well-dressed gentleman with a kind face. He appeared familiar, and because his eyes met mine, I sensed that he too was not Japanese. He then whispered, "Hello."

"*Sumimasen?*" I answered.

"Hello," he repeated and gently smiled, motioning me to sit. I took the seat opposite him.

We had met before in California. He was a Buddhist minister I had seen at a family memorial service in Los Angeles. The service was one of dozens my family held during my childhood, one of thousands he must have participated in over the course of his ministry. His voice remained gentle. He asked why I was in Japan. I explained that I wanted to learn the language and see the real Japan.

"Where is your family from?" he questioned.

"From Kumamoto and Hiroshima," I responded. I smiled at myself. This was the first time I had thought of my Japanese relatives as "my" family.

"No, I mean in America," the minister asked.

"Oh . . . we're farmers outside of Fresno."

He nodded and said that he was on his way back to his family. "But I thought you lived in California?"

He then explained that his father was a Buddhist priest and so had been his late grandfather. His family lived in a small village tucked within the Japanese mountains. His father had been ill for a few years, his health declining with each season. "Now, I am obligated to return to the village temple."

I stayed for one night in a small town en route to Nikko, a beautiful Shinto temple tucked in the lush green mountains. The sunlight lingered long into the evening, and the heat and humidity hung like tepid fog over this small village, surrounded by farms in a small, narrow valley. Rice paddies crowded the flatlands, while the terraced hills were covered with green row crops, low hedges that looked like tea plants. These fields clung to the hillsides like a series of steps, carefully groomed to the original mountain contours. As I walked through the town, I noticed that even in the vacant lots, farmers had planted *daikon*/horseradish and *napa*/Japanese cabbage, utilizing almost every piece of open ground. Then the drum began to beat.

Don-don, don, don. Kara, kara. Don-don, don, don. Kara, kara. A *taiko*/drum pounded in a nearby neighborhood. A scratchy recording blared from a tinny public address system. The twangs of a *shamisen*, a stringed guitarlike instrument, called others to the town's center. I joined a stream of villagers following the drumbeat, heading to a small manicured park. Paper lanterns illuminated the dusk; the round spheres were suspended by electric cords and contained light bulbs. Through the colored paper, the light glowed red, pink, and lavender, and white ribbons decorated posts of a large platform that stood in the center. At the corners of the stage hung a set of music speakers, dangling from a dark tan rope stretched and frayed in some places.

Accompanying the music, an older man beat a large stationary *taiko* planted next to a platform. His hair was white, but he had a taut thin body and muscular arms. He looked like an old farmer, with tan lines along his neck and on his forearms where rolled shirtsleeves ended. He wore a *hachimaki*/headband, a red-and-white cloth strip tightly rolled around his forehead. He had no shirt, and already the summer heat had caused him to sweat. His lean chest and shoulders glistened as he lifted his *bachi*—drumsticks—overhead and swung them, tapping the drum with a powerful but delicate stroke.

Some women were dressed in *yukata*/robes, with *obi*/belts. The *yukata* were white cotton or linen printed with bright pastel reds and blues, and the *obi* were ornamented with gold or silver thread. These dancers dotted the field. They took small steps, their robes securely wrapped around their bodies yet the long arm sleeves creating a fluid, moving sensation as if they floated above the earth.

Most participants were in everyday clothes, denim shorts or pants with cotton shirts, and many of the men wore white T-shirts. Around the platform and the *taiko* drummer, we marched single-file and created an oval. We were led by a Buddhist priest, and when a complete oval was created, the remaining participants broke off and began a new oval. Eventually a series of concentric rings was formed. As I walked, my slippers scraped the sand and gravel, creating a "shuu-shuu" rhythm, another percussion instrument.

Three young women were helped onto the platform by youthful men who had quickly volunteered to lift the petite and nimble bodies up to the three-foot-high stage. Once the three straightened themselves, they spontaneously broke into a dance. The crowd clapped in unison—*choo-choo-cho*—as everyone watched for the cue, then we too broke into step.

I found my feet moving almost without thought. I knew most of the dance, the patterns were familiar, the hand movements I had done hundreds of times before during the summer Obon in California.

The Obon season had begun, annual *matsuri*/festivals that

honored family with folk dancing under the summer moon and stars. The memory of ancestors was revived as bright lights and lively music attracted their spirits back to this world, even if for only a single dance. Through the clapping of hands, the beating of a *taiko*, and the twirling and spinning of dancers in colorful dress, I imagined seeing a glimpse of smiling ghosts who had returned to this village and reunited with family. A fusion of motion and spirit, Obon created an illusion, as the entire community danced in unison.

During the months of July and August, thousands of Japanese left the cities and returned to their native villages, an annual pilgrimage back to the land. For a few days, small rural towns churned with family reunions and a renewed sense of home. As I scanned the faces of the dancers, I could not distinguish the farmers from those that had departed for the cities. The smiles and laughing sounded the same.

As the music grew in intensity and more and more dancers joined the circles, I was transported someplace else. I whirled and clapped and found myself at the Buddhist temple in West Fresno, dragging my slippers along the black asphalt road, surrounded by my family and friends. There I danced alongside my cousins and aunts. We were grouped by communities, Fowler, Parlier, Reedley, Caruthers, with the largest contingent from Fresno. Those of us from Del Rey created a small but friendly gang.

I remember smiling at my *baachan* while she watched from the sidewalk, squatting or sitting on old *Fresno Bee* newspapers, smiling and clapping or holding my half-eaten Sno-cone as I completed my last dance before intermission. The warm summer night of the Central Valley of California was filled with folk songs, beating *taiko* rhythms, and the whirl of colors and movement. Our Obon broke the monotonous work rhythm of peaches and grapes; it was an opportunity to celebrate in the midst of harvest, to escape the fields if only for one evening and dance in the streets.

Along one edge of the park, I felt a cool breeze stirred by a small creek. Light from the dangling lanterns reflected on the shiny rocks, dampened with mist. As I turned away, a warm, humid wind stroked my face. I was sweating, my shirt damp and sticky; the scent of others joined with mine in the air.

Some dancers had stopped and stood to the side. They flapped with their hands, trying to generate a breeze on their faces. Others had paper fans beating quickly back and forth. They looked like a collection of moths fluttering their wings. I had seen this before, at the Obon festivals of my childhood, the Issei pulling out fans and waving them to push air over their warm faces.

The song repeated over and over, then was replaced by another record with no intermission. Participants spontaneously joined in or dropped out. They danced the same movements; a few added a different turn, but the basic motions were repeated. American Obon dances differed. We used five or six songs during the program, each with unique steps. We began most with a clap, watching the stage and waiting for the leaders to begin. When a song ended, we stopped, bowed to the audience, and paused before the next performance began.

I remember hearing Mrs. Kubota, Fresno's *odori-sensei*/Japanese dance teacher, sometimes helping us beginners by counting for us, then saying, "Now turn, turn and clap, clap." Her shrill but gentle voice became part of our songs, blending with the foreign-sounding Japanese instruments and folk songs on the records. Mrs. Kubota took pride in our movements because she choreographed each number, taking some movements from traditional Japanese steps, inventing others to create a showy, more open Japanese-American style.

"We should have fun when we dance," I recalled her saying. "And smile! Learning to be Japanese shouldn't be like work!"

The music grew louder, the beat faster; more and more dancers joined my circle. The ring swelled larger and larger. Then suddenly I sensed a gap had grown behind me. A section of dancers had broken off to form another outside circle. Stepping back, I regrouped with others, and we closed our ranks and became an inner ring, with the new one quickly forming around us.

FOR MONTHS, I had delayed meeting my Japanese relatives. I wanted to improve my Japanese language skills and make a good impression. I hoped that by studying very hard I could prepare myself for the visit and talk with family.

My mother's side of the family once called Hiroshima home. The rebuilt city, devastated after the atomic bomb during World War II, lay several hundred miles south of Tokyo. I wrote my mom, and she had to ask my aunts and uncles for names to contact. "We're not sure who's who," she wrote. "Maybe we can piece together something from a few old letters."

Using an incomplete listing, I sent letters to Hiroshima introducing myself, hoping to arrange a visit. The lone response confused me. The language was polite and formal, from a stranger to another stranger. I was told to write to another address, that the *ojiisan*/grandfather that I wanted to meet was not well. The daughter-in-law who wrote the note said she would be happy to meet me and accompany me to the Nomura house. Perhaps this woman could also help me locate the rest of Jiichan Sugimoto's family.

My father's parents immigrated from Kumamoto-ken, a province on Kyushu Island far to the south. Baachan Masumoto remembered images of her farming village outside the city of Kumamoto, but she had no idea of the address or street names. Nor did she know much about Jiichan Masumoto's village. We had had no contact with his family since his death twenty-five years ago.

My mother wrote that Baachan kept a few old letters from the Tanakas, her brother and his family. The delicate paper had faded yellow, and when opened, it cracked along the folds. Parts of the old address had crumbled into tiny pieces.

In my dorm mailbox, I found a letter from Kumamoto. At least I believed it was from there; I could read only some of the characters. I opened the envelope. The handwriting was awful, the strokes scribbled and uneven, perhaps from the shaky hand of an old man. According to the return address the letter originated in the little village called Takamura. It had to be from Baachan's brother, Tanaka-san. The envelope and paper felt familiar. I realized I had seen letters like this before.

Playing in Baachan's room, we kids sometimes sneaked a peak into her dresser drawers. The dark wooden chest had four drawers, the bottom one rarely used because of a broken pull handle. The dresser was not a valuable antique; the wood was a cheap pine or fir, and the joints had loosened. The drawers squealed when opened and often jammed in place, wedged against a side that was no longer squared. Buried beneath heavy shirts and pants, Baachan had carefully wrapped some letters and documents in cloth or newspaper. Her few letters from Japan intrigued me. The stamps had images of wild-looking warriors. The odd writing in vertical patterns looked strange and mysterious. The rice paper felt delicate and fragile, thin and frail, with black strokes painted into characters. Now I held a similar letter, quite possibly written by the same person.

I sought help from a Japanese student down the hall. Nishimura-san was studying to be an engineer and was one of the few upperclassmen living in our dorm. He was from a rural province in central Japan and had once attended an American college for a year as an exchange student.

"*Heeeiii*. Masumoto-san, who wrote this letter?" he asked. I told him the story, and he nodded his head. "This writing is beautiful. I have not seen this in many, many years, since leaving home."

"*Honto?*"—Really? I blurted and swallowed hard.

"These characters are the old-style Japanese writing, *mukashi, mukashi*"—old times, old times. "Since the war, we no longer use many of these *kanji*, Masumoto-san. They are too complicated. We all learn a simplified version, with fewer strokes. But this writing is like art!"

He stopped and wrote a few characters in the air with his finger, trying to identify meanings and translate the sentences. He then grabbed a pen and experimented by writing a few on paper, massaging the characters and adapting them to their modern-day equivalent.

Nishimura-san reread the letter out loud, and I took notes. "Tanaka-san invites you to visit in the spring. They are alone now with lots of empty rooms in the farmhouse." On the top of one page there was a hand-drawn map of Japan and the location of Kumamoto, far to the south from Tokyo. Tanaka-san had sketched another drawing showing that their village lay to the west of the town. I chuckled, because the distance from Tokyo to Kumamoto on his map appeared to be the same as from the city to their village. He wanted me to come visit, to stay with them. His children were now spread out across Japan. A daughter lived nearby and was married to a farmer, a son lived in Kumamoto city and owned a small appliance business, and two other sons were elsewhere.

Nishimura-san finished and said, "Too bad you don't know enough Japanese to read his writing. This is quite an honor. Masumoto-san, you should go stay with this *ojiisan*."

six

VILLAGE
CHILD

A SUITCASE CRASHED AGAINST THE BACK OF MY LEGS. MY KNEES
buckled and I stumbled forward before regaining my balance.

"*Sumimasen,*" said a small woman tumbling out of the train.
She followed an oversized case into the crowd, its weight pulling
her along like a large dog on a leash. She quickly dipped her
flushed face, gesturing an apologetic bow as she brushed past. I
watched her weave through the crowds, the suitcase slicing a
path, wedging itself between bodies, her head and shoulders rocking up and down bowing to each victim as she disappeared into

the mass of travelers that had poured into Kumamoto station.

Away from the train door people began to crush around me, surging toward the few exits. All I could see was the backs of strangers, arms squeezed together, shoulders and heads swaying with the shuffling crowd. A deafening noise rose, individual voices blurred into a single fevered pitch, swelling with the movement of bodies. I tried to stand motionless so as not to contribute to the crazed energy of the mob, but was pushed forward by unidentified hands and bodies. It seemed as if everyone had direction, knew exactly where to go.

The gray of the concrete platform slowly became visible as the crowds filtered out. People began to cluster into groups as friends reconnected and families reunited. Directly under the Kumamoto station sign, one group huddled, a tight cluster of bodies packed together warding off the rush of the unloading passengers. Their heads turned and eyes darted from body to body, scanning the station in search of someone. A college-age boy broke from the passenger mob and faced the group. Both sides stared at each other for a few seconds across a five-foot gap, a silent moment with passing bodies cutting between. Then a flurry of bows broke the trance— deep, low bows, a welcome-home gesture by a Japanese family— and two small children raced to the boy with broad smiles.

Travelers continued to fill the station, spilling from the train and flooding the platform. Gradually when the confusion passed, I began to study the few passengers sitting on a wooden wall, then the faces of others standing around a magazine and candy stand in one corner of the station. White cigarette butts dotted the gray floor along with trampled sheets of newspaper. An old custodian worked his way behind the remaining few, sweeping up the trash.

A steel roof jutted out over the platform and partially enclosed the station. A band of blue sky covered the tracks and trains. Iron braces rose along the dull concrete walls and supported the roof. Small ticket windows broke the monochrome gray, along with an occasional travel poster coated with the grime from the trains and crowds. Soon, with the arrival of the next train, the platform again teamed with life, then the gray returned as travelers journeyed onward. Evidence of their passage was left behind in smoldering cigarette butts and new smudges on the posters and walls.

Somewhere in the station a bell rang. A voice over the loudspeaker blared a warning, and a few late passengers ran and leaped onto the departing train. The doors slid shut and sealed each car, and the train pulled away. With my back toward the train, I stood on the station platform near the edge of the concrete. As the last car swished by I turned and watched it shoot into the glaring light at the end of the station building. The train continued on schedule, journeying to the south.

I had left Tokyo thirteen hours before, at one in the morning. As my train pulled out of the station, Tokyo was illuminated with a strange luster, the orange glow of city lights reflected off the smog-filled night sky. Unable to sleep, I settled into my seat and leaned against the cool window glass. For the first few hours, outlines of buildings raced past. With the morning's light, a transformation began. Nestled between the houses and crammed into any open space stood vegetable gardens; a blur of green swept by my train window, breaking the gray of the city. Gradually the lots grew into fields as the train journeyed deeper into the countryside, more and more of the land returning to farms. A patchwork of rice fields extended over the horizon and was crisscrossed with low earthen borders that divided the land into plots no larger than a barnyard. Families were plowing, breaking the winter seal, turning back the black soil with their small grass tillers.

I thought, "Like home in California, the spring work had begun." Living in Tokyo, I had forgotten the meanings of the changes of seasons. In the city they were little more than temperature fluctuations.

The train passed through small towns without stopping, the wheels clicking louder as the cars sped past the signs and the concrete loading platforms of these rural outposts. The train swayed methodically as it raced on. We first circled Mount Fuji, dwarfing us at its base where its slopes began gently to rise. After a stop in Kyoto, the journey continued south, through the mountain lands and their tunnels. I began to doze.

I awoke in Kyushu, the southern island of Japan. Near Kumamoto, the train entered a valley enclosed by mountains and low coastal bluffs. The rice fields with their miles of dikes and hundreds of irregular shapes stretched on both sides of the tracks; they created a design in the land, a pattern of family farms etched into the valley floor over the course of generations.

I thought of Highway 99 and the drive into the Central Valley of California. As you near Fresno, family farms with their small vineyards and orchards multiply and dominate the landscape, each with its own size and shape and diverse collection of fruits and soils. Both in California and Japan, these family farms are as varied as their owners.

Standing by myself in the emptying station, I began surveying the faces of the few old men. What if no one was here to meet me? What if I was wrong and Kumamoto was not the right area? What if there was no Tanaka family? But I had the letter as evidence. I patted my breast pocket and heard the reassuring crumpling of an envelope. In order that we might recognize each other, Satoru Tanaka had written in one of his letters, *"Mune ni, shiroi hankachi demo tsukette itte kudasai"*—please wear a white handkerchief in your breast pocket. I felt embarrassed by his idea and instead mailed a photograph of myself. I scanned the station, studying the various faces. This often resulted in a stranger awkwardly staring back at me, before we could quickly turn our eyes away.

I had practiced the greeting I would use when first introduced to Satoru Tanaka. Japanese employ a variety of honorifics, each with reference to a specific status and relationship. Elderly men are often referred to as Ojiisan, or Grandfather. But Ojiisan is a formal term. Ojiichan is less formal, reserved for family, and Jiichan is the most casual, most relaxed.

From across the station, a skinny, short-haired boy about ten or eleven began weaving his way toward me. At first I didn't pay any attention to the boy, but when he stopped and stared from a few feet away, I turned to face him. He was dressed in soiled tennis shoes, light blue jeans, and a white T-shirt that said "Havard."

The boy quickly dipped his head and shoulders, a gesture vaguely resembling a bow, and took a step toward me. He again hesitated, then raced for my suitcase. Japan does not have many thieves, at least very few that were ten years old. I returned the bow and watched the boy try to lift my heavy bag. His young muscles strained and gradually the case began to slide. He pulled the case and me toward one of the distant exits. In the doorway at the end of the station, half in sunlight and half in the station shadows, stood an old man clutching a photograph.

I froze. For a moment I believed I saw the features of my *baachan* in America. The old man was short, barely five feet, with a small build, not fat nor muscular. His hair was silvery white. His dark face contrasted with the white shirt he wore.

As I drew nearer, I saw facial wrinkles that cut deep into a weathered face, miniature channels etched into his skin as if each passing year had left a scar. This man, like Baachan, had spent a lifetime in the fields. The old man looked at me and the boy. His wrinkles moved in unison with each motion, a gentle shift of expression, a subtle look of curiosity punctuated by a slow closing of his eyes as he tried to peer through the bright glare and into the dark station interior.

He was wearing a dark suit that looked uncomfortable. The sleeves weren't quite even, a part of the shirt collar was outside the jacket, his dark brown-and-black-striped tie was crooked. Peeking from the bottom of his pants cuffs were wooden sandals and yellowed toenails.

A rehearsed scene flashed in my mind. I bowed, a low, deep bow and said, *"Konnichi wa Ojiisan Tanaka. Watakushi wa Masumoto desu keredomo. Hajimemashite."*—Good day, Grandfather Tanaka. I am Masumoto. It is good to meet you."

The old man studied my face, reexamined the photograph, and returned a stare. He nodded and said something in Kumamoto-ben, a country dialect of the region. I did not understand a word he said. The white-haired man concluded with a deep "ummh," nodded his head again, and turned toward the outside.

The young boy reached for my suitcase and herded me toward the passageway where other relatives stood waiting. *"Jiichan! Matte!"*—Grandpa! Wait up! the boy cried, struggling with the case and me. *"Matte Jiichan!"*

"Jiichan," I said to myself and weakly smiled. *"Jiichan."*

THREE PLATTERS OF *sushi* covered the surface of the low wooden table. I delicately set my *sake* glass in a space between the *makizushi* and *kappazushi*. My uncle immediately refilled it as we welcomed another guest into the farmhouse. I was not sure if I should rise with each new visitor. I heard them tap at the outside door, calling out a greeting as they slid it open. Then they walked into the *genkan*/entryway, slipped off their shoes, stepped up into the interior, and bowed.

I did not stand. We sat on *tatami*/straw mats, legs crossed with heaps of food spread before us, and large green liter bottles of *sake* scattered around the table. My head spun even while I was sitting. I could not understand every word and instead responded only to simple questions. "Welcome to our village, Masumoto-san." "How was your train ride?" *"Heeeiii*, you do look like one of the family." I dipped my head and bowed when it seemed appropriate. These guests spoke with heavy accents and word combinations I did not completely understand. Fortunately conversations quickly turned to Jiichan Tanaka or my uncle as more *sushi* was served and even more *sake* consumed.

I had no idea who most of these people were. I assumed they

were village neighbors. The majority were old men with dark tans and sharply defined wrinkles in their foreheads and temples. They sat and talked about me and my family, and I occasionally heard "Kariforuniya" in the middle of a sentence. Then they talked about the weather, the village, the rice planting, or life in Kumamoto city. Most of the visitors were farmers, peers of Jiichan Tanaka. They still worked the land and lived in the farm houses that made up the village of Takamura. Their hands were all very rough, callused from years in the fields.

I asked if they knew Jiichan Masumoto. Some had met him but didn't say much more. He was from a nearby village; the Masumotos were a hardworking family. "Do you know the village? Do they own a farm? Is any of the family still living?" None of them knew exactly. They did not know of a Masumoto farm. Jiichan Tanaka was silent. Baachan Tanaka said she would ask others later. I kept thinking of their phrase "hardworking." It must mean the Masumotos were poor.

A man in his forties dropped by. He was accompanied by small children, the only ones I had seen. The village seemed deserted of youth. Later, another man in his thirties tapped at the door but refused to come in. In the entryway, he stood in his dirty workclothes—straw clung to his black pants and dried sweat stained his gray workshirt with a band of white salt crystals. He smiled broadly with a mouthful of crooked teeth, dipped his head as we were introduced, then sounds burst from his lips so fast and rough I was not sure if he was speaking Japanese. He gulped a shot of *sake* and spoke with even more authority as his small glass was refilled. He abruptly ended, mimicked some movement to depict the farmwork he had yet to complete, then bowed to me and raised his cup. We toasted each other, and after another gulp, he trudged out the entryway into the glaring late-afternoon sunshine and greeted the outdoors with a loud, high-pitched, "*Saaaaa. . .*"

As the brilliant sun set, only half of the *sushi* had been consumed and three or four large bottles of *sake* sat unopened. I excused myself and asked where the toilet was. Baachan Tanaka took me outside to an adjoining outhouse. Behind a narrow door lay a cemented hole with a black pit below. Sunlight angled in through cracks in the walls. The smell was overwhelming. I held my breath but I could not remain within the small closet for very long. I stepped back outside and heard Jiichan relieving himself into a small round cement basin set into the ground that connected to the outhouse pit. I followed his lead and urinated with a sigh. A gentle breeze tickled my face and the smell of blooming flowers filled my lungs. Behind me I heard a set of voices and shoes and slippers tramping along the dirt and gravel paths toward me. My head still was light from the alcohol, and I could not and did not want to stop. And what option did I have—quickly turn around and greet the voices? But the party turned into the farmhouse and passed by me. No one knocked before entering, and I overheard a different, very informal set of greetings—the rest of the family. Another uncle and aunt and some cousins had arrived and entered the farmhouse to await my arrival.

"You have our family's face," said the aunt, the only daughter of Jiichan Tanaka. She had married a farmer and lived in a neighboring village within walking distance. She knew Baachan Masumoto only from a few photographs, but I too could see a family resemblance in her face. Her husband was drinking glassfuls of *sake* and smiled at me. His son and young wife also sat to the side, along with another set of cousins, the young boy I recognized from the train station and his sister, who leaned against their mom. Baachan Tanaka served dinner and we devoured the remaining *sushi*.

After dinner I remembered my *omiyage*/gifts and passed out the raisins. This began a series of questions about our farm in California. I tried to explain how raisins were made and ended up showing them by laying a large sheet of paper on the *tatami* mats and pouring a box of raisins on top. They could not believe that each berry was sun-dried.

"Too much work!" said my cousin, who was running the family farm of twenty hectares of rice and barley and a small herd of twenty milkers.

Baachan said something, but I could not translate her term. After consulting a few dictionaries I discovered she had said "risky."

"Only a farmer will do such a thing. They're such fools!" said an uncle who had drunk too many gulps of *sake*. "I guess that means me too!" We laughed and made a toast to all the foolish farmers in the world.

The evening unfolded with a series of half conversations about and half pantomiming of farmwork. When I ignored the parts I could not translate and instead focused on what I did understand, I seemed to comprehend much more. We tolerated each other's incomplete descriptions and thoughts. We seemed to speak the language of family and farms. As we relaxed and slipped into long conversations, I whispered a thanks to the aunt in California who had convinced me to lug these raisins to Japan.

The fifty-year-old eyes of the farmer uncle who drank too much drooped farther with each gulp, and his grin renewed with every sigh, a soft, low and contented moan—"Aaahhh."

Baachan brought us a bowl of steamed crab, the red shells and white underbodies swimming in a small pool of hot water. The uncle proudly explained these treats were from a nearby waterway, a local harvest. With his fingers, he drew lines on the *tatami*, attempting to create a map of the area and orient me. His rough movements looked as if he were writing *kanji*. We turned our attention to the crabs, and he struggled to pick out some of the meat with his blunt fingers. I imagined after years and years of milking, his hands had grown stiff.

As we both tried to break open our crab legs he said, "What work to get only a little meat." He then added a phrase, *"Mendookusai!"* With a growling voice, he abruptly shoved the entire leg into his mouth and bit down, crunching the shell and all.

We all chuckled. Others yelled, "Uncle, how rude!"

He repeated, "*Mendookusai!*" I correctly translated his Japanese: "What a pain in the ass!"

My aunt tried to explain something about music and a *kimono* and asked if I'd like to see some dancing. As soon as I said yes, she scrambled out the door. She returned in a few minutes, out of breath from running home. In her arms was a bag and a small portable record player. She was beginning to unbutton her clothes when someone interrupted, "Uchida-san . . . you should change someplace else!"

My aunt suddenly looked up, giggled, and said, "Oh, I guess so," and giggled again as she dragged her clothes and the bag behind a screen.

She emerged in beautiful silk and strolled around the table, a graceful "swoosh, swoosh" accompanying each stride as the folds of the delicate fabric gently rubbed together. Her chubby frame was lost behind the layers of kimono dress, her face patted smooth with a white powder. She put a warped record on the player, and a scratchy folk song began. *Taiko* pounded and a *shamizen* and *koto* harmonized with an upbeat shrill voice. We followed the graceful movements of my aunt while her round frame whirled and spun and her strong hands twisted and rose. She rotated her head and turned her face, her dark brown eyes staring into space as she performed the dance.

The record skipped a beat or two from a scratch, but it didn't faze my aunt. She shifted forward, swinging her arms to the right, where they momentarily locked in place, then stepped back, dropping her arms and eyes to the left. Then as she looked up, her hands rose and extended outward to each side, shoulder-high. We were mesmerized by the fluid movements and the many glasses of *sake*.

Then she suddenly froze, her body locked in a classic dance pose, palms down, arms spread like wings, long sleeves dangling and shimmering, her face tilted with a contemplative expression.

Her legs shifted beneath the colorful silk, and she turned her hips in a slow, smooth motion as if she were suspended in midair, drifting above us. She broke into a grin and blurted, "*Ara* . . . I can't remember the rest!" She quickly bowed and stopped the record. We burst out in both applause and laughter at her abrupt finale. She beamed proudly.

From the darkness outside, I heard a tapping. A soft voice said, "*Sumimasen*," followed by a grating squeal of wood scraping wood as the outer door was opened. Two people entered the enclosed porchlike entry room, the *genkan*. I could see the silhouettes against the *shoji* screen as they removed their shoes and stepped up into the house. The door slid open and an old woman dipped her head and slipped inside. Behind her was a middle-aged man. The others greeted them and moved to make room for their new guests at the low table.

She sat with her frail eighty-year-old legs tucked beneath her. Her hands rested in her lap, clutching a small cup of hot tea that had been handed to her. She had a pleasant face with deep wrinkles cut into her dark skin. She said in broken English, "Hal-lo. How are ryooou?"

I paused, and she took a deep breath.

Slowly, she enunciated, "I am Mrs. Honda. I know your *ojiisan* and *obaasan*." She gently smiled and then shifted into Japanese. "We worked together many years in Selma and Fowler. Our families knew each other. Your Jiisan was a hard worker. He always did his job *isshokenmei!*"—with all his effort.

I was shocked by her use of English. My head spun and I tried to force myself not to translate her words and instead simply to listen to her. "Outside of work, what was Jiichan Masumoto like?" I asked.

"Oh, I can't tell you that. It was so many years ago!" she answered. "Both your *ojiisan* and *obaasan* were quiet and strong. I only knew them until the war."

She then relayed a story I had thought to be rumor. Some very devout Buddhist families from the Fresno area had organized protests during evacuation. They rallied behind a Buddhist minister who was a strong Japanese nationalist. He felt that no country should treat its own people like prisoners and convicts. He preached that if they had no secure place in the United States they should repatriate back to Japan. Mrs. Honda's family was among the protesters. She returned to her native village and became a field worker. But life following the war was very difficult. She repeated, "*Muzukashii*"—difficult—and paused.

After a long silence, she added, "But you have a Masumoto face, neh!" She nodded her head and then, with a slurping sound, took a long sip of her tea.

Farmhouse

The Japanese *kanji* for house is written in two sections. The top ideograph is a long straight line with small squared angles at the ends and a very short line, more like a dot, on the center top. This represents a building or structure, and if you stare long enough, the lines resemble a flat roof with curved eaves. The bottom is a series of seven lines that don't really look like anything except perhaps a collection of twisted feet and legs and a body. I am told this represents a pig. Home means a pig resting beneath a shelter, protected and secure.

Jiichan's farmhouse looked like the face of an old man with wrinkles and age spots. The wood had weathered into a dark brown, and the siding was cracked and split. Knots had worked loose and left behind a series of holes. Some were patched with rusting tin-can lids, others remained uncovered, allowing sunlight to pierce the interiors like a natural spotlight. When I rubbed my fingers against the siding, the decades of dirt and dust stained my fingertips. If I rubbed too hard, fine slivers from the weathered grain drifted downward like ashes. A rusting corrugated red steel roof covered the house. In spots the sheet metal had worked loose and flapped in the wind. Along the roof edges, I saw remnants of the thatch that had once protected the interior. The overall structure was not large. A wooden veranda ran along on the southern exposure, and there, along a rail, Baachan Tanaka aired colorful *futon* and blankets in the warm sun.

The entrance door was located in the southeastern corner. Propped open, the doorway could accommodate objects five or six feet wide. When the door was slid open, I was initially surprised by the screeching rails. I expected the wood to be worn smooth from decades of use, but instead, stubborn knots scraped against the runners. The gnawing wail served as an unofficial doorbell. The bottom of the door had once been a solid panel of wood. Multiple splits were now evident, and a series of horizontal planks had been nailed over the gaps to prevent them from growing. The top half of the door was formed of vertical strips. Air, wind, and sunlight passed through the slits and into the entryway. There was no lock, only a worn handle and grooves where generations of fingers had found a grip. The door should have been replaced years ago, but it still worked, and we tolerated the morning and evening squeal as Jiichan opened and closed his home for the day.

The *genkan*/entryway could be called a halfway place, half inside but not yet in the interior of the house. In all Japanese homes, the *genkan* is like a welcome mat, inviting guests out of the weather while they wait to be greeted. Traditionally, on farms, this area is large enough to keep a few animals, especially during the winter months. I was reminded of a few old Midwestern dairies, where the milking parlor is connected to the main house. Cows and family are on equal footing.

The floor of our *genkan* was packed earth. Much of the space was cluttered with old boxes and piles of junk. String and twine filled three cardboard boxes. Short wooden stakes were piled near an old workbench where dust-covered tools were scattered. Some tools hung from the wall; most had been shoved aside to make room for a stack of small wooden boxes. Used burlap bags with a faded emblem of a seed company were shoved near the door, and a gathering of old milk cans were stacked precariously against a wall. More boxes were stuffed to overflowing with old newspapers, rags, and random pieces of wire. A gathering of old trunks huddled together. The leather straps had dried brittle and curled along the edges; the boxes were locked, and I was sure the key had been misplaced. I knew the value of this collection of farm junk: farmers will always claim it has a future use, if not for them, then for the next farmer.

While the rest of the house was elevated two or three feet high and covered with *tatami* mats, the kitchen and *ofuro*/bath area shared the same earthen floor with the entry. Baachan prepared meals on a series of small gas burners. Long ago, an indoor fire area had been used, next to the bath, which was still heated with a fire beneath a cast-iron tub. Huge gray sheet-metal containers, three feet wide and four feet high, lined one wall of the *genkan* and were filled with rice. Above them a horizontal flat plank had some carved line marks. I asked what they meant, and Jiichan said something about counting, but he did not recall much more. It reminded me of a farmer's simple bookkeeping method to track his harvests.

A collection of shoes sat on shelves beneath the step into the house. Jiichan's old tattered sandals and worn leather shoes rested on the top shelf. On lower shelves sat some guest slippers, along with Baachan's odd assortment of canvas slip-ons and flaps. On the bottom shelf the hierarchy was jumbled, with dozens of pairs piled atop each other. I recognized a few work boots that must have belonged to the nearby aunt and uncle. Dust had formed a powdery veil over most pairs, and on the sandals, spiderwebs mummified the toe openings. The shoes belonged to a generation that had once called this place home. I imagined during occasional visits, even the far-flung sons and daughters rediscovered their old shoes and slipped into them. I found a spot for my slippers by stacking them atop a child's pair of faded black tennis shoes, long ago abandoned but never removed. Now others could tell if I was at home.

A series of *shoji* opened into the main living area. These rice-paper-covered screens separated the private interior from the entryway, but they did not prevent sounds from escaping outside. I could easily see shadows of Jiichan and Baachan at their low table. The panels represented a dividing line between the outside and inside, the public and private. Long ago small fingers had punched holes into the paper, and smudge marks stained the delicate white membrane a dark brown. I knew soon I too would become careless and tear a hole in the *shoji*.

The sweet smell of *tatami* greeted me as I entered. The entire house was composed of a series of these straw mats, each about three by six feet with a stitched fabric border that held the straw ends in place. Beneath my bare feet I felt the smooth natural texture of the cool matting. When all the interior panels were opened, I could see through the house. A cool spring breeze wandered inside and visited. The bright glare of the outside illuminated the interiors with soft, natural light. Open beams exposed the architecture of the structure, ancient wood timbers stretching overhead in a complex series of trusses and rafters hidden in the shadows. I asked Jiichan how old this farmhouse was, and he did not know. He said this was the only home he knew.

There were no chairs and very little furniture. Sleeping *futon* were rolled up and stored daily. For meals and conversation, we all gathered around a two-foot-high table. Jiichan was seated on the *tatami* at his table spot, I sat across from him, and because I had a wonderful view outside, I felt I had the prized location. But Jiichan was framed by the powder-blue sky of spring, the lush green garden, and the weathered shed and outbuilding. He occupied the honored space as the head of the household.

Along one wall, an alcove housed a *butsudan*/Buddhist altar. The hand-carved wooden pillars and vinelike lattice had an uncanny similarity to the one my folks had in California. Jiichan Sugimoto had crafted our *butsudan*; he was a devout Buddhist and had tried to make a *butsudan* for each member of the family. Mom told me that after a workday in the fields of California, he'd spend hours whittling and carving, nailing and shaping wood into Japanese pagodas, temples, and altars. The Sugimoto family had a Japanese garden of his art—a miniature Japan he visited daily. *Hakujin*/Caucasian neighbors admired his wood crafting. They even asked if they could have it during the final moments before relocation. Mom said men came and took it away. They never saw it again.

Each morning Jiichan Tanaka knelt before the altar, lit incense and tapped a small chime, then silently meditated. The incense danced in the morning stillness and the high-pitched bell resonated throughout the house. Jiichan chanted softly, a whisper that awakened me from my sleep.

A large wall clock hung in a corner, surrounded by layers and layers of calendars nailed atop each other. The clock's wood had aged into a dark chocolate brown, and while winding it, Jiichan Tanaka told me that my *baachan* in America knew this clock. "One of the few things she will remember," he added. At night, the ticking filled the silence. I lay under layers of *futon* blankets, wondering if this was the room Baachan Masumoto had slept in as she dreamed of her journey to America. And did the chimes keep her awake at night too?

Art of the Ofuro

As the steam rose from the hot water, I slipped into the *ofuro*/bath. I soaked in a heat that penetrated muscles worn from farmwork. I grew light-headed and flushed, enveloped in the simple purity of water warmed by a fire tended by a *baachan*. The Japanese perfected the hot tub centuries ago.

Nightly I enjoyed a bath in an ancient metal vessel that resembled an inverted bell. Baachan made a small fire beneath it and we took turns stoking the flame until the embers glowed red. I then stepped up onto a narrow landing, shed my clothes, and kneeled next to the tub, scooping the first tepid water with a shallow wooden pan. The liquid poured down my hair and splashed onto my shoulders, then ran down my back. The second pan sent a wave of heat shimmering down my body, the water cascading down my face, then running over my chest, coating my lower torso and trickling to my feet. I immediately shivered, as the chill of the evening air met my wet skin. Picking up a bar of soap and an old, stiff rag, I washed outside the tub, rinsing off with a third dip of heated water. Another chill quickly followed, nudging me to the tub edge.

I gingerly dipped my toes, testing the water temperature and gently putting pressure on the round wooden raft that floated on the surface. As I transferred my weight, the wooden board sank and protected my feet from burning on the hot metal bottom. By curling myself into a fetal position, I avoided touching the hot metal tub around me. I sighed long and slow, as I'm sure others had done before while they too eased into the cleansing water.

Following a day in the fields, an *ofuro* tempered worn and broken spirits. The soothing water fostered a benevolence and a feeling of optimism. My best thinking was done during and right after an *ofuro*.

Ofuro water was shared. By washing outside first, one kept the water clean for others. A male bias determined the traditional order of bathing, the head of the household first, followed by the other men and finally the women. The origins of this hierarchy may have been related to farmwork, aching muscles needing the massaging heat before they could relax, yet it seemed on many days, Baachan worked harder than any of us men and she still bathed last.

The honor of bathing first was based on the faulty premise

that the new water was the best. But the initial bather must be careful, for the heat from below created layers of water of different temperatures. The uninitiated usually waited until the surface temperature reached perfection, only to jump in and scorch their toes as they sank deeper and deeper. The water had to be mixed. Either you leaned over and stirred it with one arm and hand while the rest of your body grew chilled outside the tub, or you sacrificed toes and stepped in, mixing the layers of temperatures with your body.

I discovered this after a week when, as a guest, I was allowed to bathe first. I felt awkward, disrupting a farmhouse rhythm that was decades old and watching Jiichan sit at his table spot, waiting for me to finish before he could enjoy *his* bath. By the second week I asked Jiichan to go first, an honor we both readily accepted.

Every night, I shared my *ofuro* with a hundred ghosts who once used this bath. Most were family from generations before me. We participated in a simple tradition, heating water for each other, soaking while thinking of harvests, enveloped by steam that rose and danced with the smoke overhead. We bathed together in a place my family once called home.

Many older Japanese-American houses had their own *ofuro*, before rural electrification and running hot water. They made their tubs from galvanized sheet metal folded into a rectangle two and a half feet by three feet and about thirty inches deep. The edges were rolled into a curl to prevent cuts, creating a smooth surface. No different from in Japan, each had a wooden raft that sank under the bather's weight and protected feet from burning on the hot metal bottom. Over the years, the nails that held the raft in a simple lattice pattern often worked loose from the constant swelling with moisture. Usually more nails were tapped in, holding the raft together for another year or two. After two generations, few bare spots of wood survived for another round of repairs. Eventually the metal bottom deteriorated from the daily fires. I remember, while I was growing up, dozens of these discarded baths resting in farm junk piles next to discarded disk blades and broken spring tooth shanks and bent pipes. One ingenious farmer used an acetylene torch to cut an old *ofuro* in half, added a grill, and made it into a huge, portable barbecue pit for community picnics and *teriyaki* chicken.

The *ofuro* seemed like the one luxury the Issei allowed themselves. Life in the fields was harsh, and many dreams quickly melted in the San Joaquin Valley's hundred-degree days of summer harvest or froze during the tedious pruning on cold, damp, foggy mornings. The blazing fire, the hot water, the soothing steam—the *ofuro* connected Issei to a Japan they left behind and the hope, excitement, and fears they had carried across an ocean.

I can remember visiting neighbors and watching their grandfathers and grandmothers head out for an evening bath. The *ofuro* was often located in an outbuilding with a worn path from the main house. In the cool evening air, seventy-year-old legs shuffled through the dirt and sandals flopped against the bottom of feet, creating a pat-pat, pat-pat cadence. They walked with a slight slouch, leaning forward in a gentle, almost graceful bend. In their arms they carried a small towel and clean night clothes. Later I heard the sighs of comfort as they talked to themselves, whispering in Japanese. Sometimes I could hear them humming a Japanese folk song like "Akatombo," "Red Dragonfly." "*Yuu-yake, A-ka tom-bo . . .*" Perhaps they were singing with ghosts.

In my childhood, I enjoyed taking an *ofuro* with my brother and sister, all of us literally swimming in the tepid water. The three siblings were required to bathe together in order to create enough weight to sink the raft and avoid the hot metal bottom. With only two, we were tossed and jolted. With only one, the raft precariously floated on the surface. Baachan stoked the fire for us, and in between giggles and laughing we'd scream about her making the fire too hot (we had all seen the roasting chicken at picnics). But she'd answer us in Japanese and toss another grapevine stump onto the red embers, waiting for our clamoring response of joy and protest.

When Jiichan Tanaka took his *ofuro*, I usually tended the fire for him, stoking the flames and gathering kindling wood for Baachan's bath. I discovered two approaches to building a good *ofuro* fire. One was to burn the wood gradually and methodically until healthy embers glowed in the firepit. The deep red color indicated a deeply penetrating, even heat, toasting the metal tub and simmering the water.

The other method required less attention and very little patience. I often stuffed the hearth with thick logs and odd pieces of lumber, initially fanning the small pile of coals until they ignited the rest of the fuel. Smoke rose from my pile, overwhelming the small ventilation pipe in the roof, gathering into a small cloud in the eaves, layering as a fog a few feet above the ground. Jiichan, sitting in the *ofuro*, sometimes opened his eyes and saw the world in a haze and loudly growled, as if clearing his throat. Following his signal, Baachan opened a screen door and window to circulate fresh air. I'd then stop jamming green wood into my fire and try, without success, to stop the smoldering smoke.

My impatient fire-building methods eventually created a raging blaze that scorched the bottom of the metal tub and rapidly heated the water. Being a novice, I assumed this was good for the *ofuro*, making for a good, hot bath. I'd ask, "How's the water?"

Jiichan answered with long groans, "Uhmmm . . ." which I interpreted as a positive affirmation of my work.

But once I sensed my rapid fire method overheated the water and he grumbled something about the heat. He then pretended not to mind the rising temperature as I pumped in more and more wood. Finally he stepped out with a beet-red body. I thought I had scorched him from the neck down. Fortunately, Baachan started laughing. She said something with a very heavy Kumamoto accent—possibly a shared phrase between a wife and husband, a familiar bantering between a couple married for over a half century. Jiichan answered her with a loud grunt accompanied with a half grin. I quickly went to bed that night.

Another time I made the water too hot from the beginning. As Jiichan stepped in, he was forced to jump out to avoid burning his feet. I laughed. Jiichan turned a handle and added cool water. "Now the *ofuro* will be too cold for Baachan," he said dryly.

One evening I found the bath filled with green stalks and some leaves. I asked Baachan, "What's floating in this water?"

She grinned while adding more wood to the fire and said, "It's for your health. Get in."

As I squatted in the tub, the water rose and the stalks floated around me, encircling my chest. I felt as if I were bathing in tea.

"What will this grass do?" I ask.

"For your family," said Baachan.

I didn't understand. "How will it help my parents?"

"No. For *your* family." I detected a subtle smile on her face. "The grass will help you get married."

My thoughts raced wild. Was this some sort of aphrodisiac? If so, this village would frustrate me—in weeks I hadn't seen an unmarried woman, and the average age of the entire village was well over fifty. Perhaps Baachan was insinuating that I needed to visit town. But that would have been risky. If Baachan's potion was powerful, she might trick me into marrying a Kumamoto girl and remaining here on their farm forever. She always told me that "country girls" were safe and to watch out for those girls from the big cities like Tokyo. "They don't understand the country folk and will take you away," she warned.

Baachan never explained what kind of grass I bathed with. When I stepped out of the water, the stalks clung to my back and legs. I peeled them off and asked if they still had enough power for Jiichan. Baachan laughed and chuckled, "Oh no. He's too old."

When I first bathed in this farmhouse, it felt odd to stand naked outside the *ofuro*. Often, as I finished drying myself,

Baachan stood only a few feet away cleaning up the kitchen area. When she took her bath and I prepared kindling for the next night's fire, I'd catch glimpses of her nude frame and quickly turn away, embarrassed.

Both she and Jiichan had a modest way of washing. They usually stood with their backs toward me and turned to scoop the rinse water without baring their private areas. Then with a swift turn and step, their bodies would slip into the bathwater. They bathed without exposing themselves.

I tried to copy their methods and still acted too self-consciously. I washed with a hand towel covering my genitals as if I were hiding something. Of course, I was, but from whom? The Japanese seemed to be very modest about revealing themselves, especially in public places. Young women hid giggles with their hands and adults dressed very conservatively, as if to conceal their bodies. But when I disrobed, Baachan and Jiichan seemed to ignore me and continued tending the fire and finishing chores. Initially I felt invisible. Then I realized they acted unconcerned because in this context, nudity was normal. Soon I was stepping from the water with a lack of inhibition. Toweling myself dry and slipping into a *yukata*/robe felt natural. The *ofuro* was a private, family time, integral to becoming part of this family.

During one *ofuro*, I asked about Jiichan Masumoto. Baachan Tanaka spoke about some photographs and later showed me a collection of family portraits sent from America. I had seen some, but others were new. We both tried to figure out who was who as I struggled to imagine my uncles and aunts as toddlers. In the first two portraits, Jiichan Masumoto proudly stood with his new wife, then later with their first child. He wore the same suit in each photo, with a watch chain hanging from his vest pocket. But by the third photo, Baachan sat holding a baby in her arms with four children surrounding her. She looked weary. Jiichan was nowhere to be found. We joked that he probably was at home, happily working in the fields.

Later, we sat at the small table to study the collection of family photos. I asked why Jiichan Masumoto had immigrated to America. Neither knew, and both shook their heads.

Finally Baachan Tanaka answered, "For a better life."

Jiichan Tanaka seemed to nod a confirmation, but I could not clearly decipher his response. His arms were crossed in front of him, his body rocked slightly forward and backward, his eyes slowly blinked two or three times. His eyes lifted from the table and photographs to peer outward into the darkness of the house. Then he abruptly yawned, sucking air into his lungs, and, with a sigh, exhaled.

Ohakamairi/*Before the Graves*

We drove into the countryside, along narrow roads I did not recognize, then turned into a neighboring village where a concrete-and-steel building hugged one side of the street. The dull gray structure rested in the shadows of the late-afternoon sun. Though the grime of the street traffic dirtied the sign over the entry door, I recognized enough *kanji* to read "hospital."

Baachan sighed, "How unfortunate," and rambled about how families were changing, even here in the *inaka*/countryside. "This is where people who are alone must live."

The smell of urine struck me even before I entered the doorway. Inside there was a shrieking voice wailing in the back room, and a few patients in wheelchairs sat in the hallway. Most stared blankly at walls and the bright light of the entryway. A few turned to us as we walked by, reaching out as if to see if we were real. Baachan chatted with a nurse, and we were led to a large room with a series of beds along one wall. There an old women lay resting. Her frail body shook and her sunken eyes appeared large and round. When she turned her head and her eyes scanned the room, she looked like an owl surveying the landscape.

Baachan leaned over and whispered to the woman. She seemed to stir and blinked rapidly three or four times, perhaps a sign that she was pleased to have visitors. I heard Baachan say, "Masumoto," and the ancient eyes turned to study me. I watched dry, cracked lips move as she tried to utter some words. Mucus and saliva stuck to the insides of her mouth, creating weblike strands attached to her top and bottom lips.

She then whispered something to Baachan with a raspy voice. Baachan waved me closer and said, "This is Obaasan Masumoto."

I bowed and realized this old woman was the first Masumoto in Japan I had met. I wanted to ask her dozens of questions, about our family, the native village, and about Jiichan Masumoto. Instead I blurted, "How are you, Obaasan?"

The woman opened her mouth and attempted to speak, but I heard only a long garbled sigh. She held her eyes closed for a long time before she tried to reopen them. A semiliquid pus stuck to her eyelashes and kept her right eye sealed.

I was still unsure who this woman was—my grandfather's sister or an aunt or cousin? Baachan Tanaka did not know either and could not explain it to me. She simply called the old woman "family."

I was leaning over to ask another question when the Obaasan reached up with her trembling hand. She grabbed my arm tightly, and I could feel her bony joints. I imagined this woman had spent many hours in the fields during her lifetime—her grasp was strong, and she did not let go. I dipped my head to her, and the grasp became tighter. I felt awkward and uneasy, suddenly wanting to step away. One of the moments I had hoped for in my search for family would now be etched in my memory as a chilly grip. The old woman's face suddenly broke into a smile, a toothless grin that made her look like a giggling infant.

Months later, in the middle of summer when the rice fields stood high and the countryside was filled with lush green growth, we went *ohakamairi*—to visit the cemetery. I knew this ritual from my childhood. Our family visited a small mausoleum in Fresno, a white stucco building with a Spanish tile roof. Opening the wooden doors, we located the little bronze plaque with Jiichan Sugimoto's name on it and bowed before it. Then we'd drive out to the cemetery in Selma where Jiichan Masumoto was buried. I enjoyed the cemetery visit more. A breeze often accompanied us as we walked the grassy rise. A silence enveloped our family as we carried flowers to the headstones, placing a bouquet at Jiichan's grave and then later at my Uncle George's. I could sense why they called this "a final resting place"; the open air felt soothing, and the solitude calming. I often took Baachan Masumoto to the cemetery, and when she grew older, she sometimes became disoriented and asked me to help find Jiichan and her son. We walked and read the names of all the other Japanese families. She nodded and said little. I became curious and wondered what she was thinking. Then she showed me the empty plot next to Jiichan that was for her.

The Takamura village cemetery sat in the exact middle of a field. The slender and narrow headstones were tightly clustered together. From a distance, it looked like a compact island of miniature skyscrapers floating in a green sea of grass. Like most things in Japan, cemeteries are designed for optimal efficiency of space—each stone belonged to a family and names were added as needed. My uncle joked that he visited the cemetery often, and with each pass down his field, he dipped his head and bowed out of gratitude. "How thankful I am for all those ancestors. They don't take much space! Japanese always thinking of the next generation, *ne?*"

Jiichan and Baachan showed me the Tanaka family column. I read their family *kanji* but did not recognize the list of names etched into the surface. Baachan pointed out the Masumoto family stone. The old-style *kanji* looked peculiar and strange but familiar. I would not have recognized it if Baachan hadn't helped me. We put our hands together, bowed, and chanted a Buddhist prayer, *"Namu amida butsu"*—I entrust my life in the Buddha of immeasurable life and light.

The summer breeze rustled the stalks of rice and scurried past us. Hiding in the cool shadows, the fragile morning dew quickly evaporated with the wind. On the granite stones, the ashes of incense others had burned were scattered. The Masumoto family was buried in this small country cemetery, but I could not help and wonder about my family in America. As I visited these graves, I thought of the living and not the dead.

seven

F I E L D
W O R K

WITH BOTH HANDS CLUTCHING THE BURLAP, JIICHAN STUMBLED
while walking backward, dragging a bag of seeds from the shed
to a borrowed pickup. He stopped every few feet to rest, leaving
behind a crooked trail etched in the yard dirt. I took his bag and
heaved it onto the bed. Each sack kicked up a small cloud of dust
when it landed. A neighbor hopped into the cab and delivered our
load to the fields. Jiichan and I followed on foot.

A series of small roads zigzagged through the countryside. At
times we took short cuts atop the dikes that separated the rice

paddies. We both wore flat straw hats, the kind I used to call "Chinese hats" from my childhood images of Asian peasants. The land around us was flat. To the east, beyond the town of Kumamoto, lay a mountain chain with the volcano Aso still steaming and smoldering. I was surrounded by rice fields and a maze of water channels connecting every plot with another. I had never before stood on ground that had been farmed for centuries.

I tried to imagine Jiichan Masumoto growing up and working here. I still did not know if the Masumotos of Kumamoto owned a farm. But even if they did, since he was a second son, Jiichan Masumoto was not in line to inherit the land. Had that changed how he walked and labored in these fields?

I asked Jiichan Tanaka where we were going.

"To a field," he answered.

"To plant rice?" I asked. I was eager to dirty my hands with real farmwork. I wanted to learn more about rice, how it grew, the traditions of planting and harvesting; I wanted to retrace the steps of Masumotos in these fields.

"No, buckwheat," he answered.

The sacks of buckwheat seed were dropped next to a fallow field. Jiichan ripped open a bag and filled the pockets of his apron. He stumbled down an embankment into the field and began scattering the seeds in a random pattern. I had never sown seeds before. Our orchards and vineyards were perennial crops—once you planted a peach tree you expected it to last twenty years, a grapevine, several generations. Our plants were the oldest living things I knew in California. I copied Jiichan Tanaka as we walked side by side, our arms swinging back and forth. The buckwheat looked like waves suspended in a comma shape before they hit the earth. As we trudged back and forth, the seeds arched into the air and plummeted downward, nestling in the soft dirt where next we'd rake and stir them in.

As we neared the final section of the field I realized Jiichan was walking faster. Was he trying to race me? I noticed the empty bags and realized we had been too generous with our seeds and now had to stretch the last batch. I flung my last handful to cover a large area. Months from now, this far corner of the field will look sparse. Few will notice, and if they do, Jiichan can always say that "family from America was responsible."

I was much better at driving a tractor than sowing and soon got my chance. A field needed to be plowed, the ground opened and prepared for planting. But everyone else was behind with work and a borrowed tractor sat idle, awaiting a driver. I volunteered, and since Jiichan could not drive, he reluctantly agreed. I was pleased to discover a red Massey Ferguson 135, similar to ours in California. The old black seat cushion, with a torn seam and crumbling foam padding, felt comfortable as I climbed on board. My legs straddled the transmission and drive train, and I gripped and regripped the steering wheel. The diesel engine roared and a familiar vibration I knew well tickled my spirits. I easily shifted into gear, dropped the plow, and began the work. Jiichan squatted along one edge of the field and shaded his eyes to supervise my work. Of course, I could not hear him as he barked instructions to me at the end of each row, so I nodded as I turned and assumed he was pleased.

With each pass, I moved from the edge of the field toward the center, veering closer to Jiichan's position one row at a time. I planned to pause in front of him and ask his opinion. As I approached to begin my turn, I lifted the plow and pushed the clutch. The tractor should have gradually rolled to a stop, but instead the machine whipped to the right and the plow swung wide. Clumps of dirt showered Jiichan like flying ice from a hockey stop. I jerked into a 180-degree turn, and by the time I regained control, the tractor was heading in the opposite direction, down another row. I then lifted my right foot and realized I was "thinking in Japanese." Even though the Japanese drove on the opposite side of the road and the steering wheel on cars was on the right, the tractor clutch was still on the left side. When I had pushed what I thought was the clutch, I hit the brake, locked up the right wheel, and spun around. Bewildered, I kept pushing harder and harder, expecting the clutch to engage. Instead I whirled and turned around.

I glanced over my shoulder and thankfully saw that Jiichan was still standing. Instead of halting to apologize, I continued on down the row, pretending all was well. I felt like a child in trouble, foolishly convincing himself no one would notice an error in judgment, hoping that in a few minutes the incident would be forgotten. I imagined Jiichan was angry, but he did not yell at me. No fist waved menacingly, no scowl grew on his face as he brushed off the dirt in disgust and slapped dust from his pants. Squatting a few meters away, up the embankment, he watched me from his new vantage point. He badly wanted the field plowed.

By the late spring, I had become a fixture in the village. Neighbors bowed to me as I walked the roads and paths out to the fields. I frequented the village's single small convenience store, a four-meter-wide and five-meter-deep room in front of the shop-keeper's home. It sold a few hardware items, beverages, sweets, and dry goods like cigarettes and batteries. During my evening walks, I'd stop for an ice cream bar. Once I forgot money but the shopowners insisted I take my snack anyway. They held up a hardcover blue notebook and under the Tanaka household I saw *Masumoto* scribbled, their first new account in years. I now had credit.

One warm April day, Baachan and I rode to a nearby village where a series of large greenhouses rose in the distance. Inside, humid air lingered over the low, glistening plants. Bright red strawberries lay ready to be picked. I had picked strawberries as a child. It seemed every Japanese-American neighbor grew them at one time or another. Berries were a highly valued cash crop, produce that rewarded large families willing to work, and as annuals, they could be grown on just a few acres of rented land

until farmers purchased a place of their own. Ingenious Japanese-American farmers made small wooden carts and wagons that
wheeled up and down the closely planted rows, speeding the harvest, increasing efficiency and profits.

In this region of Japan, only a few farmers grew strawberries,
but more and more were experimenting with such high-value
crops. "We have no choice," said my uncle. Because so many people had left the countryside, farmers and rural communities
lacked the political power they once enjoyed. Domestic rice, once
highly protected with tariff and trade barriers to imports, soon
would face foreign competition. "Bad rice from Kariforuniya will
arrive on our shores," he lamented. "*Dame!*"—No good! He
pounded his fist into the palm of his other hand.

"*Soo ne!*" I agreed with him, squinting my eyes and nodding.
"*Kariforuniya, dame!*" Probably in another culture or country, we
would have then both spit on the ground.

My uncle believed crops like strawberries would be a new
option if he were ten years younger. I told him I should immigrate
back to Japan and bring all the secrets of Japanese-American
strawberry growers. He laughed, because he thought growing
berries was too hard for most of the younger Japanese. "Young
farmers don't know hard work!" he said with a grin that exposed
a missing tooth.

I felt as if I were back in California and listening to an Issei or
Nisei grumble about a loss of the work ethic in the younger generation. I added, "*Wakai hito, wakaranai, ne?*"—Young people just
don't understand, no?

BAACHAN AND I picked the plump strawberries for several hours.
Our fingers were stained red. My arms grew heavy, and both
knees ached from stooping. After I had filled a flat, it was quickly
taken away for cooling, depriving me of any sense of accomplishment. The owner, a family friend, later joined us and chatted with

Baachan as they both picked. Their hands danced among the berries, sliding between the green leaves, cradling a juicy berry, searching as if their fingers had eyes. I tried to recall how the Issei and Nisei picked berries—what was their secret for working fast and conserving energy? It must have to do with how hungry you were—I was too fat and only thought of my sore back and cramped legs. I once read an article about Asian immigrants working in California's fields in the early 1900s, their short stature considered perfectly suited for "stoop labor." "Little yellow men" had a genetic advantage and unfairly competed with Americans, the racist author of the article proclaimed. Yet I felt no benefit from being only five feet six inches. Strawberries and field work were democratic when it came to pain.

By afternoon, I grew lazy and less selective. I wondered if we were going to get paid for our labor and began stuffing my mouth with the best fruit, ensuring myself of some compensation. Then the owner stopped Baachan and handed her three empty flats. They bowed to each other, and I picked with renewed energy and discretion. That evening we served Jiichan fresh fruit, and he smiled with a broad grin. I was rewarded.

During the spring and early summer weeks, I had met almost everyone in the village and many from neighboring towns. I managed to engage in a few stumbling conversations, but I had yet to grasp the local accent and dialect. Once, though, when Jiichan and I were shoveling weeds along an irrigation ditch, a neighbor began to fertilize his field using a small machine with steel shanks that slit the earth and dropped small pellets next to each plant row. Two gray-haired brothers struggled with the machine, trying to calibrate it, then the older one climbed onto the tractor and nervously drove forward, straddling the rows of green seedlings. The younger brother watched and waited. During one of my breaks, I wandered over to him to observe. We bowed to each other and I asked in Japanese about the kind of fertilizer he was using.

He scratched his gray stubble, ignored my question, and

instead pointed to me and said, "Hey, man, you Masumoto?" He spoke so quickly the first two or three words were slurred together as if a single word.

I was shocked by his use of colloquial English, almost accent-free. I nodded and stammered, "Uh, yeah."

"How long you stay out here?" He poked his chin out at me as he spoke, part of his intonation and body language.

I gestured with my hands, holding them up, and said, "*Shiran*"—I don't know. We paused, allowing me time to collect my thoughts. Behind me the noise of Jiichan's shovel scraping the ground announced his return to work, across the field a tractor grunted, and the rest of the land was filled with a silent stillness. "Hey," I said, "you know the Masumoto family?"

The neighbor shrugged his shoulders in a way that was not Japanese—shoulders slowly rising, head tilting to one side, face gradually melting into a frown. He told me the story of his family. They had immigrated to Los Angeles, where he was born. The family returned to Kumamoto for a visit in the fall of 1941. "I kinda got caught here." He described listening to the news about the bombing of Pearl Harbor as a great military victory for Japan. "We try and get back to California, but no way. The war keep going and Papa-san wanted to keep family together."

He then told of their difficult decision after the war. His younger brother and sister, who had been infants in 1941, didn't want to stay in Japan. "We were all hungry. Everything bad here," he said. He looked down at the ground, pawed the earth with his foot. On the tractor, his brother had completed the row and turned to return. "The younger ones go back to L.A. I stay with my brother to farm." He looked up past the approaching tractor, squinting his eyes at the distant mountains.

"Do you regret what happened?" I asked.

"Oh no," he said. "Man, I only wish I talk more English." He grinned, dark wrinkles curling around his smile. "I still L.A. boy, you know!"

The Cart

Jiichan tightened the rope against his waist. His crusty hands lifted the wooden cart tongue, and he took a step forward. The rope snapped taut, he grunted, and the wagon wobbled. But it didn't move forward. Loose boards creaked, and dust and dirt trickled downward like sand in an hourglass, making a small pile on the ground. The two were frozen motionless, the wagon stationary while the old man leaned forward, pushing with his legs, blood vessels bulging on his forehead.

"Matte, Jiichan! Matte!" I yelled.

Baachan came running out of the house. "Ojiisan!" she snapped, with a subtle grin and chuckle only I could see and hear. "You need help. You can't do that by yourself!"

I reached for the other rope and fit the noose around my waist. I stepped forward, the rope tightened, and the wheels shifted and began rolling. Jiichan's rope slackened and he continued to walk, holding the tongue, more for balance than steering. I guided the cart out of the yard toward the road. A broken wheel provided a rhythm—pull, pull, jerk . . . roll; pull, pull, jerk . . . roll. We began our journey out to the fields.

The cart had served generations; the abraded and twisted wood commemorated the seasons of work. The splitting planks allowed sunlight to pass through slits and cast a pattern of lines and shadows beneath the bed. The top edges of the sideboards were gnawed from countless loads, and deep gouges marked the surface where heavy cargo had been shoved and dragged. The tongue had weathered spots, and splinters flaked off. A few smooth places defied the years and weathering—for decades work animals must have rubbed against these surfaces and polished the wood. One of the two wheels was badly warped and angled outward, causing the cart to rock with each revolution.

The other was splitting and a flat metal plate was bolted onto the break, preventing it from expanding. Every few paces I was reminded of this patch as we bounced over the trail. Occasionally, puffs of dust lingered in the air as fine dirt slipped from the cracks. We left a trail behind, marking our course.

Along a winding path we passed through the village. The cluster of thirty or forty homes huddled together, along with a few small businesses, a *sakanaya*/fish store, and the shop where I had my new credit account. At six in the morning, some farmers were leaving for their fields, others tended livestock in sheds a few steps from their houses. Two carts could pass each other along our path. But when a car approached, Jiichan guided us far to the left, sometimes off the road.

While pulling, I became conscious of our pace. Too fast and I feared Jiichan would tire, too slow and the cart lost momentum. I tried to maintain a smooth and steady stride, a rhythm in step with Jiichan and the cart's cadence. Our path turned and curved like a flowing stream as it meandered into the countryside. The final village homes slipped by, and before us the landscape opened to broad horizon of farms and fields. I took a deep breath, and a silence penetrated with the morning air. The only sound was the grating of the wooden wheels rolling along the packed earth.

Jiichan had loaded the cart with a collection of various shovels, some with flat faces, others pointed and narrow. I also could feel the gentle rocking motion of liquid sloshing back and forth in the dozens of buckets I had loaded the day before. I preferred not to think about them.

Yesterday, stepping outside, I had discovered a row of well-used buckets resting in a line like a column of exhausted soldiers awaiting duty, some leaning against a neighbor, others lying on their side, sprawled on the ground. Their galvanized metal had long ago lost its sheen. Baachan asked me to remove a stone next to the outhouse. The stench quickly rose, and I was repelled by the rank stink. Baachan wrapped a towel around her nose and mouth and dipped a long stick with a scoop into the murky liquid. Over and over she dumped the watery slime into the buckets.

Gradually the cavern was emptied, but the deeper she went, the heavier the load became. I relieved her and carefully raised the utensil, avoiding splashes and drips. As with most menial jobs, I was faced with two approaches—either to go slowly and meticulously, which would require an excruciatingly long time, or to work fast and sloppy and finish the task before I started thinking about it too much. I increased my pace and slipped into a cadence, scooping, lifting, and slopping another heap. The gushing, splashing, and plunking created an orchestra of amusing sounds. In the sunlight the oozing mass of green, brown, and gray glistened with an amazing array of natural hues and tints. Searching for my grandfathers, I had traveled to the farmlands of another nation, which had led me to this—I was shoveling shit.

I could not write home and tell my parents that I had come all the way to Japan just to clean an outhouse or that my college tuition was being spent mired in bodily waste as I became skilled at slinging it (although I could rationalize that such a metaphor could be useful in other situations). There must be some lesson I could glean—why else was I living in this small village with an old couple three times my age? Perhaps the lesson was that I was part of a chain of Masumotos who were only commoners, peasants who had worked the land for generations, dirtying our hands and enriching the earth. Somehow I had hoped this moment would be a bit more grand and I would have something more to show for my journey. Emptying sewage bucket by bucket was not what I had had in mind.

Jiichan and I stopped pulling the cart when we reached a fallow field. We began emptying the buckets across the open space. A truck passed and the driver leaned out of his window, smiled, and yelled, "Say, you have a new son working with you?" Jiichan waved and grunted some remark. The farmer added, "Ojiisan, with your new help, you can keep farming! *Ki o tsukete*!"—Be careful!

WE RESTED ALONG one of the endless dikes that divided the rice fields. I called them endless because I didn't know any better; to me all the dikes looked the same. If I had lived years or a lifetime in that place, each one would have individual stories buried in its earthen walls. I scratched the dirt and heard nothing.

At first glance, Jiichan looked as if he was sleeping, but his chest rose and dropped too fast. He was trying to rest before we started again with the spreading. Baachan brought lunch out to us. She handed me a bundle of rice cakes with pickled plums inside. She served us tea from a canister that kept it steaming hot. We ate quietly. The rumble of a truck or small tractor could be heard, then faded. I was tired too.

A soft, high-pitched voice danced in the spring breeze. I looked up the dike and saw a child bounding along the earthen trail. She wore a school uniform, was perhaps a kindergartner or first-grader coming home, one of the few children of the village. A bright red scarf was loosely draped over her shoulders, almost like a jump rope that she could effortlessly grab and skip over without missing a step. She sang a nursery rhyme and with her feet played a game of tag, tapping the green clumps of weeds and occasionally kicking a dirt clod.

As she neared us, I heard the song, *"Otete tsu naide no michi o yuke ba . . ."* Then she turned away from me and took a shortcut down another dike. I saw the back of her hair briefly catch the bright sunlight and shimmer.

"Jiichan, did you hear what the girl sang?" I asked. He kept his eyes closed, seeming to insinuate that I shouldn't bother him. Then he opened his eyes, hunted for and found his cup, slurped some warm tea, and resumed his restful position.

"Baachan, did you hear the girl?"

Baachan smiled.

"Baachan? What did the little girl sing?"

She smiled and almost laughed. "Oh, just a child's song. 'Holding hands together, walking on the field . . .' Something like that. Something every Japanese child knows."

I turned to look for the little girl, but she was far away, a red dancing ball in the distance.

Hiroshima

My mother's family emigrated from a rural village outside of Hiroshima. Neither she nor my aunts or uncles knew the exact name of the village. Growing up, I heard very few stories about these relatives. We had no photos, and Baachan Sugimoto had received only a handful of letters. She kept them in a drawer, tightly bundled, with yellowed string around the flat envelopes. Most were dated before World War II.

When I first arrived in Japan, I had written letters to the addresses I had been given. I heard no reply and asked my mother to contact relatives for help. Finally, an aunt from Los Angeles forwarded me a new address. I sent another letter and received a brief but courteous reply from a family named Nomura.

I arrived in Hiroshima early in the morning, hours before my time to meet with the relatives. I wandered through a beautiful city, the windows of new buildings glistening in the rising sun, the light gray of the cement sidewalks swept clean, the smell of the nearby ocean filling the air. I strolled accompanied by the sound of a series of rivers that ran through the town, making their way to the sea. While most cities in Japan were relatively free of litter, Hiroshima seemed spotless and shiny. In front of the train station, I watched taxi drivers wipe and polish their vehicles. They all wore white gloves, and I saw a few change into new ones after cleaning their windshields and chrome.

I spent hours at the Peace Memorial Museum, shocked, moved, and overwhelmed by the story of the atomic bomb blast. I found it impossible to believe that such a force could be unleashed against a city and its civilian population, killing thousands instantly, and within days, tens of thousands. Radiation poisoning lasted for months and gene pools were damaged, wounding families for generations.

Near the epicenter, a simple white monument had been constructed, and thousands of colorful origami paper cranes were draped over the base. An elementary school class was touring the memorial, and a class leader, a young girl about eight years old, stood before the sculptured white arch. She bowed and laid her classmates' wreath of cranes atop a low platform, then stepped back and bowed again. The children all stood in silence.

As I returned to the train station, I read a brochure for a new city and province museum. On the cover, shrouded behind a delicate veil and soft lighting, was a beautiful pregnant woman, her hands cradling her swollen stomach. The pamphlet described plans for an exhibition about those Hiroshima people who had left and settled in other parts of the world, including California and Brazil. This was the only time that I had seen reference to emigrants from an area of Japan still considered part of that homeland region. Perhaps because of the devastating losses from the atomic bomb, the designers of the museum sought to reclaim the stories of all the city's former citizens.

A distant cousin met me at one of the stations in the outskirts of town. As we walked, I had expected to find a rural village, but the once fertile farmlands now grew houses. I was met by a slender old man in his sixties. He introduced himself as Nomura, a younger brother of my Baachan Sugimoto in California. He then began to talk about a Yamada family, which meant nothing to me except that I knew we had relatives in Hawaii with that name. He tried to explain, "We were born into the Yamada clan and have a brother and sister in Hawaii. Your *obaasan* and I adopted the Nomura name and have used it ever since."

I did not understand and asked for clarification. Instead he offered me green tea. During the long moment of silence, we both peered out of his open window at the blue ocean to the west. I felt the sea breeze stroke my face. We loudly sipped the tea.

Nomura-san closed his eyes, and I stared at his face and was reminded of my Uncle Mas in Southern California. "Did you know Jiichan Sugimoto?" I blurted.

The old man blinked once or twice, startled by my voice, stirring from his drowsiness. "I . . . I don't remember much about him," he answered.

"Do you know the Sugimoto family well?"

He shook his head. The remainder of the visit was quiet, punctuated by long pauses of silence.

As my cousin and I walked back to the train station, she apologized over and over. "I'm sorry Ojiisan did not know about your family." She bowed, then whispered with her face looking downward, "We have lost much."

eight

HOMEBOUND

I'M FORTUNATE THAT FARMS DON'T MOVE. AFTER COMPLETING Berkeley, I return home and say to myself, "Little changes." Just as when I left years ago, old farmers still work the land, their children run off to the big city, and the peaches and grapevines need pruning. My parents have adjusted to a house void of children, and I find myself alone. They've slipped into a routine as a couple, talking, eating, doing house chores as if I'm not there. Following dinner, they clear the table and pair up to do the dishes, talking about the day as Mom washes and Dad dries. I sit in solitude at the table listening to their conversations.

I drive down roads and wave at my neighbors the same way Dad has done hundreds of times and perhaps as my grandfather did during his weekly trip into town. I struggle to learn the proper method, the slow movement of the arm up, a broad sweep of the hand in an arching motion, a suspension of the palm outward, pausing for recognition, a quick snap of the wrist acknowledging the return of a wave. Some of the neighbors have waved to a Masumoto for decades.

Every year, a few of the old-timers die. Their once meticulously kept farms have deteriorated in the last few years. Overgrown weeds and broken equipment are scattered across their yards, and dead stumps that should have been removed now litter the fields. Along the roadside I'm shoveling weeds. Kaz, a neighbor in his sixties, stops his pickup to talk. He pulls himself out of the cab with a mumbled groan and leans against his dusty vehicle, resting his tired legs. We begin with talk about the weather and the crops, complaining and bitching in the way farmers often take comfort.

"Too hot. Not normal for this time of year."

"Gonna hurt the grapes."

"Wish we'd get some rain. The peaches could use a drink."

"Heard the South has a bumper crop. Another one of those years with too many damned peaches."

After a series of these exchanges I realize we share a certain optimism—we worry about elements out of our control while in the same breath we allow ourselves to anticipate future harvests.

"Heard Mr. Nakagawa passed away. How old was he?" I ask.

Kaz answers, "Not that old." I can see him calculating the years in his mind. He writes 1915 with his index finger in the dust on his pickup hood. "Little older than me."

"Figured something was wrong. His place didn't look right," I add. "I drove by and saw all these dead vines and bad johnsongrass. Not like him."

Kaz nods with a frown on his face.

"Sad to see his lifetime of work looking so bad."

A pickup lumbers by. We wave to the driver, then a silence joins the conversation. I run my fingers through my hair, made uneasy by the pause.

"At least he could keep working to the end," Kaz answers as his voice fades away.

I CAME HOME to help Dad—that's what I told myself. I had finished my final year at Berkeley, qualified to start a few graduate programs with the possibility of specializing in rural sociology. But one evening a good friend and I conducted a mock graduate "orals" exam over a few beers and decided I was not Ph.D. material. Later, when my family gathered for Dad's birthday in Fresno, before I could tell them my plans to come home and not enter graduate school, Dad joked, "I'm a Ph.D., a proud, happy dad." I was heartened—perhaps my advanced education degree could be earned back on the family farm.

Initially, I set out to prove that you can go home again. I started by tackling the hardest, most physically demanding jobs, like hauling hardpan out of the fields. Hardpan is a hardened layer of clay and minerals that feels like rock. It forms in pieces ranging from small, palm-sized chunks to huge plates three or four feet across and weighing hundreds of pounds. Hardpan restricts vine and peach tree roots from spreading and taking hold, blocking their access to water and nutrients.

Ironically, Dad was able to purchase our farm because of the hardpan, a gentle fifteen-acre rise in the middle of the eighty-acre farm which we called "the Hill." The hardpan made a quarter of the property virtually worthless, and so made the farm affordable to a beginning farmer. Dad spent years hauling out the chunks of pan one by one and tossing them onto an old flatbed Chevy truck. Dynamite assisted him with the oversized plates too large for one man. He cleared the land and brought in a bulldozer to rip the fields, only to watch tons of new stones surface, dislodged by the four-foot steel shank. A field teeming with hard-pan tested the will of a young farmer.

He spent another year clearing his land, and now lush green vines grow on that hill. "I guess you'd say I was hungry to make the place work," Dad says with a grin. With each chunk of hard-pan removed, he claimed a small piece of the earth and planted roots.

Hardpan will always be part of our farm. Despite Dad's work, in some places chunks still rise and announce themselves when disk blades scrape against them with a shrill grinding sound of metal against stone. Half-submerged rock icebergs, the hardpan chunks are occasionally so large they shove the disks out of the soil, abruptly jolting the tractor and driver.

Clearing the worst areas, I toss the stones onto a vineyard wagon hooked to a small tractor. Thousands of rocks lie half buried in the ground, a few baseball-size, others flat and up to two feet long and wide. I cannot lift some of them and use a pick and sledgehammer to break them into manageable pieces. The pounding crushes me—my hands grow weary and my spirits sink. Smashing a huge plate creates dozens of stones where there was only one. With the large rocks I must use my body for lever-age, pulling the stone up to my waist and upper thighs, propping the mass against my frame, and waddling to the wagon. With a deep grunt, I heave it onto the pile. It lands with a heavy thud, dust flies, and the wagon bed rocks with the jolt.

By the end of the first day, I am exhausted and my back is sore. I walk like an old man, hunched over and in small steps. I am not in farm shape. My hands shake that evening, too stiff to grip a pen, aching with deep pain. Worst of all, they are badly blistered and shredded, despite my using leather gloves. I lack callous hands to work these lands.

Fortunately I can alternate clearing hardpan with other less draining work. The peaches need irrigating, and for three days I walk and check the water, monitoring the flow down the rows, regulating the streams from the concrete pipes and valves. When a college friend comes by for a brief visit, I explain how we farmers irrigate our fields, tapping water from the Sierra snowmelt and delivering it to individual farms through a maze of canals and ditches. Even on our small farm, furrows are cut in each row, earthen borders plowed at the ends. Then frantic work begins, adjusting the valves to maintain a good "head" of water so that it reaches the ends of rows, directing the volume by opening and closing channels, connecting the ends of rows so the liquid turns down another row and irrigates the other side of a vine or tree, and constantly repairing breaks in the borders and furrows, cursing and pleading with the water to cooperate.

My friend says, "It's much more complex than I ever imagined. Where did you learn everything?"

I stop shoveling and look up, surprised by the question. For the first time in my life I realize how much I know about farming just because I grew up in these fields.

Bolstered by this revelation, I contemplate how to become one of the best young farmers in the valley. Even though my sociology degree from Berkeley has little to do with eighty acres of sandy loam soil, it sounds impressive when I chat with neighbors and hear them repeat, "That Masumoto boy has a University of California degree and now is back to the farm. His father must be happy." I believe them for about a month until Dad and I talk about the coming peach year. I have to stop and ask simple questions: When do you know when to water? What do you look for in a healthy orchard? Which weeds are bad? I really can't explain how a peach grows or grapes thrive. I know, though, every year the blossoms will bloom, trees push leaves, the hard green fruit grow fat and juicy. Then we pick them. The rest I must leave up to nature.

I hesitate to call myself a farmer. Few of my friends work the land; others from Berkeley question why I returned to the valley.

They cannot hear my unspoken language that describes my need to "care for my folks" or "give farming a try." They feel that I'm tossing away my education, stepping backward into rural America, closing my mind to new thoughts and meaningful futures. The weight of family obligations will crush my spirit, I'm warned. Sometimes while pruning or weeding, I find myself again thinking about my grandfathers. Each left the farm in Japan so there'd be one less mouth to feed. I came back to our family farm so there'd be another set of hands to work.

ALMOST EVERY MORNING I have coffee with my father. He rises earlier than I do, follows a routine of starting the coffee, getting the morning paper, and setting a breakfast table of toast. I join him by asking, "What's up, Pop?" He answers with a light sigh, not a grunt but more of an acknowledgment that says "Same old, same old." I find his consistent response a comforting way to begin our day.

We talk about the chores. Usually I begin with my schedule: "I'll be disking the Hill later this morning. Gonna try and water by the weekend."

He listens, waits for me to finish, then answers, "Planning on mowing the weeds soon?"

At first I wonder if he's criticizing me for allowing the weeds to grow dense, then I believe he may be hinting that I should mow instead of disk. I pause before saying, "Ah . . . no. I hadn't planned on it. Why?"

"Some of the fields can be mowed this morning." He nods with his answer. Two days later, he'll have the entire farm mowed and looking freshly groomed without interfering with my disking. Then when I irrigate, the water will run smoothly and quickly, unimpeded by overgrown weeds.

Dad rarely uses the pronoun "I." "The vines could use a drink," he says. "The ground is starting to get hard and needs to be worked up. The big Ford's oil hasn't been changed in a while. A storm is heading our way—better off if we shred before the rains." According to Dad, it's the farm that needs the work, the fields that request his labor. He acts in response to nature.

I often ask about his work history with a specific field. I want to know, did he always need to irrigate the young trees in early spring? What kind of furrows did he cut in the Riffel vines? Are the sections near the road prone to have a worm problem? Some mornings, the stories expand as we talk.

"What was planted on the Hill before our Thompson grapes?"

Dad slowly sips his coffee, squinting as he searches his memory, then answers, "Muscats and Ribiers." He grins as if congratulating himself for remembering. "They were planted at an odd angle along the old Garfield line."

"The Garfield line? Ribiers?" I ask. These are words I only vaguely recall.

"The Garfield irrigation ditch was piped just after you were born. It ran diagonally across our land, slicing it in two. So we buried it with concrete pipes. Then we could work the land on top it. That's when I cleared the Hill of hardpan. . . ."

For the next few days, we discuss how a concrete pipe, buried a few feet, retards the growth of vines. Other times we reflect about the art of farming uneven lands and explore the history of crops that once tried to grow on the rocky surface without much luck. I notice Dad rubbing his hands and massaging his fingers when he tells stories of the hardpan. Later, while shoveling weeds on the Hill, I wear a pair of gloves with a worn hole in the palm and think of the hardpan that Dad cleared and the translucent green of fresh young grape leaves all around me, basking in the morning sun.

"Ribiers were good for cheap wine," Dad adds. "A good old variety."

I cannot remember their taste but know they were a dark red grape that stained the cheeks of toddlers when we snacked on them while playing in the vineyards as our parents worked nearby. When I was four or five, I inherited my older brother's grape-juice-stained hand-me-down T-shirts and promptly initiated them with my own dribbles and natural hues.

I grew up with the Muscats and know their tangy flavor well. We kept a five-acre block for years until the demand for them declined and we replanted with Thompsons. I recall gorging myself on those Muscats, first wiping dust off the bulbous bunches with the waistband of my T-shirt and gently blowing over the grapes as I cradled them in my hands. In some years, the berries were tightly squeezed together and I'd bite into a bunch from the side instead of individually pulling a berry for a taste. The juices would ooze onto my cheeks, drip from my chin, and occasionally squirt into my eyes with a burning sting. Other times the grapes hung loose and the berries grew into large marbles. I'd pop one or two into my mouth, feel the crunch of their thick skin and the sharp taste swishing in my mouth before spitting out the seeds onto the ground.

On mornings when Dad and I are not rushed and can enjoy a second cup of coffee, some of our best conversations revolve around sports. Because I never grew more than an inch in high school, my athleticism peaked in eighth grade, when my short legs could outrace all the Caucasian kids who were caught in adolescent transition, growing too fast for their bodies. But a year or two later, the lanky and muscular boys caught up with and easily surpassed me. Dad never coached me—we rarely threw a ball back and forth, and he never taught me the proper stance for batting or how to focus on the ball. Nor did I ever expect or long for such lessons. Instead we spent many long hours out in the fields, where he taught me how to use a pruning shear, shovel weeds, and drive a tractor. He shared with me everything he knew about work. Now, though, when we talk about sports, we enjoy the simple pleasures of play. We support the same teams, biased toward those on the West Coast. When a rare Asian player joins a roster, we'll root for his success. We definitely support the underdogs. Our best conversations often occur the day after an event. During our coffee, we relive the plays we enjoyed and share in the successes.

I ask if Jiichan participated in sports. Dad chuckles and says, "Jiichan was just too damned tired from field work to even think of playing a game." Dad can't recall many Issei who played American games well, though Japanese sports, *sumo* wrestling and *judo*, flourished in the community, with numerous contests and tournaments. I can't picture an Issei farmer hanging a basketball hoop on the old barn and working with his young son on perfecting his free shot. Yet the Nisei seemed to understand the meaning of sports—it was the American thing to do. They held track meets culminating in a statewide meet. Rival Japanese-American communities played each other in baseball leagues, and sometimes a team from Japan toured to compete against local ones. Occasionally an all-star lineup played other teams of different ancestry, some Nisei wanting to prove that they could play this American game. But the most popular sport seems to have been basketball. Nisei boys and girls played both on school teams and in their own leagues and tournaments. There were Buddhist teams, Japanese Christian teams, and divisions for women's and children's teams. In the relocation camps, basketball was played on the rocky slopes of Manzanar as well as on the desert soil of Gila River. Champions were crowned behind barbed wire.

As Dad and I exchange sports stories, our histories parallel each other not only on the court (he too peaked at the age of thirteen) but also off the court. Jiichan didn't understand American sports very well but tolerated his sons' desire to play the game. "Besides," says Dad, "Basketball games were played during the day at school, so we farm boys could get home to help with chores." Dad let me play for my basketball teams and faithfully picked me up after practice. I don't recall him ever attending one of my games, and as I grew older and shorter (relative to the other kids), I was glad—I didn't want him to see me on the bench. I never played baseball—practices and games conflicted with summer farmwork.

Dad and I enjoy the meaning of an athletic event, the contest of spirit and body. We often lament that our heroes on the field have been replaced by businessmen, and money controls much of the game. Winning at all costs seems to be the new ethos, and individual performance more important than teamwork. Yet the power of play still attracts us. Sports allow a father and son to participate in a common language we can share during our morning coffee.

A few mornings extend into a third cup of coffee and our range of topics expands. Sometimes I share my observations about farm life. The best ones evolve into stories, and Dad adds character and history.

When a newspaper story reports on a union vote of farmworkers, he'll show it to me, awaiting my response. "Seems like the people who do the real work rarely get paid what they're worth," I say. Dad listens intently; he nods, but I can't tell if he agrees with me. We never debate, but he may answer by not continuing the conversation.

Later I wonder aloud, "Since we do almost all the work on our farm, when they boost the minimum wage, we'll give ourselves a raise!" Dad cocks his head to the right, ponders the idea, and shakes his head.

"When you were a farmworker, did you ever think about organizing yourselves?" I ask.

"Japanese stuck together. We worked in a crew, shared the work, and spoke the same language," he answers.

I ask questions that prompt his memory: How big were your work crews? How did you find jobs? Did you have a crew boss? Who'd you work for? Were you ever cheated? Did you migrate with the crops?

He answers in short statements. "Small crews, maybe a dozen. We'd hear about Rosenthal's needing pickers or pruners and show up at a meeting place, like Tori's grocery store in Selma. Then we'd hitch rides and work all day. Lots of times the crew boss was a family friend, like the Kimuras or Hondas from Fowler, or the Miyatas or Matsuis from Selma, or even the Matsumotos of Del Rey. They'd take care of the Masumoto family."

I pick a subject and ask follow-up questions about the Rosenthal farm, Tori's store, picking grapes or peaches, the Miyatas' or Hondas' work crews. The stories stream forth.

"So why didn't you workers ever organize yourselves?" I ask again.

"We didn't want to keep working for someone else. We wanted our own place," he answers.

"What about Jiichan or Baachan? They couldn't own land, because the Alien Land Laws prevented them," I remind him.

"But Issei rented land," Dad answers. He then tells about a field located on Leonard near Central Avenue. "Jiichan rented that place for a while, I was only a kid."

I picture the vineyard and wonder why Dad never mentioned this before. We've driven by it numerous times without any reference. I guess Dad had no stories to tell.

"Farmers have been notoriously independent and can't organize themselves," I conclude. "Too damned independent."

Dad responds by pointing out that we belong to three farmer cooperatives and explains how right after World War II, when tensions ran high, Japanese banded together to create a supply co-op. And later, during the violence in the fields in the seventies when unionization of farm workers swept the valley, many of the farmer neighbors organized themselves into night patrols.

"Why don't farmers demand better prices? They're always at the mercy of nature and the market. You seem to accept everything," I blurt.

Dad pauses and fills the room with his silence. "Wait till you've farmed for a while," Dad concludes.

We also often talk about family over our coffee. I update Dad about Shirley, my older sister, and Rod, my older brother, who both live and work in Los Angeles. A few times a year they drive the 250 miles home, but our slow farm pace must feel like an alien world compared with their big-city rhythms.

A quiet and reserved man, Dad does not talk very much with his children over the phone. When he listens to their voices through the receiver, they can't see him nodding or frowning and much communication must be lost. I relay my conversations, though, trying to explain as best I can about Rod's latest computer engineering project or Shirley's frustrations with her nursing job and her career change to computer work. Dad patiently listens, wincing as I tell a story about egotistical doctors treating nurses like second-class citizens and raising his eyebrows as I describe the process of harvesting silicon and the potential profits in the computer industry.

I share a conversation I had with Shirley. I wrote a short essay about farming and the summers we had spent as kids packing peaches in the shed, working with our cousins, spending long hot days with peach fuzz and glorious summer evenings with extended family.

Shirley joked, "That sounds like a wonderful story. I can't wait to read it! Too bad it's not exactly how I remember it!"

A grin breaks onto Dad's face.

When neighbors ask about his oldest son, Dad says, "Rod's doing pretty good working with computers." Dad doesn't understand exactly what is involved in Rod's job as a computer integrated circuit designer, but when Rod showed Dad one of the tiny, postage-stamp-size microchips that he had designed, Dad squinted and studied it with a magnifying glass for a long time. He then nodded his head in approval and set it aside.

"Think Rod would ever come back to the farm?" I ask.

"Hummm," Dad answers slowly. "Don't know why he should."

We take a final sip of coffee. The morning's work awaits us outside.

Old Peaches

The winter fog settles near the earth in the evening, drifting downward in descending clouds. First the lowlands are blanketed, then the rest of the landscape is enveloped. Daylight is cut short. All wind currents are abated by the mountain ranges that surround us. The stillness allows humidity to collect and the fog to linger for hours, even days. We can go for weeks without seeing the sun.

I return to pruning our peaches, beginning with our old Sun Crest orchard, an old variety with a wonderful flavor that takes people back to the peaches from a grandparent's farm or backyard. When I'm picking these fruits, the peach aroma grabs my attention and my mouth waters in anticipation. With the first bite, the juices gush over my lips and down my cheeks. I grin with delight as the nectar dazzles my taste buds and I lean forward to avoid dripping on myself. We've farmed these trees for over twenty-five years; they are ancient by industry standards. Newer varieties have been introduced, with redder color and longer shelf life. Most farmers replant a field with new varieties every ten to fifteen years in order to "keep up," as a neighbor advises me.

A month ago, the orchard leaves fell and created a golden carpet of fall colors. Now the leaves are brown and withered. Left behind are naked limbs and branches and a stark forest of growth that needs clearing. I carry one of Dad's new pruning shears with me and can feel the morning's cold in the clean wooden handles. The light tan wood hues contrast with the shiny gun-barrel-gray metal of the cutting head. These shears have never been used; the pivot bolt is snug and tight, and opening and closing the blades creates a sharp grating sound of metal scraping metal. They feel powerful in my hands, and I am ready to slice through the thickest of branches.

Peaches bear on second-year wood. Growth from the last summer becomes the healthy foundation for the next harvest. First, from the ground, I start clipping, wandering around the tree, chopping branches back to the new growth, leaving behind "hangers"—small, short branches that gracefully loop down and out. I try to imagine the delicate pink peach blossoms blooming along these stems, but since I have not seen a valley spring since before I left for college, I cannot picture the scene. Instead, the cherry blossoms of Japan fill my imagination, with their clusters packed together so thickly the wooden branch is hidden.

Before I climb a ladder up into the canopy, I step back to study the overall structure of a peach tree, trying to recall the form we'd like to achieve. I want to shape our trees into a wineglass sculpture, five or six main scaffold limbs rising from a common trunk bending outward in a gentle curve, then straightening with a top lip ten feet off the ground. Each scaffold will have smaller branches stemming off the main line; they in turn produce the second-year wood I search for. But the stark silhouette before me appears to be a jumbled mass of branches.

Did I ever learn how to shape a tree properly or did Dad simply let me prune the easy ones? As a teenager I'd prune every winter, but by the summer I worried more about Saturday-night dates and volleyball tournaments. Our classroom in the fields was the last thing on my mind, and I rarely returned to review my winter's efforts. Now it will be months before I see the results of today's test. I prune with the winter fog, in the spring watch for growth, and finally judge my work with harvests. It may take me years to understand the significance of pruning hard or leaving lots of hangers, of allowing trees to grow high and stretch to over ten feet or sawing them low, of bowing branches outward into a goblet shape or tightening them into a champagne-glass form. I wonder how much longer we will keep these old trees and if I'll remain on the farm that long.

Out of the five or six main scaffold limbs, many trees have one or two dying. The wood is brittle, with little or no new

growth. In bright sunlight they are almost black with cracks in
the bark, life drained from them during the summer heat. In the
fog they are hard to distinguish, though. I study their lines against
a gray sky, trying to identify those with stunted growth. The dead
sections are expensive; each season we waste money on fruitless
branches. When I irrigate or fertilize or treat for worms, expenses
remain the same whether or not only half a tree is producing.
These old trees cannot compete—they're obsolete and of no value
in the business of farming. Yet what if only one large branch is
dead and the rest of the tree remains healthy? Where do I draw
the line of productivity? No one talks about keeping old orchards.
The industry seems to look only toward the future with new
plantings.

I talk with the manager of our fruit packing shed, where we
take some of our peaches to be sorted into boxes and shipped. He's
in his early forties, a large man with a huge desk decorated with
golf trophies. "If you've got an old orchard, then it means you've
got an old variety," he says, shaking his head. "You've got to stay
competitive with the new varieties. Besides," he jokes, leaning
forward to me, "you're too young to be thinking like an old
farmer."

At the bank, I run into a fruit broker who has worked with
our family for years. He's glad to see me back on the farm and
says, "Say, you're a bright young guy. Maybe you can convince
your father to get rid of those old peaches." He lights up a cigarette. I wait for him to continue. "No one buys fruit by the flavor—they make decisions with their eyes. Besides, how much
longer are you going to accept price-lowering adjustments with
that old variety?" He chuckles oddly and shakes his head, then
my hand, before he turns away. I believe he's sincerely trying to
help our family by offering us good advice.

I tell Dad about my conversations while he's shoveling old
weeds from an irrigation valve, clearing the brown tangle of dead
stems and leaves from the summer before. For a few minutes we

dig together, I on one side and he on the other. Our shovels never hit each other but occasionally scrape against the concrete stand. I explain my dilemma. He agrees, resigning himself to the fact that farming continues to change and we have to find different ways to survive. But I sense he wants to keep this orchard. He planted the trees, sent us kids to college with the profits, remembers more good years than bad. "Yeah, you'll probably need to get rid of 'em," he finally says, flinging a shovelful of roots to the side. He stops, leans against the handle, lifts his hand and runs his fingers through his thinning gray hair as he looks down the peach row. "They're not as useful as they once were. . . ."

He stops. I wait for him to continue. He returns to his shoveling and weeds.

I sharpen the blades of our chain saw and mix five gallons of fuel, preparing for a long week of work. I pick out my first target, a tree with stunted branches and tired roots—its stubby limbs have been infected by wood borers. The saw easily slices through the soft bark, and the wood chips fly in a stream of dull tan sawdust. The scaffold tumbles to the earth with a muted thud, splintering upon impact. One of the forks, where the branch divides into a Y shape, snaps with the fall like a brittle bone. I discover most of the trunk is dead, and I feel redeemed—the limb needed to be cut.

But the next tree feels different. As I cut, the wood resists, the blade grabs hold of healthy tissue, slowing with the denser bark. The wood chips sailing into the air are light in color, with a tinge of pink; a breeze casts them onto my hair. I can smell the aroma of fresh-cut wood, a damp scent almost like pine. The limb falls with a huge thump. Moisture bleeds from the smooth surface of the saw cut; I can feel it with my fingertips.

I count the years' growth in tree rings and am surprised by their consistency. The early years of rapid growth with fat rings are followed by another decade of even widths. The gradual narrowing of the last few years does not necessarily imply bad growing conditions; the trunk was over a foot in diameter by then and maintained a uniform growth. But peach trees and their rings are not necessarily accurate indicators of weather. Farming is all about fooling nature. The rings record our irrigation and fertilization practices—no matter the rainy winter and droughts or the poor market price of peaches, these trees were watered and cared for year after year. I wonder if the few narrow bands were from my teenage years helping Dad, perhaps indicators of overdue irrigations and delayed fertilizing when the chores of a farmer's son were neglected for a summer romance.

As my saw bites into the bark of the next limb, immediately I realize I've made a mistake. Within seconds the engine whines as it struggles to chew the living tissue. I stop, but it is too late. Instead of removing the one bad limb, I have severed a good one. Before I continue with the next tree, I stop the saw engine, and a silence returns to the orchard. I walk from tree to tree, trying to single out damaged limbs. A quarter of the way into the field, I look back, and out of eighty trees, I estimate twenty have just one unproductive scaffold limb and two or three have multiple ones. This is how farmers make crucial management decisions. Perhaps I need only remove a few trees, in which case most of my work lies in identifying the individual diseased limbs and extracting them from the fields.

"Like keeping an old car for an extra few years," Dad responds when I share my plan only to cull limbs. "They lose most of their value the first few years, then they become valuable."

We discuss the costs of replacing an entire orchard with new trees, then the pruning and care for three years before a single peach is harvested. "With young orchards, we're in a race to reclaim our investment," I explain, as Dad nods in agreement. "But old orchards just need maintenance . . . and a different level of expectations."

Dad peers out into the field. I wish I could see through his eyes. Maintaining this orchard requires his vision and sense of history, his intimate knowledge of each tree—which ones have dying limbs, which grow languid with each passing year, which few are near death. I want to know the stories from the many seasons that have passed. We walk and begin to talk, mapping the field with his memories.

No ONE HAS researched how to regenerate an orchard. If you remove the old, will healthy wood grow and renew? How exactly does one sculpture old trees?

I begin by circling each tree, studying the growth revealed by naked branches. With winter dormancy, unproductive limbs cannot hide behind leaves. But against the stark gray background of the overcast winter sky, these branches can fool you and look quite healthy. I struggle to recognize which old limbs I need to remove.

My new technique was an accident at first, a lack of focus and concentration. Mesmerized by the stillness of the overhead fog, I caught myself staring beyond the treetops, lost in the vast expanse of grays. In the foreground lay the silhouette of a dying peach limb. I shook my head, then turned and gazed at another branch and another and found that much of the sky was concealed—a veil of denser, healthier stems and branches obstructed my view. I completed my circle around the tree and revisited the first feeble branch where the sky opened beyond the limbs. Weakness was revealed not by the growth but by negative spaces—what was not growing. I flagged the branch with a bright red ribbon for later chain-saw work.

With the next tree I repeated the process and found no injured scaffolds. On another, three major limbs were stunted, and I felt that no matter how much care I invested, the tree could never completely come back and would remain terribly frail and suffering. I would have to remove the entire tree.

For the rest of the day, the winter sky became my partner.

Where the gray passed through the tree unfiltered, I tagged the damaged wood. Fortunately, most of the tree canopies diffused the light and I would keep them for another year. I walked faster, marching down the row with confidence. In the winter shadows of these ancient trees, I could see the growth.

Now, with my chain saw in hand, I advance from tree to tree, ribbon to ribbon. I weed my orchard. The sawblade dances through the dead wood, reinforcing my decision, the crosscut revealing only a very small edge of the bark that was alive.

As I cut, I look for new wood to replace the old. Usually there are neighboring young limbs that can be retrained. Because they are young first- or second-year branches, I can gently push or pull them to the side and redirect growth to fill the empty gaps. Some require a short band of rope to pull them into the open space. Two or three years from now, I hope these will develop into main scaffolds, fulfilling the potential I am learning to identify, so that these trees will have generations of new wood, scars of my chain-sawing overshadowed by new, vibrant greens from the young, vigorous growth.

I can see the past and future in these old peach trees, Dad's work of planting an orchard alongside of my labor to regenerate the old. I will keep this old orchard—and work with timelines necessarily measured in years. With my contribution, these might become family trees.

nine

RAISIN
TRADITIONS

WE FARM EIGHTY ACRES, TWENTY IN PEACHES AND SIXTY IN GRAPES.
Once, at a friend's wedding reception in San Francisco, someone
heard I grew grapes and became curious about my work. He
wandered over and introduced himself. In one hand he held a
dark red Merlot, which he kept swirling, leaving behind vivid
leg streaks on the glass with each roll.

In the course of our conversation, he renamed my farm an
"estate" and inquired if I operated my own winery. I politely said,
"No," laughing to myself. I had never imagined the Masumotos as

part of a grand wine family and Jiichan as a first-generation wine baron. But by the end of our ten-minute exchange and with a second glass of wine, my new friend believed I had a "vineyard." I didn't want to destroy his romantic image by explaining that most of our grapes are simply dried into raisins—our riskiest venture.

We prepare for this challenge in late July with our last irrigations and when the ground has dried but not become parched. We enter the fields with tractors and disks, chopping all weeds and pulverizing chunks of earth into fine particles. Our goal is to leave behind a thin soil layer, a few inches of powdery silt and sand that will cure in the heat. For the next two months, moisture becomes an enemy—sprinkles, thunderstorms, rain, even heavy dews are not welcomed, for they will bond with our earthen powder and spawn dirt clods, creating an uneven texture. During the last weeks in August, I terrace the ground, making it smooth, with a slight angle of just a few degrees sloping to the south. The surface looks like a polished tabletop. When a small dirt clod gently rolls downhill from the top, it leaves behind a light trail in the dust. Overnight, all farm creatures leave evidence of their presence in their footprints. The sun further bakes the land; my bare hand burns when I press against the topsoil. The earth is now ready for raisin drying.

In the final days of August and early September, crews of pickers arrive and lay sheets of brown paper on the ground, each sheet about two feet wide and three feet long. Green grapes are hand-picked into shallow pans, then spread over the surface of the paper trays. For a week, I'll have as many as forty workers in the vineyards. The total count for sixty acres can be over sixty thousand trays, each tray beginning with fifteen to twenty pounds of green fruit that will dry into four or five pounds of raisins. With luck and three weeks of dry weather, I expect to have over two tons of raisins per acre, as much as 120 tons from our farm.

A neighbor, an Armenian grape farmer, tells me stories about harvests from his past. He is a small but heavy man, shorter than my five feet six inches but with a stocky build, which he claims is perfect for working under a grape vine. He speaks with emotion, with eyes that can be laughing one minute when we talk about family farms, then glaring the next as he curses the low price of raisins. He first greets me with a firm, hearty handshake, then begins a story by waving his hands and raising his voice as if I were hard of hearing. Just as quickly, though, his expressions grow quiet and he completes sentences with a dangling silence, leaving me to fill in the blank spots.

His tales vary with each season's weather. The most recent summer had the "worst heat" or "darkest clouds" or "wettest rain" he'd seen. "Almost like the time," he'd begin, "back in the thirties when the summer was so hot, grapes withered on the vine. Or when it rained so hard, the wooden trays floated in the puddles." Compared to my family and our conversations, he speaks with a thunderous passion—a loud, intimidating bellow that makes me nervous. He explains, "The weather in September cannot be trusted." As I prepare for our harvest, I believe him.

When we finish picking, the trays lie exposed to the elements. I feel vulnerable. A sudden rainstorm can destroy a crop, breaking the skin of the delicate berries and allowing rot to fester, or creating humid mornings conducive to mold. All we can do is wait and hope.

When news of an impending cold front scares us in a long-range weather forecast, I ask Dad, "What can we do?"

He answers with a different emphasis, "What *can* we do?"

I am not used to leaving so much to chance. Instead, I start researching weather patterns, studying long-term projections for rain in September and the charts of historical averages. But when a sudden late-afternoon thunderstorm in the nearby foothills surprises all of us, including the weatherman and his noon update of sunny, hot days, I realize no one can predict the weather even a few hours in advance.

Some claim grapes dry into raisins by "baking" in the sun.

Vineyards do feel like an oven in the summer—the twelve-foot space between the rows acts like a natural dehydrator tunnel, blocking any breeze while trapping the warm air. In some years with intense heat well over one hundred degrees, we broil the berries with the overhead sun—the top side of a bunch quickly wilting, leaving the underside green. We then have to turn each tray, flipping the bunches and exposing the juicy side to the heat.

During the weeks of drying, I walk my fields often, checking for dampness, sometimes stirring the raisins to blend the wet with the dry. Shadows from the vine shoots can shade the trays and create a "cool spot." I pull trays up into the direct sunlight. At the row ends the grapes do not dry as quickly, possibly because cooling air currents stroke the berries. I move them into the interior where the heat collects. I'm the type of cook who needs to keep opening the oven door to check on the food. A friend says, "Why do you spend so much time out in the fields? There's nothing you can do." She's right, but perhaps that's precisely why I walk the fields.

Drying raisins does differ from cooking—our oven temperatures are never the same nor exact. Each year brings variation, scorching heat waves over a hundred, slow baking in the mid-nineties, high-altitude clouds that diffuse the sunlight, northern cold fronts that suddenly drop temperatures twenty degrees into the mid-eighties as if someone had opened the oven and let out all the heat. Since I cannot control any of this, I cook "from scratch" with every new year. I may follow a proven technique, but the kitchen conditions vary tremendously from one year to the next. I can only rely on experience to guide me in anticipating how the grapes may wither like overcooked vegetables in the searing hot spells, or knowing how many days I must add when clouds linger overhead with heavy dews and excessive moisture that can ruin a half grape/half raisin and make for a soggy soufflé.

Creative chefs and bakers understand the uncertainty of nature. We both work with chaos and add a dash of fun and adventure when we experiment. With raisins, I follow a family recipe with a necessary ingredient of unpredictability, combining new elements with each season, hoping for pleasant surprises. Farmers are not fast-food workers—we don't manufacture meals.

During the raisin season, all my senses are stimulated. I listen to the flapping of the edge of a paper tray during a late-afternoon wind and smile—the breeze will help cure the grapes. While picking crews harvest, I can walk down rows and hear the grape bunches dropping into the steel pans, followed by the tinny sound of the metal sliding along the dirt, then the muffled unfolding of paper as trays are spread and filled with grapes. Later, I listen to the rhythm of turning trays, a cadence with a few seconds' pause between the crinkling of paper as a worker finishes one roll, then moves to the next, often silently sliding on his knees in the soft dirt. They complete a row with an audible sigh, preparing themselves for the next one. Occasionally I hear voices and an exchange of numbers between workers—" . . . *cuatrocientos treinta y ocho* . . ."—as one man writes the piecework tray count for all of them on a small piece of paper torn from the corner of a tray.

The air is filled with the smell of drying grapes—a caramel fragrance mixed with an earthy aroma. At first, the odor is subtle, as if the dust carries a subtle bouquet. As the days pass it gains in strength, especially during the evenings when the warm air settles and compresses the candy fragrance into a layer hugging the earth. I drive through the countryside with my car windows open, breathing the air, knowing when I pass a vineyard by the scent.

Following days of stress as I watch the sky for rain, the grapes dry into raisins and we roll each paper tray by hand. Farmers employ different techniques when rolling. In the "biscuit roll," raisins are collected in the middle of the tray, then the paper is folded from the sides around the mound, and finally rolled into a spiral shape starting at one end, resembling a cinnamon roll. This seals out moisture and heat, protects the berries, and halts the drying process. In the "cigarette rolls," the raisins are raked into a line in the center and the paper is then rolled around the pile like a giant hand-rolled smoke, allowing air to circulate through the open ends, curing the crop with continued heat. A few farmers experiment with "flop rolls"—the bottom portion of a tray, which becomes shaded in the late afternoon, is flipped up toward the top, turning bunches "over easy," exposing the green berries to the sun and toasting them caramel brown.

It may take days or weeks to bring these rolls in from the fields, and the biscuit rolls can withstand the heaviest rains. But before I roll, the raisins must be completely dried. I can roll my crop days earlier with the cigarette roll, but must monitor the raisins' curing. While rain is not a major threat to my thousands of cigarette rolls, the raisins can absorb moisture with a storm or can overdry if left out too long. Flop rolls must sit out longer, and the temperature needs to be hot for the heat to penetrate. (A modified version of a flop roll will only flip the bottom green bunches over for rapid drying but leave the rest of the tray open and exposed.) With a cool spell, flop rolls become a headache, the farmer kicking himself because the moderate temperatures would have been sufficient if the trays were left open, but now the raisins will take much longer to dry, adding days and weeks to the farmer's worried, sleepless nights. I can pay workers to unroll each tray and after a few days of heat reroll them, which adds to my expenses. One neighbor claims, "That's really why they call them 'flop rolls'—they can really be a flop."

We match our rolling with our personalities. Dad had always been a biscuit-roll man, waiting patiently until the berries were completely cured, then rolling and securing his crop. I tended to like cigarette rolls—they were faster and I could still control the drying process, securing the crop a few days earlier than by Dad's method, though I was forced to keep on top of it until the raisins were properly dried. Other neighbors had their own systems, adjusting to the weather conditions, access to labor, and level of stress management.

Conversations become animated when farmers discuss the

merits of the different rolling strategies. We take sides and cite successes and failures as if we were arguing over whose sports team is better. The old farmers inevitably bring up history during their rebuttals: "Remember the rains in '76? That year I saved my crop because of biscuit rolls."

A friend then reminds us, "Yeah, it was your wife's idea to pick and roll early, if I recall." Chuckles undermine the defendant's testimonial.

Another memory centers on '78, "when nothing helped at all." A moment of silence follows as many share a painful moment.

By the end of the season, coffee-shop exchanges and side-of-the-road impromptu debates flourish. Farmers joke and banter with each other, knowing they have claimed another harvest.

After rolling, we "box" the raisins, dumping the trays into containers, and deliver them to the packing plants, where they are washed and packaged. Our family has worked with three generations of containers used to haul the crop out of the fields. From the 1900s to the 1950s, farmers used "picks," wooden boxes about two feet in length and one foot wide and deep. Each held about forty to fifty pounds of raisins and could easily be carried around in the fields. Some farmers boxed the raisins directly from the wooden trays (paper was introduced after World War II), while others first loaded the trays onto wagons and filled picks at the end of the row, sorting out rotten clusters and removing leaves.

Picks could be hand-loaded onto trucks and large wagons. They were individually lifted by one worker and "swamped," or tossed upward, into the hands of a waiting stacker. When stacking, timing was essential to maintain the momentum of the box. The ground worker swung the pick upward, hurling it into the air. For a brief moment it was suspended, rocketing to the sky. Then a set of strong hands caught the wooden crate, directing the momentum toward the stack. A smooth cadence not only required the least amount of energy from the "swampers," it also avoided spilling the valuable harvest.

The biggest change occurred when electricity arrived on farms. Electric hoists were used and larger boxes were introduced. We called them "sweat boxes," wooden flats about three feet long, two feet wide, and a foot deep, capable of holding over two hundred pounds. The larger boxes allowed us to blend raisins that were at different moisture percentages so the "wet" raisins could cure alongside the drier ones, "sweating" to even out the quality of the bunches. Too much moisture and raisins could mold while stored, too dry and the farmer lost tonnage and ultimately money, since we were paid by weight.

I know of some farm couples, husband-and-wife teams, who used these larger boxes without the electric hoists. Some had chain-and-pulley systems. Others did all the work by hand. Mrs. Mura said, "Yes, it was hard work. Oh, how about raisin time . . . I helped carry those sweat boxes, we had to load them onto the truck by hand. We didn't have equipment in those days." She unconsciously wrings her hands, and her small five-foot frame seems to sink deeper into the living-room couch she shares with her husband. "Those boxes must have weighed over a hundred and fifty pounds. I'd carry one side, he carried the other. It was hard work, but working together for your own place, we didn't think about it. But those sweat boxes, oh now . . . I can't believe I did it."

After a few seconds, her Kibei (born in America, educated as a youth in Japan) husband added with a smile, "She a powerful woman there!"

All autumn, while I was in school, my parents brought in the raisin crop. I remember Mom and Dad walking up and down each row, rolling a few trays that had dried, leaving others to cure for a few more days. As a child I sometimes could not locate my parents as they worked in the autumn vineyards. Shading my eyes, peering down along a row, I could not differentiate them from the background as they kneeled amid the long column of dark brown raisins.

When they boxed raisins, Mom drove the tractor and Dad stacked the rolls on the vineyard wagon. The trailer had planks of wood set into a bed four and a half feet wide by fifteen feet long, with each axle on a turntable so that the wagon could follow directly in the tracks of the tractor and easily slip into the narrow avenues between vine rows. There was an art of stacking the rolls on the bed into a pyramid shape, hundreds of biscuits per load. After a few rows, the wagon became full with the top rolls precariously balancing, held in place by a neighboring roll. My folks then parked under a large walnut tree and spent the rest of the day dumping each roll into a sweat box, mixing the wetter raisins with the dry, blending and stirring to create a proper mix. In the late afternoons when I came home from school, I'd find them talking and working. I helped by gathering the paper trays to burn and playing with the sparks and embers until nightfall.

Later, Dad would stack the sweats in a long column, using the electric hoist and a homemade rig that looked like a sailing mast with a metal beam jutting outward at a ninety-degree angle. After attaching a set of metal clamps to the box, he yanked on a control and the box rose. He then pushed the box, which swung the mast around, dropping the box into place on the stacks. Later, after he covered the tops with paper and wooden trays, our entire harvest sat in a row. As neighbors drove by, they compared crops and exchanged waves.

In the 1960s, large bins were introduced and adopted. These wooden crates are four feet square and three feet deep and hold a thousand pounds. They can be moved only with forklifts. On part of our farm, we once had a huge old red hay barn, with loft and a second-story swinging door where bales were lifted with a pulley system and stored for the winter. But our forklift could barely fit under the entrance doorway, and the pillars and support beams often blocked our path. We tore it down and built a rectangular pole shed where bins and raisins could be kept out of the weather. Across the countryside, old barns were discarded, victims of raisins that needed to be moved and stacked and the larger machines required to do the work without many pairs of hands.

Once the crop is out of the fields, we sigh with collective relief—another harvest completed. We celebrate our Thanksgiving in mid-October.

The process of making raisins has remained virtually the same for centuries. I use no machines to pick the grapes, no chemicals or drying tunnels to cure the berries into raisins. I depend on the sun and trust the weather in September, no different from my father and my grandfather.

We are fortunate that our valley lies precisely at the longitude and latitude ideal for making raisins. When high pressure builds off our California coast, the heat easily rises into the upper nineties and above a hundred, with little morning dew. Alaskan cold fronts track to the Northwest, showering Seattle and Portland with early fall rains but leaving us alone. We also dodge tropical depressions—southern hurricanes swirl off the Pacific coast of Mexico, and should they make land, they break up over Southern California and twist into the Southwest.

But perhaps it is not luck. During Jiichan's lifetime, farmers learned how far north and south they could dry grapes and still avoid storms. Generations before me passed down hard lessons. That's why almost all the nation's raisins are made in a fifty-mile radius that includes our farm.

Historically, raisins were harvested by families. In the first half of this century, in hundreds of small, ten- or twenty-acre vineyards, the father and mother picked the bunches into pans and the older children pulled the containers from under a vine to a waiting tray laid open by the youngest child. Small hands were well suited for gently spacing each bunch so that none were piled atop each other. By the time one tray was completed, another pan full of grapes lay ready. Working as a team, a family could pick three to five hundred trays a day.

Even today, Mexican workers often work as a family unit.

Brothers and their wives, cousins, and nephews team up to work a patch. Labor laws prohibit children from working, although at times they sneak into a vineyard to help their parents. While I am concerned about the working conditions, I sometimes question the message new regulations seem to convey. Are children not supposed to help their families? Is it better for them to be left locked in a hot car? Child care is too expensive for their parents. In the fields, reality is often seen differently than from the point of view of laws and regulations.

THE FIRST YEAR I am back on the farm for raisins, just as they are cured and ready to be rolled an oppressive heat wave settles in our valley. The forecast is for days, perhaps even weeks, of hundred-degree days with evenings remaining a hot seventy degrees. The raisins begin to overdry, hardening into "beans." I can still deliver them, but with each passing hour, my raisins lose moisture and weight. I am not alone—many farmers are in the same situation—and suddenly rollers are at a premium and cannot be found. One crew promises to come in a week. In the meantime my crop literally shrinks daily and so does any chance for profits.

I roll early in the morning and stop only when I am dehydrated and overheated by the early afternoon sun. I hide inside, recuperating and replenishing fluids, preparing for the evening work session. At night my legs cramp badly, my body drained of electrolytes, causing muscles to contract wildly. The next day I feel as if I had bruises inside my calves and hamstrings.

I cancel a visit with an out-of-town girlfriend, Marcy. But she insists on coming, despite my protests. I will have no time for relaxing and entertaining.

Marcy was raised on her family's goat dairy in the high desert of Southern California. She understood the meaning of hard labor, inheriting a strict work ethic from her parents, a hardy Wisconsin German couple who sought redemption as they toiled and sacrificed. Marcy had daily chores of milking and feeding. If she worked twice as fast as normal, she could go to an evening event. Even throughout her undergraduate years, every weekend she returned home to help with the chores.

Despite it all, her blue eyes still sparkled when we talked while both of us attended graduate school in Davis. We traded stories about growing up on a farm, and I concluded her teenage years of milking twice a day was purgatory compared to my life with deciduous crops. At least I had an "off season" I could count on.

"It wasn't that bad," she said, then paused and added, "I guess I didn't know any better."

I agreed—ignorance can be bliss.

She is a small woman, just over five feet tall, with strong forearms and wrists from her "chores." She arrives during my afternoon rest and we briefly visit over dinner. I explain the situation with the raisins and oppressive heat, why the harvest is in jeopardy.

"I understand," she answers. "It is scary."

She then asks to accompany me out into the fields, and I'm impressed when she dresses appropriately in jeans and work boots. Having never seen raisins drying before, she wants to learn all about the process. I end the lesson with a demonstration of a biscuit roll and a hands-on exercise. She quickly learns and insists on helping. We start with a very short row, less than a hundred trays long, and stop at the end of the row as a glorious orange sunset stretches over the western horizon.

I slap at my pants and shirts, dusting myself off.

"Why do you dust yourself when you'll be going right back into the field?" she asks.

I shrug. "Maybe because for a moment, you feel good." We both smile.

A small cloud of dust hovers around us in the still air of dusk. We share a swig of water from the canteens I've placed at both ends of the field.

"You can wait back at the house. I'll try not to be too late," I announce. We both know I'm lying. I'll be out as long as I can, trying to save as much of the crop as possible from tomorrow's hellish inferno.

"I'll help if you let me," she answers.

We each take another short row. I drop to my knees and crawl from tray to tray, saving my legs from the wear of constantly standing and kneeling. The paper rustles and crinkles as I roll a tray. In the next row I can hear her working too. As the sun sets and the temperature slips a few degrees, I can feel the heat dissipating from the earth, radiating upward. The change seems to invigorate my spirits.

We complete another hundred trays and another. The first stars peek out to greet us as we look upward when we gulp water at the end of a row. Even in the darkness, a full moon illuminates our way. But by this time, we're not using our eyes as much. We can almost roll blindfolded, kneeling in the soft earth, grabbing the tray and flipping the raisins inward and quickly rolling the paper. We glide to the next tray and feel for it with open hands.

The sounds at night seem to carry. I know where Marcy is by the sound of her working. She has slowed slightly but does not complain. When I finish my row, I start working in hers. We crawl toward each other, closing the distance between us until the work is completed. Our knees are aching and our backs are stiff as I help her stand up. In the moonlight I reach for her hand and pull her to me. We kiss and exchange dust on our lips.

As we walk home hand in hand, we feel the silence of the ghosts of families who have worked this land. Just as artists must create, farm families must harvest. The work continues no matter the price of our produce. Grapes have to be picked and raisins delivered. And each season will be followed by another year. Marcy returns to Davis and promises to help next season too.

Dad always picks a few trays of raisins for himself. They're from the grapes the workers missed. We find them a week later

when the berries have turned amber and yellow and are so full of
sugar they shatter when tapped, tumbling off the stems and into
a picking pan. Dad dries them in his yard, using old wooden trays.
Every evening he goes out and covers each with another tray in
order to protect it from heavy dews or a sudden early-autumn
rainstorm the next day. This last crop becomes his private reserve
for the family to enjoy. Months from now, in the middle of winter's fog and cold, we'll savor the taste of the past year.

Occasionally, while working in the shed, I'll discover an old
coffee can and shake it. Inside I hear the light tapping of the contents, a soft, muffled knocking unlike the sounds of nails or bolts
clanging together. I pry off the cover and immediately the sugary
scent of raisins perfumes the air. These were from various harvests of the past, Dad tucking away a few bunches in cans, perhaps to have as an afternoon snack as he repaired a tractor or
welded to build a new trailer or packing stand. Now the cans are
scattered throughout the shed, a surprise treat as I labor in the
space where he once worked.

During the short wintry days of fog and cold or the early
spring rains when he can't work in the fields, Dad stems his late
harvest by hand. He spreads newspaper on the kitchen table,
unrolls a tray of raisins, and begins to pick off the tiny dried stems,
first collecting them in his hand and then piling them along an
edge of the paper. He works quietly, sometimes listening to the
radio or pausing and crooking his head in order to read a newspaper article upside down.

A sweet aroma fills the room, and all the family is gradually
attracted to the table. Initially I stand looking over Dad's shoulder,
watching him work, then I take a seat as the sugary morsels
become irresistible. I stem a few and pop them in my mouth.
Grabbing another handful, I study the caramel treats more closely.
Sweet raisins have tiny wrinkles and are plump and meaty. They
look almost black, the dark, rich color of good quality.

Stemming becomes contagious. What began as a brief visit

extends into a family gathering. Before I realize it, my accumulation of stems grows into a small pile. Dad moves his bowl closer to me and I add a handful of cleaned raisins to his collection. Mom and my sister join us, and we each mark our spot at the table with an assemblage of stems. We chat, exchange stories and news, laugh and joke with each other. I eat more than I save, but no one notices. Mom and my sister make plans for baking with the raisins; cookies, cakes, and breads top their lists.

Baachan wanders over to help and sits in her corner chair, silently pulling and piling. She removes her thick glasses after a while and gropes for the berries with her fingers, working by touch only. All the while, the family bowl of raisins continues to fill.

ten

S W E A T

E Q U I T Y

I ENJOY SWEATING, PARTICULARLY DURING FRESNO'S SUMMER DAYS
when you awaken to a glorious sunrise filled with promise and by
noon your shirt is drenched with perspiration and rows and rows
of fields still need weeding. I feel as if I'm breathing through my
skin; heat oozes from every pore with my panting. Drops dangle
from the tip of my nose and run down the sides of my face and
forehead. I wipe my palms as the shovel handle slips in my hand.
Even the bottoms of my feet are wet; I can feel the heat and dampness when I rub my toes together. Despite the blazing sun, a pecu-

liar chill tingles my flesh where the sweat has thoroughly soaked my work shirt. I lean forward when I drive my truck, trying to keep my back away from the seat, but with each bump in the road, I feel a moist lick and cold tickle along my spine.

My baptism of sweat is repeated with each work trip out into the fields. Despite the dust and dirt of a farm, I feel purified as I peel off another drenched T-shirt and feel the rush of heat over my chest. Sweating on a farm instills a sense of freedom. I challenge myself to care for the thousands of vines and trees on my land, and accept the responsibility to succeed or fail based on my own labor and ability to sweat.

Tractor work coats my skin with a blanket of sweat and fine dirt. I can blink and see puffs of dust dance in front of my eyes. At the end of the first couple of rows, I'll pause to pat down my pants and shirtsleeves, shaking the silt from my clothes, slapping my hat against the side of my legs. By the third row, though, I'll stop, ceasing my futile battle to keep the dust from settling upon me. When I finish the field hours later, I drive back to the yard in a mummified state, wrapped in multiple layers of dust. On the inside of my elbows and along my neck I feel the blend of moisture and earth; delicate lines of mud outline the creases of my skin. At home I refrain from sitting, so as not to leave a dust imprint of my rear on any and all surfaces.

I perform a ritual at the backdoor sink. Removing my shirt, first I rinse my fingers and hands. Then I hesitate, debating if I want to completely wash up. I cannot simply splash my face— the water will mix with the dirt and create patches of mud under my chin. A streak will drip down the front of my neck and onto my chest, leaving behind a trail of grime. Instead I immerse my arms under the faucet and dip my shoulders into the steam, watching a brown muddy column run off my skin. With my parched mouth so close, I'll quickly turn my head sideways, cupping my lips below the faucet to gulp the liquid and wastefully let it dribble over my cheek in a satisfying moment of decadence.

Then I immerse my face and feel the heat drain from my cheeks and swirl downward with the water and dust. I blink and stare through the water; only my forehead and eyes are enveloped, yet my mouth opens and closes like a fish's with each breath. I pause before inserting my entire head beneath the faucet. The water falls in sheets through my hair and dribbles down the back of my neck. I shiver with the striking coolness, a reward for washing up.

In the end, I realize I should have taken a shower, but it is not the same. A shower implies the end of work; washing up is just a break. I toss my head back, and a trail of water whips behind me. I feel like a dog shaking itself and wish I had the creature's loose fur and skin to fling off the moisture and watch it sail away around me in an instant cloud of mist. Within a few minutes, though, I will dry in the arid heat of this farm valley, renewed for more work.

I want to return to my fields and sweat more. I lick my lips often and enjoy the tangy taste left on my skin. The sweat, dust, and cool faucet water all merge together and make me feel real—this is honest work. Occasionally, when I drive through town, I'll pass one of those gyms with windows that open to the street. I study the faces of pain and blank stares as people strain and sweat while bouncing on machines and pumping devices up and down or back and forth—a poor substitute for farmwork.

Technological progress in agriculture has reduced the need to sweat, eat dust, and wash up at backdoor sinks. With new innovations, as farmers get older and wiser we're supposed to ease gradually into retirement. Yet most of the old men I call neighbors want to keep working—they may slow down, but to stop work is to become weak and helpless. Farms provide them with lots of opportunity to plug away. Their sons and I will nod our heads and wink at each other when our fathers miss a few rather large clumps of weeds or when we notice a trail of crooked furrows behind the dusty tractor of an old-timer. The vocal grandfathers will defend their driving skills and make sure we know there's a good reason for everything they do: "There's a damn big chunk of hardpan right over there, right there where the furrows swing back and forth." We know better than to walk down the row and try to locate and remove the rock. Surrounded by family and neighbors, old men can work without worry.

Veteran farmers enjoy sweating. As one old-timer explains, "Reminds me that I'm still alive."

I FIND AN old shovel. The blade is browned by rust, but I am struck by the fine old handle. A sheen is reflected in the wood despite the shovel's sitting outside unused and hidden over the winter. Wiping off the grime and dust with my bare hands, I stroke the tight grain and feel a coolness in the sleek surface. Sweat and body oil from working hands has polished the wood tens of thousands of times.

I am intrigued by the fact the handle is broken about a third of the way down. Rarely does useless equipment stay protected in the barn—usually it's tossed onto a junk pile that grows with each farmer. The rough grooves where the wood once snapped off are now quite smooth. Even after the handle was broken, someone still used the shovel until the splinters were abraded and burnished by work.

Why would someone keep a damaged tool? I know Baachan uses the shovel. In her old age, she often rescues broken things and puts them to use. Her favorite phrase is "Can't be wasteful." Her tiny four-and-a-half-foot frame matches the shortened handle. She seems to enjoy digging weeds. I watch her trudge into the fields and spend hours claiming the land from the wild grasses.

Only when I try the shovel do I understand its value. As I poke at some yard weeds, the brown steel slides easily into the dirt, cutting just below the surface, slicing the weeds in a single smooth pass. The rust is deceiving; the metal is still sharp, with a filed edge. But it's the shape of the blade that makes the difference. The shovel face—a relatively flat piece of steel gently bowed upward at the sides—has two crescent-shaped curves that glide through the moist ground of spring and the damp earth of freshly irrigated summer furrows, swimming just below the surface, slicing through delicate roots. Nature has sculpted the correct slopes and angles from solid metal, generations have honed the proper shape so that each pass in the sand and silt acts like a natural whetstone. I can't tell if the original shovel had this shape or if years of use have slowly ground the metal to half the size of a new shovel, leaving only two rounded cheeks instead of the point.

I imagine that once the power of this tool was discovered, it became a favorite of my grandparents and parents. Many times as a child I raced to the shed in order to beat my brother or sister to a special rake. I often see farmworkers wrestling for a favorite picking ladder. Field work marries laborer with tool. One lives with early-morning decisions for hours, intimately getting to know nuances, cursing when the shovel doesn't want to dig deeper or the pruning shear doesn't want to cut faster.

As I sever weeds, the brown rust of the shovel gradually disappears, replaced with the polished gleam of steel, scoured by sandy loam and an occasional fibrous root. I work with a piece of my family's past, a gift I inherit.

By accident I leave the shovel at my folks' house and Dad begins to clear his yard. The next day, piles of weeds lie scattered, and I can hear the scraping of the blade against the dirt behind his shed. "Works damn good, doesn't it?" I say.

He grins and nods his head, then turns and shows me his contribution. I gasp. He has removed the old, broken handle and added a longer one, borrowed from another old shovel. The wood is also smooth and polished with a light stain of oil from his palms and years of his life. "Now it should work even better," he says.

Natural Farming

I want to farm naturally. That sounds odd, because all farming in one way or another is a manipulation of nature. When I first returned to the farm, I found myself working less and less *with* nature—I sprayed chemicals to kill unseen pests for months, applied synthetic fertilizers according to soil tests, mass-marketed my grapes and peaches as a commodity with the highest priority given to volume and bottom-line economics. In the technologically dominated business of agriculture, a natural farm had become an oxymoron.

But as I search for alternatives, organic farming demands I accept a natural uncertainty, a daily dose of chaos. As I walk my fields, I stop worrying about irrigation timetables and days to harvest. I force the voices of pesticide salesmen from my mind. I begin to work in silence.

Natural farming methods require time. Compost takes months, even years, to work into roots and plants. Biological controls (good bugs eating bad bugs) are not quick fixes; generations of lacewings and ladybugs may need to call my farm home before their population levels can challenge worms. In the meantime, my peach trees look weathered and my vines stressed. I begin to doubt myself.

By chance I meet a second-generation-Italian farmer, the father of a friend of mine. He is not that old, perhaps in his late fifties, with thin brown hair, a light complexion, and a quick smile. The exchange takes place in a few minutes, farmers passing each other and talking through rolled-down pickup windows.

He comments, "Good vines don't grow too much. Just enough for the best grapes."

He licks his lips as if sampling the dry wine from his grapes. He peers over his vineyard, a field of mixed greens, some leaves slightly yellowing, others a lush, dark green. Deep red grapes hang under the leaf canopies. A light coat of dust covers the berries, creating a darker hue, a noble color much like velvet. Weeds also find a home in his fields, along with other wild life.

Before he drives down the dirt avenue to check water, he adds: "Vines that struggle make the best grapes."

But the Masumoto vineyards were all Thompson seedless, a grape with high sugars and neutral taste, perfect for raisins or blending with other, higher-quality grapes, but not suited for high-quality wines. Since our crop was sold by weight with little reward for quality, my Italian friend's philosophy seemed out of place. Yet some of our vines grew vigorously, with huge grape leaves that stretched over eight inches wide, and dense leaf canopies that cast long shadows and prevented sunlight from penetrating the interior of the arbor. These vines had poor crops—the green bunches were stringy, the berries scattered instead of nestled tightly together, and many of the canes bore no crop. We wasted fertilizer and labor on these vines, growing shade instead of grapes.

I checked Dad's fertilizing records scribbled in a small notebook with a tiny calendar on the back and the emblem of the local farm credit association where we annually borrowed operating money. Dad followed an old strategy—in good years when we made money, he took care of the farm by repairing equipment, replanting an orchard, retrellising a vineyard, and purchasing fertilizer. When we happened to have a string of good years, Dad followed a fertilizer salesman's advice and served hearty meals of synthetically formulated "triple 15" to all the crops. Our "shade" vines grew lush without any corresponding rise in grape tonnage; our inputs did not increase production. "The vines are growing fat instead of me," I said to Dad and decided to stop using fertilizer.

After returning to the farm, I kept a daily journal of work. After a few years, I realized my calendar system was virtually useless—little was replicated from one year to the next. Only the seasons and their accompanying work—winter pruning, early-spring fertilizing and thinning, late-spring irrigating and fighting pests, summer harvests, fall plantings—were repeated. The exact timing of work varied from year to year according to conditions and circumstances. Some years were "wormy" while others were conducive to brown rot pathogens. Wet springs saved me from irrigating, but the weeds grew wild with the moisture. Mild winters led to early peach bloom in February but not necessarily an early harvest. I began to try to respond to nature rather than manage her.

Our farm belongs to an irrigation district created in 1921 when an entrepreneur obtained water entitlements for the Kings River and organized a group of farmers. Fed by the vast snows from the nearby Sierra Nevada mountains, the Kings was an untapped source of water for thirsty fields. The farmers paid taxes to a district, their lands were granted water rights, and through miles of canals that crisscrossed through the east side of the San Joaquin Valley, water was channeled to new lands. Each of these conduits was monitored by a team of ditch tenders who tried to maintain an even flow of water while scheduling farmers with their turn and monthly allotment.

"Old man Mitchell" was our tender, a slender man in his fifties or sixties with weathered skin etched with wrinkles, especially around his neck. Whenever I saw the gripping Depression-era photographs of Dorothea Lange, I thought of Mr. Mitchell. I don't know if he was a Dust Bowl immigrant from Oklahoma, but his deep-set eyes and hollowed cheeks created shadows across his face and gave him an expression that seemed hardened by tough times in his past. As he drove his old, dusty dark green pickup along the ditch bank, checking the water level, he rarely smiled nor frowned. His bony hands seemed to twitch a little as they gripped the steering wheel. His eyes were glassy, locked in a blank stare. Because he often had to drive through our yards and farms, he had trained his eyes not to roam. It was better to ignore

MASUMOTO FAMILY KANJI.
The *kanji* is written in two characters. The first, Masu translates as "a wooden box used for sake." The second character means "origin." This is not a common Japanese name.

VACCINATED

(Signature or Stamp.)

Keep this Card to avoid detention at Quarantine and on Railroads in the United States.

Diese Karte muss aufbewhrt werden um Anfenthalt an der Quarantäne, sowie auf den Eisenbahnen der Vereinigten Staaten zu vermeiden.

Cette carte doit être conservée pour éviter une détention á la Quarantaine, ainsi que sur les chemins de fer des Etats-Unis.

Deze kaart moet bewaard worden, ten einde oponthoud aan de Quarantijn, alsook op de ijzeren wegen der Vereenigde Staten te vermijden.

Conservate questo biglietto onde evitare detenzione alla Quarantina e sulle Ferrovie degli Stati Uniti.

Tento listek musite uschovati, nechcete-li ukarantény (zastaveni ohledně zjistění zdravi) neb na dráze ve spojenych stětech zdrzeni byti.

Tuto kartocku treba trimat' u sebe aby sa predeslo zderzovanu v karantene ai na zeleznici ve Spojenych Státoch.

合衆國ニ於ケル檢疫所又ハ鐵
道等ニテ停留ヲ免カルル、タメ
此札ヲ保存所持セラルルペシ

IMMIGRANT CERTIFICATE.

U. S. Immigration Service,

Under Dept. Circular No. 159, 1893.

Sept. 11, 189 .

This is to certify that Hikozo Masumoto
a native of _____, who arrived at the port
of _____, per steamship _____
on the ____ day of ____, 189 , has been duly inspected
and registered, and will be admitted into the United States upon presentation and surrender of this certificate to any customs or immigration officer at the frontier. His description is as follows: Age, ____ ; height, ____ ; color of hair, ____ ; color of eyes ____
Remarks ____

Commissioner of Immigration.

2—1781.

HIKOZO MASUMOTO QUARANTINE CERTIFICATE.

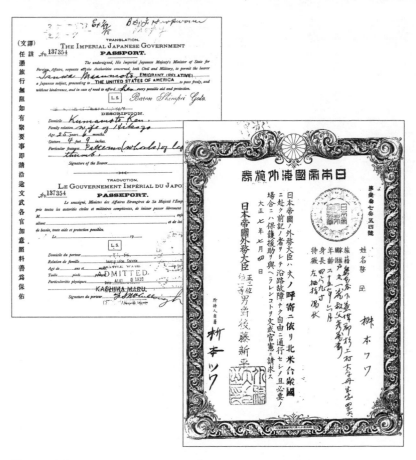

Tsuwa Masumoto passport, 1918.

Tsuwa Masumoto is my grandmother (on my father's side). She too immigrated from Kumamoto, Japan. My grandfather had journeyed back to Japan in 1916, married, and traveled alone back to America. Two years later, he earned enough money to send for his wife, Tsuwa. She traveled on the ship *Kashimaru* during the summer of 1918 and arrived in Seattle.

The couple, whose marriage was arranged, were introduced to each other through pictures. Many Japanese women who immigrated to America were "picture brides," their marriages determined by families who exchanged pictures of prospective brides and grooms. Many couples did not meet each other until they arrived on American shores and were married shortly afterward.

The photo on my grandmother's passport, facing page, was her "picture bride" photo.

熊本縣指令保移甲第　九四〇　號

渡航許可證

一身長　四尺九寸
一特徴　右
髻
右第壹指關節跡
右手金如傷痕

熊本縣下益城郡杉上村大字丹生宮四百六番地

戸主一藏叔父彦藏妻農

桝本　ツワ

明治三十年十壹月貳拾日生

右
　北米合衆國
渡航チ許可ス

大正七年十二月九日
熊本縣知事
太田政弘

This is to certify that the photogra...
attached hereto is a likeness of t...
person to whom this visa is issu...
In witness whereof the seal...
the American Consulate Gener...
Yokohama, Japan, is impre...
upon the photograph.

ERICAN CONSULATE GENERAL,
Yokohama, Japan.

...ON. No. 6088

Vice Consul of The
United States of America.

Dated.

MASUMOTO FAMILY PHOTOS. A series of three photographs of the Masumoto family.

In the first, at left, the young couple poses soon after the arrival of Tsuwa Masumoto from Japan. In the second, below, the couple are photographed with their first born, a son in 1918. In the final photograph, facing page at top, the family has grown to five children. My grandfather Hikozo chooses not to participate in this family pose. My father is sitting on a chair in the sailor outfit. He is the third child, the second son.

UNCLE GEORGE ARMY PHOTOGRAPH. My Uncle George was drafted into the U.S. Army before December 7, 1941. While his family was interned in relocation camps, he fought and was killed in Italy during World War II. This is the photograph my grandmother holds during a memorial service honoring Japanese American soldiers at the Gila River Relocation Center in the Arizona desert.

SNAPSHOT, 1944.
A memorial service for Japanese American service men killed in action.
The location is the Gila River Relocation Center. My family is to the
right—my grandfather holds the American flag, my grandmother the
photo of her dead son. My father is far to the right in uniform—he was
drafted into the U.S. army a few months earlier.

HATSUJIRO SUGIMOTO.
My grandfather on my mother's
side. He was the first to die at
Gila River Relocation Center.

JIICHAN AND BAACHAN MASUMOTO.
My grandfather, just before his death in 1953, and my grandmother.

FAMILY PORTRAIT.
Jiichan and
Baachan
Masumoto with
three of their chil-
dren. (The oldest, a
son named George,
is not pictured.)
Standing in the
center is Tomiko,
their first daughter.
My father, Tak, is
held by my grand-
father, and my
Uncle Stan is in my
grandmother's
arms.

MARU TANAKA.
My grandmother's sister-in-law from Kumamoto, Japan. She tends the fire in the *ofuro*/Japanese bath.

BAACHAN MASUMOTO.
My grandmother peeling a piece of fruit. She was in her early eighties. She and my father held the knife the same way while peeling—gently rotating the fruit as the skin fell away from the blade.

Mas Masumoto.
Harvesting peaches into picking buckets. The wooden sticks are called props and are used to support sagging branches heavily laden with ripe fruit.

Mas Masumoto and his parents.
My father, Tak Masumoto, stands to the left with my mother, Carole Masumoto, on the right. We have just completed picking and packing these boxes of peaches—our finest variety, Sun Crest—which we sell under the label "Masumoto Family Farm."

Mas Masumoto.
Series of farm photographs taken with our grapes and peaches. The family dog is named Jake. *Photo credit: Jeremy Green, courtesy of American Farmland Trust.*

KORIO MASUMOTO.
My-four-year-old son, Korio, enjoying a peach.

Left to right, Korio, myself, ten-year-old Nikiko and my wife Marcy
Masumoto at the summer Obon festival in California. A taiko drum
stands in the background.

work habits or things that might not look right in our fields. They were not his business.

Once, while he was informing me of my irrigation dates, I surprised him by asking, "How do you know when the vines and trees need water?"

He stopped, startled by the invitation to conversation. Then his cab door creaked and moaned as he pulled his way out. His spring-cushion bench seat was frayed, with the cotton filling popping out of the brown upholstery. As he reached back for his straw hat, some of the white fibers flew into the air and danced with the dust and sunlight. He turned a dull gray key and the engine whined, then sputtered to a stop. "What was that?" he asked.

"How do you know when the fields want water?" I said.

He nodded, tightened his lips into a frown. "Guess you go by the feel," he said.

I blinked. I had expected a different answer, like "Don't know," or "Not sure, maybe when it looks dry."

I asked, "What do you mean by 'feel'?"

"By your hand, of course," he answered. He walked over to our ditch gate, where weeks ago water had leaked and created a small puddle that dried up. He grabbed a handful of damp earth, clenched the wad tightly in his right hand, squeezed, then quickly opened his palm, and the dirt briefly clung together but crumbled. "Feels like you might need to water pretty soon," he concluded.

I practiced for a few minutes, grabbing different handfuls of dirt, squeezing, and asking his opinion. He became a teacher, instructing me on the ideal location to draw my sample, helping me to interpret the various colors and hues, sharing a story or two about pumps and deep wells and the strata of earth below us.

"Once, when they were drillin' a well, they found an ancient piece of redwood over a hundred feet below," he said. He tipped his yellowed hat, stained with sweat on the brim, and scratched his head. "Whew. Can you imagine how old that piece of wood must be?" He shook his head, lost in thought for a moment. Then suddenly he blinked and his glassy eyes stopped wandering and refocused. He straightened up, his slender frame growing rigid. "Humph," he concluded, nodding his head slightly. Before I could thank him, he strode back to his truck, slipped in, and was gone with a trail of dust behind him.

For weeks, I experimented with old Mr. Mitchell's touch method, randomly grabbing a scoop of dirt, squeezing, and judging moisture content. I discovered that dry soil would not hold together at all but crumbled in my hand and could not be formed into a ball. Moist soil stuck together and kept its shape. My fingers left notches and grooves in the dark earth and the fragrance smelled rich. Wet soil felt like mud and gushed between my fingers. It had a rank odor. Left in the sun, the gooey soil sample would harden into a rock, its crusty surface quickly becoming scarred with hairline cracks.

I also noticed that my hand was stained differently depending on the moisture. Dry dirt left little or no mark, while wet earth stained my hands. This varied according to the different soil types on our ranch. Our high, sandy ground created a light stain that quickly dried into a powder and was easily dusted off when I clapped my hands together. Our lowlands had more silt and clay and the dampened earth left a bronze hue in the palm of my hand. For hours, as I walked throughout the fields, the particles stayed clinging to my skin's wrinkles. Later, when I washed up and watched the faucet water turn slightly tan, I realized how much the stain had penetrated my skin.

Hand testing our soil for moisture is like preparing clay for ceramic work. My potter friend Bob described how he first wedges the clay, kneading it on a workbench top, massaging the lump, making it soft and pliable while removing air pockets and tiny bubbles that could shatter a pot when fired in a kiln. "You need to work the clay with your hands to get a feel for it. Warm it up as you warm up to it," he explains. "When I wedge, I think of shaking hands with the clay."

I squeeze a handful of earth, trying to get a feel for the land, unlock some of its secrets. It will take years to warm up to this place, to feel the dampness, to understand the meaning of the stains and learn the tones of the different soils. I want to know the various scents of my soils, rub the textures between my fingers and thumbs, watch and study the dust particles as they settle back to the earth, wondering if they contain a hint or clue to the mystery of this place, lessons each generation must learn for itself.

I never saw my father squeeze the dirt before he irrigated. I wonder if Jiichan understood this method or if he watched his father in Japan test their land before watering the rice. But they were good farmers, and like old man Mitchell, I'm sure they shook hands with the land many times.

A neighbor, a young farmer in his thirties, swears by tensiometers and neutron probes that can measure soil moistures. "They don't lie," he informs me. We stand by the roadside next to our pickups wearing beat-up baseball caps.

"But what do the numbers mean?" I ask. "Do you take an average, knowing the sandy ground will always be drier than clay soils?"

He shrugs, and contends that his automated drip irrigation system of hoses and pressure gauges always maintains a constant, even flow to his entire farm. "I don't worry," he concludes, grinning, crossing his arms as he leans against his pickup. The brim of his cap casts a shadow across his face. I can see his white teeth.

When I take a rest break in the fields, I squat and grab some dirt, squeeze it like a stress-relieving device, and let the earth crumble out of my palm. I want to feel when the land needs water. I rub my callous fingertips against my palm. The dry particles shift and tumble to the earth. I want to worry about my soil.

I attend a farm conference about growing cover crops to replace synthetic fertilizers. "Green manure," they call it. Planting clovers, legumes, and vetches will increase soil nitrogen, build organic matter in the earth, and provide a healthy habitat for beneficial insects. I plant a dense stand of red and strawberry clover, fava beans, and cahaba white vetch and toss in a handful of California wildflowers. I chuckle, feeling a bit foolish about the rush of free spirit I feel as I fling seeds for a random mix of poppies, mountain garlands, baby blue-eyes, and five-spots. Such frivolous behavior does not fit my image of the stoic farmer, especially the reserved character of someone raised Japanese. But my act is private, and I have until next spring to think about how I'll explain the golden poppy petals and the pink and lavender stocks of garlands to my father.

I learn that when he was younger, Dad also planted cover crops as well as spread manure to build our soils. "We couldn't afford the modern synthetic fertilizers," he explains.

He planted a variety of berseem clover that grew low to the ground and easily reseeded itself, going for years without replanting. He also purchased tons of manure to augment the soil. I remember the autumn smell of manure. With the harvest safely picked and sold and if the peach and grape prices were high, farmers banked their profits in the land. I could smell the fortune of my neighbors with each gentle shift in an evening breeze.

Cover crops, manure, and compost—they require a different time line. I can't see their results immediately; it may take years to build up the soil organically. But I have inherited the memory of good practices from my father. I wait and hope that by next spring, I will be able to smell the aroma of fresh-cut vetch, feel the soft, carpetlike texture of our clovers, and witness the crimson clover reseed itself for the future. My wildflowers will bring a new smile with their spring blooms.

I walk with Everett, an entomologist by training, who is monitoring my fields and helping me establish a habitat for beneficial insects rather than using pesticides. He's in his sixties, with long, healthy legs that take huge strides, white hair and beard, and an elfin grin on his face. He moves rapidly through the orchards, sweep net in hand, gathering samples from the weeds and cover crops. The green-stained net whisks above the canopy, occasionally dipping into the tops to capture dozens of creatures. He stops, rings the mesh with his large hands, and slowly herds his catch into the end. Then he gradually inverts the net, exposing the trapped insects as they pause for a moment, crawling toward the small opening he makes. His eyes dart, assessing and evaluating, scanning the sample before they escape. Then he reaches up and sweeps high into the tree, curious to see what's there. At over six feet tall, he can reach different life, the winged creatures that are not ground feeders.

"Height adds a new dimension," he proclaims as we walk home. At five feet six inches, I have to look up to him as we talk. "Farming is three-dimensional," he contends.

We discuss my experimentation with pheromones. From each tree I hang a small strip that's been coated with a scent. During the mating season of the oriental fruit moth, my strips contain the odor of a female moth. The males enter the area and become confused with an orchard full of this perfume. They cannot locate the female to mate. No eggs are fertilized; no worms will chew on my peaches.

"Birth control" is how Everett describes it.

"Frustrated males," I add.

We both grin.

But pheromone perfume is affected by location. The scent tends to settle low to the ground, being slightly heavier than air, and can layer in a field, exposing the top of the orchard to unprotected sex. So by trial and error, we have determined the proper height at which to hang these strips.

A field is more than just trees or vines. It includes the roots under the surface, the ground floor, and the zone at the tops of the peaches and grapes. "Think in three dimensions," Everett concludes. "Like the past, present, and future."

Buying Junk Piles

An agricultural economist writes of the changing trends in farm ownership. More and more farmland is concentrated into larger and larger operations. Less of the land is being purchased, more of it is leased and managed. This fits the character of our economy—use something for a while and then move on, throw it away. But I can't imagine working this farm and simply moving on. Too much history lies buried here. A few years after returning from college, I buy half the farm from Dad—forty acres, an old farmhouse, and a junk pile.

All good farms have a junk pile. It stays with the land and a succession of owners who contribute to the collection of odd machine parts, old equipment, and discarded but never forgotten stories.

Once I found a long round metal bar in our junk pile—taller than I, fat as a baseball bat, weighing thirty pounds, with a thick square steel point welded on. We used the tool to break up buried chunks of hardpan, especially when we discovered a slab while punching a hole to replace a vine row end post. I started by digging into the earth, clearing a passage about two feet wide. In the worst ground, my shovel often struck rock a few feet down. At first I'd try cutting around the blockage, hoping it was small and easily removed. But when my blade bounced off the stone, I dragged out the metal "hardpan puncher." Lifting and dropping, I pounded the rock, raising and thrusting the spear, chiseling a path. Eventually I'd break through, then drop to my knees in order to remove the fragments, anxiously inspecting the crevice, hoping another stone did not lie just beneath.

Between gasps and grunts, I'd lean on the shaft, stroking the smooth steel, pressing my cheek against the cool metal. I often wondered where the tool had come from. I doubted it was fashioned for breaking hardpan. Dad did not know. "It came with the farm," he said.

The farmer before us, Al Riffel, was a kindly man whose family we considered our friends. Dad says that Al was almost too kind, always willing to drop his work and help out others. "Doesn't make for the best business decisions," Dad explains. "But it makes for a good neighbor." I dragged the bar into his house and laid it on the dining-room linoleum. The retired farmer in his eighties grinned. His thin white hair and pale face contrasted with his bright blue eyes. "Well, thought I'd never see that again!" He picked up one end, unconsciously wrapped stiff fingers around the shank. He had spent hours with the implement, and as we talked, I watched his hands open and close, flexing and stretching aching muscles, gripping and regripping the shaft.

"This came from the railroad company," he explained. "They used it to set the track. A team of men stuck the point under a rail." He tried to stand, but diabetes had weakened his feet and legs. I took the bar and bent at the waist, angling the tip beneath imaginary steel. He continued, "Together they shifted the iron in place while another team held spikes and pounded with mallets. That's why the pointed end has to have a flat face—to push the rail. And a round bar for gripping."

I once saw film of railroad workers performing this task, a leader barking out a fast-paced chant or rhythm, the crew of broad, muscular men hollering together as they slid the rail, a booming sledgehammer adding percussion. I pictured my hard-pan puncher cradled in the thick, strong hands of these workers. But both Al and I had fairly small hands. We would be dwarfed by the huge workers who built America's railroads.

"Chinese," injected Al. "It was Chinese work crews who used this before I got it."

I ran my fingers over the dimples in the metal, shallow pockmarks from the years of rust. Over the seasons, with each new set of hands, the steel shined with use.

In 1964, the Riffels departed for another farm eight miles to the east. We bought their forty acres, adding it to Dad's original forty. Now I work the land of Al and his family and search through piles of junk left behind. I'm sure over the years he added stuff from other friends, materials stored out on the farm because there was no other place to put it, objects given to the farmer when a neighbor sold his ranch and parted with his collection. We've received similar gifts from a retiring farmer—his old drag disk, an old dump rake, a set of spring tooth cultivator shanks, and a homemade A-frame.

Good junk sometimes gets moved from one corner of a barnyard to another with a new owner. We shifted Al's pile from behind to the side of the barn. Dad wanted to clean up the place, but it looked the same to me, only with a different view. "I wanna be able to see what's there," Dad rationalized. Dad never intended to throw much away. He had a favorite line, "You never know when you might need something," as he tossed his own stuff onto the top of the pile. Anything metal can eventually be used, according to Dad, "as scrap iron for welding."

Since I have a forklift, my first major contribution to the pile is to restack most of it onto wood pallets. I now have a portable junk pile. I can move the stuff from place to place, sort of like a modern archaeologist using machinery during his rummage through history.

I use the junk to fix things and glean new ideas and inspiration. When a sculptor friend and I probed though the pile, he was enthralled by the variety of odd shapes and angles. We pulled out a bright orange forked steel tooth from some type of harvester, sat it upright and then on its side, and walked around and made comments. He buried part of it in the dirt and called it modern art. I left it in place for a few months, then dug it out when I needed to cultivate that area, tossing it back on the pile and calling it postmodern art.

My junk pile allows me the freedom to fail, unlike modern farming, in which we often buy a specific tool for a specific job. This odd collection of objects seems to encourage experimentation and foster a slower pace with trial and error. I enjoy farming without the pressure of a quick solution. Since my return to the farm, I've begun testing various methods, like mechanical weed controls instead of herbicides. But this requires different sets of disks and plows and cultivators. My junk pile contains potential solutions for my challenges—I just need to find them.

While searching for a different weed cutter implement, I found a pile of old disks. I mounted one of the blades on the outside edge of a tandem disk and found that it didn't cut the normal depth and instead only skimmed the surface, just enough to peel off the top few inches. But that was perfect for killing weeds without slicing feeder roots of my peaches or grapevines. Another set of blades were worn so badly they didn't cut at all, which helped me to realize it was okay to leave a strip of untilled earth behind my tractor and disk—the clover cover crops thrive in the undisturbed area, along with a horde of earthworms.

I recycle and renew the old. I feel that a used plow shear still has lots of energy left in it and mount it next to new ones. The cutting edge of an ancient French plow blade is reattached to a ridger that I use to dig a shallow trench when irrigating. The odd shapes of some tool bars create numerous possibilities. The three-inch-wide metal staffs range in length, usually five to seven feet. Implements, such as a flat furrow, plow, or harrow, are attached to these thick bars. A bent one may work with a modified berm plow—the curvature creates a natural guide to push low branches and limbs out of the way. The very short one can be attached to my weeder, providing the option of reducing the width of the setup for the dozen narrow vine rows that were planted crooked.

Treasures lie hidden. The old pieces from equipment tell me of a history of a farm. It's as if time is left behind in these relics, but not as fossils or memorials to the past. The remains are to be used by future farmers.

We sat at the kitchen table, the window open and the fresh smell of spring wandering inside. Dad and I signed the papers, and a once-in-a-generation exchange took place—he passed me the grant deed to the farm. I now owned forty acres. Dad would keep his forty until I was "on my feet," as he put it, and ready to buy the other half. I joked that I was finally committed to stay in one place for a while. Our accountant had advised us that technically, I could turn around and sell the land anytime for profit. A moment of silence followed, then both Dad and I exhaled with a "humph"—a type of sigh that we both trust.

I moved into the ninety-year-old farmhouse that came with the farm. The foundation was sound, the wood weathered, the rooms full of dreams. Vineyards surrounded the structure, and peach orchards stood to the south and west, visible from my front windows. Tractors and equipment were parked under an adjacent shed, and the junk pile remained the centerpiece of the barnyard. When I walk the land, I think about junk piles and old vines and trees.

Staking a Claim

The steel glistens in the cool air, polished with dew; the drops capture the sunlight in an early-morning dance. I lift my pounder and drive another metal pole into the earth next to the old redwood stakes. Gnarled vines have wrapped themselves around the wooden shafts, bent and leaning from years of growth. They will like my new stakes, I think to myself, straight and upright, supporting harvests for decades.

The metal does not look natural against the black of vine trunks. The redwood stakes have aged over the years into a gray tone that complements the brown moist earth. But in order to restake with wood, I would have to dig a hole for each one and tap each with a sledgehammer without splintering the top. I refuse to do this—it takes too much time and I have not yet learned the light touch required to pound delicately. Metal stakes have a sharp edge that slices through compacted dirt and roots, and they can be pounded with a metal weight. I lift the heavy pipe with one end capped and slam it downward, jamming the shaft past chunks of rock and roots. I'm told that the metal stakes will last for years. That's what Dad said about the wooden ones.

I am raising the height of the vineyard. Instead of the five-foot redwoods, I purchase seven-foot metal stakes with cross-arms that will support two top wires above the vines, making more room for a thicker canopy of leaves. The extra height will not only increase production but also lift each bunch of grapes and expose it to the breezes—the increased circulation of air will reduce humidity and help in my battle with mildew and other diseases. The old redwood stakes lasted a long time only because many were treated with now banned chemicals that reduced rot and repelled termites.

After a few days of pounding, my arms begin to ache. I take long showers before bed. By the end of the week, my back hurts and I resort to hot showers both in the morning to reduce the stiffness and in the evening to coax crying muscles into rest. Instead of blisters, calluses begin to grow on my hands, protecting them from the constant abrasion.

Through my pounder, I learn the lay of the land and can visualize the topography two feet beneath the surface, feeling the hardpan sections and the rich topsoil areas. I can distinguish between a rock that abruptly stops a stake, sending a wicked vibration through my hands, and the slicing of a thick root, as the stake inches deeper, splitting the woody fibers beneath the surface. My muscles develop a physical memory of the earth.

I fall to my knees, the vineyard spinning around me for a few seconds. My steel pounder slipped off the top of the stake as I slammed it down. It bounced high and grazed my head. I swear at the stake and then myself for being so careless. I stand, still light-headed, and figure I can work my way through the pain. But as I wipe my forehead with the back of my hand, I notice my sweat feels too warm and slick. I glance down and see the bright red of blood. "It doesn't hurt that bad," I say to myself as my fingertips make their way up my scalp. My hair becomes matted; it's hard to locate the gash. As the blood dribbles down to my forehead, I have to keep blinking to keep it out of my eyes. I realize I need to get home and see how badly I've damaged myself.

I stumble to my truck and look in the rearview mirror. Like a kid, I gasp at the sight of my own blood, the red streaking down the sides of my face and drips dangling on my nose. I ponder the worst scenarios—passing out in the vineyard, found by Dad and rushed to the hospital. Or perhaps Jake, the trusty farm dog who likes to lick strangers instead of bark at them, will find my body and lap my face, and I'll send him off like Lassie with instructions to find help.

I use an old sweatshirt as a compress to slow the bleeding and head home. I have trouble holding on to the steering wheel with my one free but sticky hand. An ache begins to throb in my head. I cannot focus on the road, and I drive by a familiar feel of the dirt avenues, recognizing the bumps that signal the upcoming turn, searching for the final potholes guarding the barnyard. I try to calm myself, imagining that a racing heart pumps more blood out of a wound.

Once home, I sit for a moment in the cab, trying to collect myself, then stumble out and head directly for the garden hose, sticking my bloody head underneath the cool water. I keep my eyes open as the liquid changes from stained burgundy to a light tinge of red. I hope the injury isn't as bad as I thought. I locate a mirror, and between my hairs I can see a long scrape where the edge of the pipe pounder sliced into my scalp. A flap of skin floats in blood and hurts when I tug at it. "But it's not deep," I keep repeating to myself as I lie on the front porch in the sunlight, waiting for the blood to clot.

The next day I return to the vineyard and find blood smears on the pounder, the metal stake, and the vine trunk. I remember as a child, whenever one of us kids got cut, we'd rub the blood on each other and mark the place where the accident occurred, making a red X on a peach tree limb or grape stump. We left smears, tagging the landscape with our blood. I will remember this spot where the stake refused to penetrate the earth and I bled, just as Dad recalls those areas where his redwood stakes would not anchor in the soil because of a hardpan layer a few feet below. He probably shattered a few posts, straining his arms and shoulders. Then, with a ringing vibration left in his hands, he accepted the fact he could pound no deeper. I have found a few of these areas too, where my stakes stand above the vine canopy by a foot or two, markers flagging the battle that nature won.

I begin pounding a new row. Tap, tap, whack, broken by a pause as I walk to the next stake. Tap, tap, whack. The rhythm is altered when I strike hardpan or thick roots. Add three extra taps and a deliberate whack, accompanied by a grunt and groan escaping from deep in my lungs. I tighten my muscles and clench my teeth. With the next vine the cadence resumes. I feel like a shoe cobbler patiently tapping away, his art noticed only when his work is completed.

Later a neighbor and I chat. "Hear you makin' some improvements," he says. He knows exactly what work I'm doing and can hear my progress across the vineyard.

I imagine over the years my new stakes will age and loose their luster. Some will twist with abuse when I hook them with a disk or snag a thick cane that yanks and contorts the metal. But unlike wood, the metal will bend and not break. On spring mornings, I will see my contribution to this land, no different from Dad when he added his redwood stakes or Jiichan when he planted a field that was once bare.

WE WAVE TO each other. A moment of solidarity between two people working, a common language of sweat and place. I may be on my tractor and look across the ditch to see another worker on a wagon or in a pickup, or I may be walking with my shovel when workers complete their rows across the street and look up. We recognize each other and connect for a brief moment.

The arm is raised slowly, allowing for recognition despite the distance. A dramatic reaching for the sky, a single hand stretches upward, fingers open. I hold it upright until seen and greeted with a like response, the space between us shrinking with each second, the blue heavens and country air linking two waves together. I nod as my tractor turns for another pass down another row or the workers slip back into the vineyard and disappear behind the lush green growth.

They may or may not speak English or be American citizens. It makes little difference. We are joined by the bond of working the land. I believe Jiichan understood the wave. I can imagine him waving, knowing little English but conversing with other laborers across a field, on someone else's land. A swing of the arm and hand as neighbors share the bone-chilling dampness of a foggy winter or the heat of a moment on a hot summer day. I also wave to the shadows that appear and disappear in my fields, the spirits of old farmers still working.

eleven

HONORED
PLACES

Brown Rice Sushi

YEARS AGO, DURING A SUMMER BREAK FROM COLLEGE AT BERKELEY,
I brought home a newly found obsession with organic foods. Not
only would I try to persuade Dad to start farming differently
using natural, holistic methods, I hoped to integrate a new philosophy into all of my family's life, including meals. One of my
goals was to enlighten everyone to the wonders of brown rice.

On the second day home I shocked everyone by volunteering

to make the dinner rice. Both Mom and Baachan looked up from their work of thinly slicing and marinating strips of beef. Mom asked, "Are you sure?" After I nodded, she returned to chopping vegetables while carefully trying to avoid bumping Baachan in the cramped kitchen.

When the family gathered for the meal at the dining table, my sister, who was also visiting from Los Angeles, and I both slipped into our childhood seats. But Baachan and my parents had changed chairs, adjusting to a childless household. It felt odd for my father to sit so far from his usual place at the head of the table with Mom seated opposite Baachan.

With serving bowls placed in the center of the table, we filled our plates with *teriyaki* beef, *tofu*, stir-fried *napa*, and carrots. I alone heaped a large helping of steaming hot brown rice on my plate. I smacked my lips aloud, trying to induce everyone to share in the new flavor. A half hour later, with a pot full of the rice sitting cold in the center of the table and people nibbling on the meat and vegetables, I got the message that my enlightenment campaign was in trouble.

Baachan finally asked, "Did someone burn the rice?" My sister burst out laughing. Mom stood and bolted for the kitchen. I sat in my chair, weakly smiled, and tried to laugh too.

Dad didn't think it was so funny. He added, with a hungry look, "You know, Jiichan ate Japanese rice his whole life and lived almost eighty years." Returning from the kitchen, Mom carried a reheated pot of white rice left over from lunch and we continued the meal.

As a child, I understood the difference between the short-grain "Japanese rice" and the long-grain, grocery-store variety we called "Chinese rice," which we considered inferior because it didn't stick together. Dad purchased our rice at the farmers' co-op that he belonged to, a local association formed by Japanese-American farmers after World War II. Our rice came in fifty-pound bags that Dad poured into a special three-foot-high round steel can with a lid—a trash can dedicated to storing rice. Many times he let me help him by steadying the can and I'd watch the white kernels stream in, raining against the metal sides, clattering with a rising pitch as the can filled to the brim. I felt as if we were rich.

Our rice sack always had bold *kanji* printed on it, signifying that the grain was grown in California by Japanese-American farmers. The large red lettering *Ko-ku-ho* was written with a distinctive Japanese style, as if painted with brush strokes. (Once I asked Baachan what *Kokuho* meant and Mom translated—"national gift." Later I learned the correct translation is "national treasure.") Like the American pioneer women who saved flour sacks and every scrap of material, Baachan had many uses for the old rice sacks. She bleached out the printing and made underwear. She dried plates and cups with rice sack dish towels. She stuffed the used bags with strips of rags and sewed the open end closed to make a soft pillow. We took naps with our heads resting against stiff cotton that rustled in our ears as we shifted our heads.

Rice was a daily symbol of Japanese traditions, one of the few that survived generations in America. But could I simply substitute one rice dish for another without disrupting the pattern of the entire meal? White rice brought meaning into our home.

When I tell Marcy my brown rice disaster story, she muses, "Perhaps it's not what brown rice is—but what it isn't. The way you served it was quite simply not Japanese."

I frown and shrug, begging for clarification.

"Japanese are not used to men cooking, especially in your family! And then there's the question of substitution," Marcy says.

Japanese seem to accept cultural differences when there is a clear demarcation of that difference. They use a different written alphabet, *katagana*, when writing foreign words. Japanese food is served on Japanese dishes, but perfectly tasty-looking Western-style dishes would look odd if presented on a Japanese-style tray. Baachan did not like the time I wore tennis shoes instead of *zori*/slippers with my *happi* coat at the summer Obon.

Marcy then adds, "I'm Caucasian and people in the community seem to accept me. But I think it's because I fortunately don't try to be like a Sansei." I pondered what she meant by "fortunately."

Finally I sigh, "Then it must always be white rice. Things will never change."

"But you married me," Marcy whispers, then laughs.

Baachan calls brown rice *inaka* food, something for peasants. Japanese see it as impure because the bran, which is refined away in white rice, darkens the grain. The stripping of the nutritious bran from rice adds a Japanese flavor, even for me: eating white rice reminds me of home, it makes me feel Japanese-American. Yet how do I mediate the health benefits of brown rice with the Japanese diet of white rice?

East meets West and the drama unfolds atop a plate. I had seen a newspaper cartoon in which the dual worlds of American and Japanese traditions have clashed. In the first two frames, a Japanese-American child asks his mother, "What's for lunch?" The mother is preparing *makizushi*, a type of *sushi* with rice rolled in black seaweed.

She answers, "We are having *makizushi*."

The son immediately pouts, "Yuck, I want hot dogs!"

Later, the mother calls her son to the lunch table. The mother wears a sage smile, and to the son's surprise, she has his "hot dog" on his plate—a wiener wrapped in black seaweed instead of a bun.

The cartoon helps me envision a solution that bridges differences and conceive of a new packaging of culture, one not American nor Japanese but a fusion of the two.

Perhaps my brown rice needs packaging, a frame that links the natural food community with a Japanese-American sensibility. I imagine a type of brown rice *sushi*, with the rice encased within *nori*/seaweed, a literal and symbolic wrapping within

Japanese tradition. Brown rice then would no longer substitute for white rice on a dinner plate but rather be a creative, alternative form of making and serving food.

My brown rice *sushi* requires a certain context to be introduced, an environment or situation open to change. My folk's dinner table contains too many other established roles and routines; the mere presence of food from Marcy and me brands it as different, even unnatural.

The opportunity for our cultural contribution to the Del Rey Japanese community occurs at the annual New Year's potluck, a gathering of twenty or thirty families, usually held on the weekend following New Year's Day. Marcy is considered new to the community. Her dishes are expected to be different, since she is not a Sansei. Sociologists could have labeled us the perfect change agents—a new generation, educated and entering the community as highly motivated outsiders. Family friends still call us "the kids."

We meet in the old hall. Long rows of tables run the length of the interior, with butcher paper spread on top functioning as clean white tablecloths. The adult men plant themselves along a row of tables against the one wall, the women sit along another set of tables hugging the opposite wall. The in-between tables are for children and younger adults. When I was growing up, we had five rows of tables to seat over two hundred people, with dozens of children running and chasing each other. Over the years, fewer and fewer come; many Issei have died, the Nisei age, and all but two or three Sansei have left the area, drawn to jobs in the city and careers with more opportunities. The *toban*/organizing committee finally concedes that the extra rows of empty chairs are no longer required.

Food remains the centerpiece of the evening. Spread across two head tables, various dishes are jammed together, salads first, then rice, followed by the main entrees, with desserts last and drinks crowded on a side table. The like foods are grouped next to each other, chicken dishes presented in a tight circle, fruit pies rubbing crusts, *wonton* and beef *teriyaki* sticks poking each other. Patterns have evolved at these annual gatherings. The "better" cooks always make the Japanese food, and others bring American foods like meatballs and fried chicken. Recently enchiladas and taco salads have become popular. The Nihon wives (women born in Japan who have married Nisei men) tend to dominate the Japanese food circuit, often in competition. Some of the Nisei women joke that they no longer have to bring Japanese food, since "the Nihon wives are so good at it." I sense a relief from many of them. American food can be served in all sorts of manners, but Japanese food demands a strictly proper appearance and taste.

Marcy and I decide to introduce our brown rice *sushi* in that setting. I am one of the few Sansei attending the gathering, one of the few farm sons who has returned to work in the area, and Marcy is the only *hakujin*/Caucasian. When we walk through the double door entry, people look up, smile, and wave. Marcy carries the *sushi*. A Nisei woman quickly takes the plate from her, commenting on how nice it is of her to bring something, and then directs us to be seated. We feel like guests in our own home. "We'll take care of all this," the woman says, smiling as she asks what food we brought.

"Brown rice *sushi*," I answer. The woman keeps looking at Marcy, smiles again, and peeks under the foil cover. After we take our seats, I glance back to see a dozen women surrounding our plate, curious and not wanting to be left out.

The Del Rey Kyowakai/Community Club president welcomes everyone, "Let's hope for healthy times in the New Year! *Itadaikimasu!*"—Let us eat! The Issei are asked to go first and fill their plates, then the rest of the men, then the children follow with the women last. Marcy, still considered a guest, and I are politely requested to line up between the adult men and children but instead wait—we want to observe the popularity of our brown rice *sushi*. Four or five plates of *sushi* are on the table. All of them except ours are *inarizushi*, Japanese rice stuffed into small pouches made from soybean curd. The *sushi* we brought is *makizushi*, rice rolled in black seaweed with strips of vegetables in the center. Our *sushi* was cut into round pieces with a brightly colored vegetable in the center and black on the outside. But instead of the contrasting white rice, we had used brown.

The lines of hungry Issei men shuffle around the head tables, scanning the dishes and selecting their food. At a glance, the brown rice *sushi* stands out from the other rice dishes because it happens to be the only *makizushi*. People lean closer as they pick up pieces with their chopsticks and hold them up to the light, seemingly studying the color. By the time everyone has a first helping, as usual, all the *sushi* is gone. Marcy won't admit it, but she is relieved.

After dinner we begin asking what people thought about our *sushi*. Some are surprised and wonder why it looks different, others comment on the slightly different flavor. I quickly survey the men but garner few comments.

Two of the older Issei didn't realize there was a difference. I ask about the darker color and they say, "I thought it looked odd. I couldn't tell for sure. My eyes . . . *warui ne*"—bad. Some other men didn't notice any difference in the flavor. At that point in the evening they are quite happy with their *sake* and insist I toast the New Year with them.

One of the men says, "No taste the flavor of the rice. It same?" He then takes a sip of very, very hot tea, smacks his lips, and sighs. His taste buds have probably been fried with a lifetime of scalding teas and bowls of noodles.

Later a friend of my mom's decides to conduct a series of interviews of her own. She approaches the keenest judges—the Nihon wives. They sit together in a corner of the room, chatting in Japanese, nodding their heads and covering their mouths when they giggle or laugh.

Their response is polite and clear: "The *sushi* tastes different."

Some say the rice was too hard and should have been cooked longer. Others are concerned about the dirty look of the rice—it isn't white and clean. But despite their minor concerns, they agree it's pleasing and enjoyable and they are happy to see "young folks" make Japanese food. In addition, for most this is the first time they have eaten brown rice. A few others wish we had brought more of the *sushi* to try.

When I explain that Marcy made the *sushi*, more praise and amazement are expressed. "Oh? She make *sushi*?" "*Heeeiii . . . joozu ne!*"—how clever!

Marcy whispers, noting how polite they seem, "Is my *sushi* that surprising?"

As the evening winds down, a few people begin to clean up, collecting their utensils. A new tradition has evolved at these potlucks. People bring much more food than before and therefore feel comfortable sharing their leftovers while filling their plates with the delicacies of others.

"This is perfect for tomorrow," claims Mrs. Morishige as she picks some *teriyaki* beef sticks and carefully places them between the potato salad and garlic bread. "With all the kids gone, it's so hard to cook for just two!"

At least a half-dozen women wander over to Marcy's empty plate and look disappointed they cannot take home a sample. Perhaps they want to taste the flavor at home in a private setting with their families. I whisper to Marcy that we should double the recipe for the next potluck. She shakes her head and says, "Yeah, right."

I help the men gather chairs, store tables, and sweep floors. A mixture of laughter and Japanese fills the old hall as chairs are dragged across the wooden floor, the stage curtains are opened, and the tables are stacked in the unused area.

I join Marcy and she shows me her dish, a flat antique carnival glass piece from her grandmother. Some of the women have carefully placed food on the rose-colored glass, the Japanese items to one side, the taco salad next to the spaghetti. Some reddish heavenly bamboo leaves create a garnish with the red *shoga*/ginger in a corner to balance the colors. A sprig from a blooming Japanese plum is carefully laid on top, the traditional white blossoms symbolizing the start of a new year. We grin and I end our meal, in Japanese style, with the words *"Gochisoo-sama!"*—An honorable treat!

The Hall

I can still hear the voices and smell the biting scent of incense. Generations walked, sat on, and danced over this wooden floor during Sunday school, funerals, and Obon celebrations. The Issei performed skits onstage; Nisei were married there and used the hall for receptions; Sansei came for community potlucks. Kids ran up and down the steps and around the outside, skinned their knees on the cement and gravel walkways, and stumbled on the uneven floor as the planks bowed with age. I always remember the floor as gray. "Navy gray," some Nisei called it, joking that all the paint the community could afford after the war was from military surplus, a bittersweet irony as they returned from the relocation camps. "At least it's painted," some concluded.

Gray but clean, swept after each use. Cedar shavings, stored in a large bucket with a lid in the back corner, were spread by hand. The men sprinkled the pale tan material and appeared to be sowing seeds or spreading fertilizer from the faded red "Dale Bros." coffee cans. With wide push brooms, they herded the scattered shavings into a small pile where another man awaited with a wide gray sheet-metal dustpan in hand. A pleasant scent filled the air and the shavings kept the dust to a minimum. Behind them chairs and tables were returned to their spots for the next service.

We call it the hall because it belonged to the entire Japanese community, built in 1919 by Issei who realized a centralized meeting place was essential. On the front gables they mounted a wood carving—a rising sun with brilliant rays stretching outward. I've only seen pictures of this, which was quickly removed after December 7, 1941.

The hall became the centerpiece of the community, surrounded by boardinghouses for Japanese farmworkers, businesses, restaurants, and gambling rooms. Tennis courts were built for Issei learning the American game. Nisei children entered the hall for Japanese language lessons. The summer Obon helped to recreate a Japan left behind. A split divided the community in the 1920s, when the Japanese Christians objected to the Buddhist services that were held in the hall.

"The fight was loud and very bad," Mr. Muira, an eighty-year-old Kibei, explained, gently shaking his head. He opened and closed his hands as we talked. "Oh, some Issei yell and argue for many hours. Not too quiet of people that night."

The Buddhists outnumbered the Christians, and the issue was settled with an awkward vote. The Buddhist services continued throughout my childhood. Yet we still call it the hall and not a temple, because the entire community built it and maintains it— it belongs to all of us.

Outside, the white paint is chipping and fading. The wood siding bakes in the summer heat and weathers in the winter rain and fog. I drag my fingers along the surface and can feel tiny splinters breaking off. My fingertips are smudged white. A few windowpanes are cracked; some have been temporarily repaired with yellowed tape that has curled along the edges. The front entryway roof sags slightly to the right and has buckled part of the ceiling's tongue-and-groove strips. The support pillar appears solid, but the trim disappeared years ago and exposed the rough edges. Spiders spin their homes along these cracks, hiding in the shadows until their webs are disturbed and they come darting out into the sunlight.

The once manicured pines and shrubs are emaciated, scraggly, and drooping from irregular watering. Some have died. Withered pine needles blanket the ground beneath the skeleton branches. Brown needles still cling to the drying wood and rain to the earth when shaken. Weeds crop up in random clumps around the large yard. In one corner, a patch of puncture vines grows profusely. The hardy seedpods will remain active for years, germinating in all conditions, ensuring the weed's survival. "Goat heads," as some people call them, have pointy needles that prick fingers and flatten tires, and, worst of all for farmers, can lodge themselves in drying raisins. Just a few found in a bin of raisins can cause thousands of pounds of harvest to fail inspection. I consider the weed evil, and am shocked by its abundance. After I walk the yard, I stop and scrape the bottom of my shoes, knocking off some of the seed heads that could have stuck in my soles and would have traveled home with me to invade my fields.

My generation will inherit this hall, but the wood feels alien. I grew up within these walls, yet they seem distant. The faint echoes of Japanese voices—the barking instructions from a language *sensei*/teacher during the many years of Japanese language school, the scratchy voice of a *shigin*/folk singer entertaining at a New Year's potluck dinner, the deep raspy tones of a Buddhist minister chanting at an *ohigan*/equinox service held twice a year—these come from a generation before me, too recent for stories to be forgotten, too far in the past for memories to be retold with clarity. Others tell me about these voices, and through them I gain a glimpse of this history. Yet I do not feel the hall belongs to my generation.

I step through a heavy set of wooden entry doors, and a large table with a green surface greets me. I'm told it was a Ping-Pong table, fashioned before the war when the game became the rage in Nisei communities. Whenever I ask about it, stories of tournaments and competitions pour forth, and I can hear the ball bouncing and clicking off the wooden paddles with their sandpaper surface and the "ooohs" and "ahs" from the spectators. The table never moved; it served the community equally well as a workbench for cooking or flower arranging classes and as a display area for food during potlucks when hungry eyes circled the table, scanning the dishes and treats, as the wealth of a community was shared.

The hall's ceiling is nearly twenty feet high. I could never figure out why the Issei built it so high, except perhaps for a natural cooling system. A series of windows border the top of the walls and can be opened. During the hundred-degree summers, as the hot air rises, cooler air drifts in from below, creating a subtle current, pleasant while the rest of the valley bakes in stagnant sordid heat.

A rudimentary kitchen area sits in one corner, just a stove and a sink. A few tables and chairs hug the walls, along with some metal storage cabinets. A large pile of chairs is stacked in a corner, most of which haven't been moved in years. We no longer need them.

An odd piece of plywood is nailed over one window where a swamp cooler sat for decades. The metal box with a fan powered by an electric motor blew air into the room, the breeze first cooled by damp gunny sacks that hung around the box frame. In our dry valley weather, the added humidity felt refreshing. Within the last year, though, someone had stolen it and we hastily nailed a plank over the opening. Since we're now spoiled by air conditioning in our homes and avoid using the hall during the heat of summer, no one intends to replace the cooler.

A row of hooks are mounted on a two-by-four that's nailed along the back wall. The hooks were once filled with jackets and coats. A set of misplaced *ojuzu*/prayer beads from a Buddhist service dangles on a peg; it's a child's set and must have hung there for years, along with a woman's yellowed sweater, unclaimed by a long-lost owner. I stop at the bulletin board which hasn't been touched for at least fifteen years. A Sunday school class attendance

list is still posted, names of children I have not seen for years. I picture them as kids, just as they once sat around a table as the
teacher placed a gold star next to their name when roll was taken.
A huge gas heater hangs in the center of the room from the
ceiling. Pull a cord, a lighter ignites, and within minutes, warmth
is produced, accompanied by the ticking sound of heating metal. I
can imagine, unfolding beneath the furnace, the New Year's
potluck celebration (still held every year until this past one, when
it was canceled because of bad weather—the few remaining families were mostly elderly and no one wanted to risk catching cold
in the damp fog and drizzle). I remember the room swelling with
conversation and the sharp smell of Japanese food, especially the
fish and vinegar-flavored *sushi*. We began with a toast and *banzai*
cheer. Everyone stood with a small cup of champagne in hand; the
kids substituted 7UP. The soft voice of the community club president stumbled through a brief welcome, then raised his cup and
boldly shouted, *"Banzai!"* Instantaneously the room erupted in a
loud response—*"Banzai!"* Arms were thrown upward and drinks
were spilled. Three times this was repeated—a leader shouting,
a community cheering, champagne splattering, and a new year
was christened in a small farm community.

"*Itadaikimasu,*" the president then barked—we will receive this
food. We all responded likewise, and the potluck feast began. As
we ate, conversations flowed and more champagne was poured.
Raffle tickets were passed out and the young children wandered
down into the basement to play. During the fifties and sixties, as
more and more Sansei were born, the hall had expanded into the
lower basement area, an unfinished room beneath the stage area.
Sunday school nursery and kindergarten classes met there, and
during potluck dinners, we played with the toys and colored in the
books until the bingo began and we rejoined the adults in the main
room. We were then replaced by a group of grinning men who
slipped into the basement carrying a bottle of *sake* and a deck of
cards for their own private games.

The stage area now feels cold and dark. I've seen photos of Issei actors in striking poses with elaborate costumes and settings up on the stage, bringing *shibai*/plays to entertain the rural village of Del Rey. I imagine the acting was quite awful and the stories very melodramatic, but I can hear hundreds clapping and bowing, grateful for the opportunity to be entertained.

I have spent time up on this stage, performing children's skits, singing Christmas songs (we considered them an appropriate part of our "end of the year" program), and reciting speeches. I can remember staring out over a packed hall of faces. Most smiled, while the older men sat with expressions I could not read. When we tried to act out a skit based on the story of Momotaro, Peach Boy, I would see bright eyes and nodding of heads, subtle statements of approval, especially when we tried to say a few lines in Japanese. Some of the *ojiisan* closed their eyes but did not sleep. They drifted into their thoughts as the Peach Boy returns home carrying treasures for his kind parents.

The Reunion

We lack rites of passage; the world seems obsessed with the new. What does that say about the old? Marcy and I and a group of Nisei help plan a Del Rey Japanese community reunion bringing generations back to the hall. We begin the event with a grand banquet in Fresno. The evening is filled with bows, hugs, and handshakes. Extended families gather, friends return to the area, and generations of stories and memories are passed around the table and served family-style.

Following dinner, the entire evening's program centers around a simple idea—we introduce all the participants to each other. As family names are called, groups of people stand. While a few came as individuals, most have extended family in attendance. At first, some hesitate, uncomfortable with the attention, standing sheepishly, shoulders drooping, heads tilted downward, eyes avoiding contact. Then, as we read personal information about family members—where a son has moved to, the profession a daughter chose, the university that a granddaughter attended— approving nods and smiles could be seen in the audience, along with pleasant sighs of "ohhh?" and "humph!" Gradually they relax, enjoying their public moment as the history of a community is revealed.

When I introduce Munabu Fukuda, who has a successful career in Washington, D.C., working with the State Department, a chatter breaks out accompanied with a chorus of "ohhhhs." As I read his life history and the detail about his once serving as the Japanese language teacher in Del Rey, I realize his honored position in the community. He is still *sensei* to many in the room.

One elderly couple rise as their name is announced. They stand upright, their heads barely rising above the seated audience. "Mr. Hideki and Yoshino Okamura," I announce, "worked for many years on the Del Rancho Rey farm just outside of town. They were forced to leave during the war and lived in Block Twenty-one at Gila River Canal Camp during relocation. During the war, they moved to Colorado and worked there. But tonight is their first trip back in forty years. All during that time, they called Del Rey home."

Then the tiny couple gently bows. The Issei *ojiisan* has his arms to his side, and the *obaasan's* hands slide down the front of her thighs as she drops her head and shoulders. The room applauds, and they stand back upright. For a moment, a pride fills their faces, they wear soft smiles and glassy eyes. Decades late, they receive a homecoming.

The next day we journey to the hall for a brunch and gathering of memories. People arrive early, anxious to see "the old place," stroll through the yard and grounds, and inspect the basement and stage.

I had created a simple display of several black-and-white photographs, including some of the hall's 1919 dedication. In one photo, over the entry doorway, a Japanese flag was crossed with an American flag. A column of Japanese immigrants stood in front of the new structure, dozens of men in black suits, and a cluster of women, some clutching infants, as well as a group of Caucasians, dignitaries from Del Rey town along with their families and neighbors. Issei and older Nisei gather around the display, pointing at faces and trying to remember names.

Some couldn't identify their own parents at first and ask older family friends, "Who's that?" All the faces are young, Issei in their teens and twenties, Nisei as infants. Many of the Sansei only knew pictures of their *jiichan* and *baachan* when they were old. They require an older neighbor to make the connection and point to a serious face with dark eyes, an immigrant dressed in a baggy suit or frumpy dress.

A young man identifies himself as a Yonsei, a fourth-generation Japanese American, from Walnut Grove. His great-grandfather Kazuo Sakamoto lived in Del Rey long ago before settling near Sacramento. He came to learn more, having only seen Del Rey on some of his family's documents. "Neither my father nor my uncles and aunts know about Del Rey," he says.

A handful of the old-timers remember his family. We find evidence in a photo of an old wooden board that listed the names of contributors for the building of the hall. These family *kanji* were posted, acknowledging donations and providing a directory of who was part of Del Rey seventy years earlier. The young man cannot read the *kanji,* and a Kibei has to point out the name. For a minute he stares at the characters, and then he runs his fingers over the writing.

"What were these marks?" he asks, pointing to a series of lines and 0's beneath each name.

"I not sure," says Mr. Muira, the Kibei. "Maybe something about how much each family gave?"

The Sakamoto Yonsei spends the rest of the day trying to deci-

pher the donation code, attempting first to determine the amount
his great-grandfather had given, then, if possible, the contribution
relative to others. As he departs, he pulls me aside, grins, and
jokes, "Maybe we Sakamotos were rich, no?"

One Nisei woman searches the yard for a spot where a tree
once stood. "There was a pump next to it where we drank water,"
she explains. "We sat under the shade and watched the Issei play
tennis. The men even wore whites and looked funny with their
dark farm tans. They tried to show off but they were pretty bad,"
she jokes. "The balls kept flying in all directions and they cussed
in Japanese—*'chukushoo!'* I think they pretended we kids weren't
around. But it didn't matter—we didn't know the rules to tennis
and clapped every time the ball actually cleared the net, even with
a couple of bounces in between. Then the rallies got really good!"

Onstage, a trio of Nisei women look for marks where they
once stood as young girls. One shows me a group photograph of
them as ten-year-olds, dressed in elaborate silk kimonos with
heavy white rice powder makeup. The image captures intense but
soft expressions on their faces. They are not trained performers.
Once a year an *odori*/dance *sensei* made a tour of the small rural
valley towns. For a week, the teacher diligently worked with the
raw young farm girls, instructing them on the arts of tea ceremony and teaching them a few dance movements. The professional photograph taken of the dancers, in kimono uniform
onstage, with makeup, was for sale at a "special price for the family of the performers"—a Japanese-American version of *The
Music Man.*

A gray-haired Nisei man with an impish grin cocks his head
and waves a finger, motioning me to follow. "Say, you want to
see something?" He scampers around a corner to the far back side
of the hall, moving with a bounce in his step. He shows me nicks
in the wooden wall where Nisei boys pitched pennies.

"When we didn't have any money," Mr. Yokoyama explains,
"we did it with stones. Just like the other poor American kids."

He picks up a small flat rock and deftly flicks it. It hits the wall near several dents. The stone nicks the siding with a backspin and falls to the ground. There it sticks in the compacted earth, a few inches from the structure. He repeats the toss, his body suddenly becoming still with each turn, his hands remembering the motion. He smiles, picks up a flat stone, and slips it into his pocket.

Farewell to the Hall

For years the community had talked about one day selling the hall. Property taxes and utilities were eating into the community's treasury, fewer and fewer members attended the hall cleanups, and people feared that a building that appeared abandoned invited problems. Then, a Buddhist church in the neighboring town was sold to an organization of American veterans looking for a meeting hall. Most of the Sansei in that town had left the area, and the offer created an opportunity; ironically, a Buddhist temple would become home to the veterans of World War II. When the news came to Del Rey, we started talking about the advantages of selling. A few conversations hinted of a desire to keep the old structure, but no one voiced a strong opinion. We placed the hall on the market just to see if we'd get a bid. A large plywood sign was hung on the fence with red hand-painted letters, FOR SALE, and the property was listed with a real estate agent. Someone began to stop and water the lone surviving pine tree, and a broken window was replaced.

I had hoped the hall would continue as some type of community center for Del Rey. First a group of women inquired about utilizing it as a child care facility, and I hoped they would make an offer. Then a Mexican-American asked about purchasing the property for use as a boardinghouse for farmworkers and their families, perhaps like the old structures that once lined the streets of Del Rey's Japan town in the 1920s and provided shelter for Issei immigrants. A formal offer was quickly made. An informal poll was taken through a quick series of phone calls. No one voiced an opinion against the sale, and an emergency meeting was held at the hall.

I arrived late and found the yard full of cars, a rare sight in the last few years. Inside a few people chatted, most sat quietly at the two long tables set up in the middle of the hall. The only other Sansei, Rod Ikeda, arrived at the same time, and as we stepped through the double front doors, heads turned and someone said, "There they are—now we can begin." We both sat in empty metal chairs in the middle of the tables. I dipped my head to the others, who nodded back. Their faces were worn from years in the fields, wrinkles molded around glassy eyes.

Yo Kimura, a younger Nisei in his fifties, was the Kyowakai/Community Club president. He had pushed for the sale, wanting the community to move on with the process. "We've talked about selling the hall for years," he began. "And now there's an offer on the table." The value of the hall in dollars and cents sounded cold and impersonal. "Last chance for anyone to speak up," said Yo. "Come on, everyone, I know you have some feeling about this." A long silence followed.

For a moment I wished we could be like other communities where decisions are loudly debated. Once, at a Portuguese community hall in a nearby town, I attended a raisin industry meeting with the farmers on one side of the room and the processors, owners of companies that washed, stemmed, and packaged raisins, on the other. Many of these plants were owned by Armenians, who bought raisins from Japanese Americans in addition to many other farmers. The processors wanted to project a poor outlook— sales were down, a huge crop hung in the fields, prices had to be low. Farmers (many of whom were Armenians too) proclaimed the opposite—it had been a meager crop, raisins should be in demand, and the processors appeared to have empty warehouses with little carryover inventory of raisins. The two sides engaged in a shouting match, as if the one with the loudest voice would be declared correct. Tempers flared; accusations of false figures and withheld information were flung freely from one side to the other.

One older Armenian farmer who was very overweight and short yelled in a deep voice, waving his hands in front of him, pointing a finger at a processor and calling him a liar. Blood vessels on his temples swelled and pulsated; beads of sweat trickled down his face and along the protruding artery. Suddenly the talk of raisins seemed unimportant to me, I simply hoped the farmer would not have a heart attack.

Nearly everyone except the Japanese Americans participated, making speeches and pounding fists, interrupting with passionate comments and breaking into smaller, private conversations while someone else spoke. The debate lasted for hours, and only after physically exhausting themselves did the debaters begin to calm down. Outside, the cool of a summer evening settled over our fields. Inside, a proclamation was made, followed by a series of reluctant nods from influential leaders. Suddenly the meeting was over. An understanding had been reached. On the way out of the steamy room, handshakes were exchanged, along with pats on the back and even loud laughter.

But silence dominated our debate about the hall. I tried to read the people's faces. Some stared forward while others dropped their heads. The men sat upright with arms crossed; the women clustered together and sometimes whispered to each other. The tension was relieved when tea was served.

At first I believed the silence stemmed from a lack of emotion. Perhaps the community was weary of caring for the old hall; most of its members were retired and wanted to rest in their final years. Later I wondered if everyone had heard the motion to sell the hall, because as tea was offered, a number of the older folks had to be nudged awake by a neighbor's elbow when asked if they'd like a cup. For a long time afterward, the only sounds came from the slurping of the refreshments. Subtle glances were

directed toward Rod Ikeda and me. We were the only two in the
room younger than fifty.

I did not feel we had a right to say much—we had not built
this hall and sustained it for decades. If anything, the exodus of
Sansei—people of my generation—from the rural community
had helped precipitate its demise. A sense of guilt rushed through
me. I too gulped my tea. I also wondered about the personal burden I'd be accepting if a decision was made to keep the hall. Maintaining the structure required time and expense, continuing to
drain the small reserve the Nisei had built up over the years. We
no longer seemed to need a physical centerpiece for ourselves—
both the other Sansei and I had married non-Japanese women, we
now worked and participated in larger circles outside of Del Rey,
we were part of many communities.

I tried to make eye contact with Rod Ikeda. We had chosen to
return to the farm with our families. But neither of us could com-
mit to maintaining the hall the way our parents and grandparents had. Those generations built monuments manifesting the
spirit of community. Our sense of community was different—
more conceptual than physical, based on history and memory
instead of the need for a structure. I tried to convince myself that
the Nisei owned the hall more than I did. Its fate belonged in their
hands, and we Sansei would respect the decision of the group.

The silence grew and Yo again asked for someone to speak up.
A few feet shuffled. I looked around and watched the faces frozen
in hardened expressions, frowns, tight lips, blank stares broken
only with occasional blinks of the eyes. Without words, we stated
our collective decision to move on with the sale. Memories of the
hall may stay with many of us, personal histories attached to a
place and passed on through stories. Yet in our silence, we also
chose to forget.

When Sansei children asked their parents and grandparents
about immigration and relocation, many Nisei and Issei answered
with silence. Many interpreted this as subservient resignation to

the power of the government and the hysteria of other Americans. But the silence of Japanese Americans was full of emotions. It signified painful acceptance, not indifference.

I am reminded of the silence when old farmers realize no one will take over their land. Children have left for the city and better, easier jobs. The old-timers seem to accept their destiny and keep on working, a few hoping that one day something good will happen for them. I asked one older Nisei, Mr. Fujimoto, "Are you disappointed with your children about leaving the farm?" We were sitting at his kitchen table, eating a juicy peach his family had propagated and patented two decades ago. No heir will continue farming his prized orchards.

He answered first with a silent pause, then a soft grin while explaining, "Not to worry. I choose what I want to remember and I remember the good times more than the bad." He sliced another bite from the peach he cradled in work-hardened hands. The paring knife glided through the flesh of the fruit and stopped just as it scraped his callused palm. He raised the blade, the metal sharp but worn to half its original width, dripping with clear juice. He held the piece up for me to sample. "Have another?" he asked.

The hall echoed with the sounds of the slurping of tea, then swallows and gulps. I exchanged glances with others around the table. No one met my eyes. Mrs. Moriyama finally pointed out that the Sansei should have a big say in the decision, "After all, it will be their hall." She was a large, wonderfully warm woman. We described her as "a Hawaiian," reflecting the friendly, caring, and yet vocal personality of her native state.

I paused and stared at my compatriot. He shrugged.

I blurted, "But it belongs to us all." Then I too answered with silence.

Rod Ikeda added, "Let's see. . . . It's getting to be difficult to keep up the place. . . . Why, in a few years, you never can tell, we may need to do some major repairs. Will it be worth it? Everyone's getting older . . . and the hall isn't getting any younger. . . ."

A few chuckled, and our smiles broke the tension of the moment. Then a vote was called for and the sale was approved unanimously. For days I kept thinking about this decision.

I TAKE A final solitary walk through the hall, my work boots echoing in the vacant structure, the dust from my faded blue jeans and frayed shirt blending with the layers of grime that have collected along windowsills. Memories of smells and sounds rush through me; the hall seems to speak as a door creaks open and the musty odors of the basement brush my face. The wood floor moans beneath my weight, and the distant smell of incense resides eternally in the stage curtains. I struggle with youthful emotions racing through my thoughts, tearing at the silence of maturity.

During the last few weeks, individuals make final pilgrimages to the hall, taking anything that belongs to them, dividing up piles of junk before they are tossed out. Tom Morikawa asks permission to take the old clock and an American flag that sits in the corner. He and his late wife donated them to the hall years ago when they first joined the community; he is a proud veteran and the old flag has forty-eight stars on it. Other members retrieve wooden benches from Sunday school that they will use for visiting grandchildren. The trophy case poses a difficult problem—how do you divide up team awards and plaques? We pass out the old awards to anyone who has children, guessing if they belonged to the volleyball team that won the 1970 tournament or the basketball team in the '61 play-offs.

We are unsure what to do with the *butsudan*/Buddhist altar. It's hand-crafted and perhaps sixty or seventy years old; it's over four feet high and three feet wide, with folding doors and elaborate wood carving. We store it in a small closet area located in the back of the stage, and many, many times I have helped wheel it out for services, opening the sets of gold-painted doors, helping to straighten candles, and preparing the incense to be burned.

Someone suggests we donate it to a museum, and initial inquiries are made. Curators from Japanese-American collections politely inform us that they already have many such artifacts. Apparently other Japanese-American communities have sold their halls. We discuss giving it to a local historical museum, but a number of people protest because, as someone says, the *hakujin*/Caucasians don't know how to take care of it.

A few propose we keep the *butsudan* in the local community, and everyone blankly stares at everyone else. All of the Nisei already have their altars at home. My house is one option, and I hesitate, unsure of where to store such a large object. Most other altars are small, desktop versions that can sit on top of a small dresser or in the corner of a room. But I accept the proposal and agree that the community *butsudan* should be kept by someone who has a history with it. I store it in my study and office, next to my desk and books. Every time I walk past it, I can smell the incense that permeates the wood grain.

A committee of women make their last visit to the hall and work for hours to sweep, mop, and clean up. A few of us can't understand why they expend so much energy—the deal is already signed and closed, we have vacated the premises, taken all valuables, and divvied up the remaining boxes of stuff, as if dividing a community junk pile. But the women want to work; they feel uncomfortable passing on the hall while it is so dirty. A few of the remaining Issei approve of the effort, pointing out that when the new owners open the doors, they will know how Japanese take care of their homes. My grandparents always stressed how important it was to leave behind a good impression. I'm told that even when departing the relocation camps, many of the *obaasan* swept their barrack floors one final time. Despite the harsh conditions and the desolation of living behind barbed wire, their one section of their wooden barrack was a sacred place. And because it was home, memories from that place mattered and had meaning. Perhaps a final sweeping became an act of closure, a recognition of changes and acknowledgment of a life that once was and will continue to be celebrated.

A message from the most recent Community Club meeting, held last month, is still scribbled on the blackboard. Dad is listed as next year's president, and there is a list of suggested activities, including a renewal of the annual picnic and luncheon party meetings funded by the monthly payments from the hall. At that meeting we all met the new owner and his family, a quiet Mexican man who spoke little English. We smiled at each other, and a few thank-yous were exchanged between the two parties, separated by language and culture. Yet with this family, the hall will be renewed as a type of boardinghouse, given another life by another generation of immigrants who will come to call this land home.

The entry doors sit open, the thick panels swung inward on old hinges that have survived decades. A bright, glaring sunlight contrasts with the now dark interiors. I can still see faintly etched initials once carved into hardwood that was later sanded as smooth as possible, to erase the defacing. The letters were not Japanese—the Issei and Nisei discovered them when they returned to the hall after relocation. The building had been procured during the war by the government and used to house temporary farmworkers. I am appalled by the thought of strangers moving into our property and violating the sacredness of our church. I grow angry when I think of men gouging their knives into walls and doors to leave their marks, as if this were property won in a war and occupied by the victorious forces. But it was wartime and Japanese Americans were branded as the enemy. I can imagine the scene as the first Issei returned to the area only to find their property abused. Sanding out the lettering was one of the first tasks begun. But perhaps the Issei did not blame the migrant farmworkers, who may have only been trying to leave a name behind, to tell the world who they were. Now the hall once again returns to a community of workers: a universal language will be spoken when laborers pass through these doors and exhale a collective sigh following a hard day in the fields.

I close the doors behind me. They have not shut snugly for decades. As I walk away, I look up and see the gables and recall the decorative emblem and can still see the rising sun suspended in the air.

Community Funerals

As the minister lights the incense, many of the farmers sit in the audience with a stern look. Deep creases are etched on solemn faces; weathered skin complements wrinkled white shirts. Some ties are loosely knotted, while others appear to be choking the men. Black suits are rumpled from resting in closets for months, and a faint scent of mothballs mingles with the biting aroma of the incense. The men keep crossing and uncrossing their arms. The women wear simple black dresses with little jewelry and clutch small purses; small, white handkerchiefs lie neatly pressed and folded in their laps. Except for the mourning family, most appear over fifty years old, gray and balding heads of men interspersed with the dark and dyed-black hair of women. Neighbors of a Nisei farmer gather in Fresno at the main Buddhist temple for the funeral of their friend.

The room is filled with quiet conversations. An hour earlier, mourners arrived and quietly took their seats in the Fresno temple. Members of the Del Rey community set up over three hundred chairs with another one hundred in waiting. The women politely whisper to each other, often covering their mouths with a hand as if to muffle their already soft voices. Occasionally, heads nod in agreement or slowly shake back and forth, followed by a tissue that wipes a tear. The men are mostly still. Scattered discussions stir through the large hall as stories are exchanged about farmwork. Since long before faxes and computers, these gatherings have provided bulletin boards for information—prices for produce, wages paid to workers, pest problems and solutions. New practices are discussed and debated, albeit in a whisper. Bad prices stimulate dialogue that circulates with the incense smoke as a farmer learns he is not alone with his problems. A lighthearted neighbor spreads a joke about fruit brokers being properly named because they're skilled at helping farmers go broke. When the minister prepares to strike the gong to begin the ceremony, chuckles are heard as another poor harvest is made tolerable.

I begin, "Minoru Tanaka was a farmer." As chairman of the service, I have the responsibility of delivering a eulogy, a task performed by community leaders.

"We've all seen the back of his dented and dusty orange '58 Dodge pickup with his shovel tossed in the bed, billowing exhaust smoke trailing behind him and puttering down the country roads at about ten miles per hour." I could hear chuckles in the audience. "And we all can picture that trademark cigar drooping out of his lips, our personal memory of the late Minoru Tanaka."

Heads nod in agreement. Minoru's widow, their five children and dozen grandchildren, and his six siblings and their spouses and nieces and nephews filled over sixty seats in the front section. Some stop crying and look up, listening to the eulogy.

Mr. Tanaka died three days ago, setting into motion the flurry of acts surrounding a funeral. The Buddhist minister was immediately contacted and conducted a deathbed service. The body was then taken to a funeral home and emotional phone calls were made to family and neighbors. Within hours the Del Rey Kyowakai/Community Club met at the Tanaka home to offer condolences and help delegate work assignments.

We gathered around the Tanakas' dining-room table, a worn dark oak oval with white rings where a hot teapot or pan had bleached the wood. The matching wooden chairs creaked and wobbled. The room was dark, the curtains drawn, and a candle at the *butsudan* in the corner flickered when someone entered the room. We sipped tea, were offered "soda water," and munched on *sembei*/rice crackers and *manju*/pastries.

Yo Kimura, the club president, started with the details. The eldest Tanaka son, a Sansei doctor named Steven, sat awkwardly in a chair, having just arrived from Southern California. His mother sat next to him but slightly behind, off to the side. As funeral details were discussed, Steven kept turning to confer with his mother—someone needed to reserve the temple and speak to the ministers, the organist and florist had to be contacted, and reservations needed to be made for the post-funeral dinner at a Chinese restaurant. Steven stumbled, his answers unsure. His mother responded with more and more authority. By the last question, Mrs. Tanaka had pulled her chair up to the table and articulated clearly and precisely the family's wishes.

We then repeated a debate about who was supposed to be a pallbearer and who an honorary pallbearer. Community members agreed to follow the unwritten rule that anyone who couldn't actually help lift the coffin must become honorary.

For the next three days between the death and the funeral, hundreds of guests visited the family, offering condolences and company. The yard was continuously filled with cars. Other neighbors drove by and immediately understood. They'd return home, clean up, and drop by for a visit to console their friends. Some volunteered to help with the farmwork; an informal schedule was created, farmers taking turns with the disking and irrigating. The youngest son, Darren, was still at home and had taken over some of the work. He tried to coordinate the help, unsure of the protocol when accepting or refusing assistance. I'd see him cornered outside, leaning against a pickup as a gracious neighbor gave him advice, mixed with reminiscences about growing up with his father.

As chairman of the funeral service, I had already helped bury a dozen members of the Del Rey community and anticipated being involved with many more burials. I found it strange, though, when neighbors approached and said, "I want to thank you in advance for taking care of my funeral!" My main task was to deliver the eulogy, a blend of life history and personal stories. The evening before the funeral, I met with the Tanaka family, again at their home, to review information and ask questions of the family. His children and widow sat at a small kitchen table with other relatives standing nearby and listening. The worn Formica tabletop and stiff reupholstered chairs were well used. I was seated on a chair with an old, worn, and faded lavender *zab-uton*/cushion. A notepad with some numbers scribbled on the top sheet lay to the side, next to the *shoyu*/soy sauce and toothpicks. A small transistor radio, the kind that fits into a workshirt pocket so farmers can listen to the San Francisco Giants baseball games as they work, sat next to the paper. I realized I was sitting in Mr. Tanaka's chair.

Everyone looked tired. Eyes drooped and many took deep breaths and sighed. They seemed ready to move on. The service would act as a closure for this initial period of mourning. I asked Mrs. Tanaka, "Where was Minoru born, and when?"

"Oh, just outside of Del Rey, on a little farm near Rosedale School in 1910," she said.

Immediately, one of his daughters, a nurse, asked, "It was a home birth? Who helped with the delivery? A midwife?" I sat back and listened to a series of questions and answers, taking a few notes for my eulogy but mostly enjoying the family stories being passed around the table.

Occasionally one of Minoru's three sisters, standing behind us, made a comment. "Right after the war he had one of the first Caterpillar tractors in the area. He'd work for others during the day and then work the home place late into the evening. You could hear the roar of the engine long after it was dark. I remember those days. We all worried he'd have an accident, it being so dark."

Haru, Minoru's wife, gazed out the kitchen window, and her

thoughts drifted into a story. "I remember one evening, he came home with blood all over his shirt. . . ."

Later, as I drove home with my notebook full of details and stories wandering in my mind, the full moon of a late-spring night illuminated the vineyards. I rolled down the car windows, and the warm evening air danced through the interior. I slowed, and I could hear the whine of a motor in the distance, the night air carrying sounds over the landscape. Somewhere another farmer was working. "His home place," I said to myself, beginning to construct the eulogy for the next day.

On the day of the funeral, the Tanaka home was filled with even more voices of siblings, children, aunts, and uncles as they gathered to honor a family member. At times, the hugs and laughter, the conversations and noise of children, seemed to disguise the somber reason for the meeting. Deaths created instant reunions. Funerals made family visible.

I reviewed the final details and procedures with the family, such as the proper order of seating at the church. Usually the immediate family members were first, beginning with the surviving spouse, then eldest son, followed by other sons, then daughters. Brothers and sisters followed, intermixed with nephews and nieces and then cousins.

Ordinarily confusion was kept to a minimum. However, in one rare case, the funeral of a Nisei man, an intense but quiet conversation was held just prior to the service. Nisei aunts and uncles huddled in a corner; each wore a serious expression broken with gentle nods and tears. As I watched the family line up, a younger Nisei man, called Uncle Harry by all, switched places and sat with the immediate family. He had been a quiet man, raised by the eldest sister of the deceased. During the chanting, my mind wandered and I read the names attached to the array of flower wreaths lined up next to the casket. Some read "Dearest Brother," others were from community groups that used the phrase "With Sympathy." Three said, "Loving Dad"—one each from the three children. But an extra said, "Beloved Father," with no name or identification attached. As the solemn organ music began I understood the meaning of the family's conversation and the sudden adjustment of seating arrangements.

"Immediately following the conclusion of this service," I announce, nearing the end of the program, "the family invites all to the Chapel of the Light for a final service." I had learned that Mr. Tanaka would be cremated, and his ashes then buried in a plot he and his wife had selected years ago. His final resting place would be near the Issei Ojiisan and Obaasan Tanaka, along with a brother who was killed in World War II and an infant sister who died just after birth. Numerous other Japanese Americans could also be found in the same general area of the Selma cemetery, including Jiichan and Baachan Masumoto. My parents have their plots selected and paid for there. I imagine Selma is where Marcy and I will be placed too. The Masumotos first lived and worked in Selma, and it's where Dad and I were born (Dad in a farmhouse just outside of town, I in the old hospital in town). Perhaps even my children will be delivered there. In the West, it's not often that three generations are born in the same place and may be found buried together. Like the Tanaka family, the Masumotos are becoming settled.

After the funeral service, I watch many of the Issei widows loudly greet each other. I've seen two women literally run into each other, squint, and bow as recognition sets in. Veterans of death, they share notes about who's still alive and the last time they saw one another. Their time lines are built around the past year's funeral schedule.

Family histories are told when a community gathers; old neighbors sit next to each other and exchange recollections. Their voices grow loud from their enthusiasm coupled with poor hearing. An elderly man approaches me with a story about not only Mr. Tanaka but also his own life. He worked side by side with the Tanaka family, picking grapes, pruning trees, planting vegetables. While we talk, another member of the original work crew joins us, explaining how Minoru and he were field partners during the Depression. "The Tanakas were tall men, " he began. "But we were all short, so it worked just fine. When we had to swamp boxes out of the field, the tall ones passed the crates to the short ones on the vineyard wagon." Then the two men demonstrate the technique, assuming positions and passing invisible lugs of grapes. I can almost see how the lanky Minoru Tanaka fit into their work detail.

Later, I hear more memories of the past, of family traditions and community events. A *hakujin*/Caucasian neighbor of Mr. Tanaka shakes my hand and says he enjoyed the eulogy, "especially the part about working late with that Cat. Some folks didn't like the noise late at night, but to me, it was the sound of real work. Made me relax, knowing something was getting done right. Perfect way to fall asleep at night."

George Fujikawa, another longtime resident of Del Rey, tells me about Mr. Tanaka's Issei father. "He worked even harder than Min. Can you believe that? Guess that's why he took the news so hard, about the cancer. They found him in the fields with the shotgun right next to him. You know, many Japanese felt that was the honorable way to go, especially for someone so strong, instead of just wasting away."

I want to sit and talk with Mr. Fujikawa, but before I can make the offer, he shakes my hand, smiles and dips his head, and turns to meet another old friend. They greet each other as if it's the last time they will see one another—a long handshake, heads that keep nodding for at least a minute, and the same phrase repeated—"*Saaa*, it's good to see you. Good to see you, *ne!*"

A Nisei woman stops and informs me that I left out a detail. "When you mentioned the Quakers and the Tanaka family during the war . . . they were good to many of us. Warned us what would happen and helped some family relocate back East. That's where Minoru spent his camp years, in Pennsylvania."

I had stated that the Quakers helped the family during World War II and the evacuation, but I did not realize the Tanakas had lived with a family. It was hard to picture the cigar-smoking Minoru living with dedicated Quakers.

I try to retain the rich details and phrases by quickly jotting down notes on the back of a funeral program. Later I'll discuss them with Marcy and question why I'm told these stories. They feel like a burden and need to be told to the children of Mr. Tanaka and other Nisei. Marcy says perhaps that's why I write.

I wear many faces at community funerals. I'm part family, friend, and neighbor. I'm part of a final act, as one generation takes care of the other, a child says goodbye to a parent. But I witness the drama over and over; a community requires a decade or two before the transition is complete. I notice fewer chairs are needed at a community gathering, and out in the countryside, I observe more and more unkempt gardens next to a barn or shed as I drive past. Many of the farmhouses I visited as a boy are now abandoned. The land is put up for sale, and I think about the years of work committed to a vineyard, only to see a bulldozer level the land for a new crop. I have returned home and am a witness to many losses.

At the end of Mr. Tanaka's service, a tiny Issei approaches and bows to me, then, in a soft voice, she shares a memory. I have difficulty understanding her words, a blend of Japanese and pidgin English. I decipher tales about working with my *jiichan* and knowing the Masumoto family. I find comfort in hearing he was an *erai*/great man, hardworking but reserved. My family's history grows by gradual accrual—story by story gathered year by year. The gray-haired woman asks about the Masumotos of Gila River Relocation Center and wonders if I'm related to the Sugimotos from Fowler. She knows me by my grandparents. For one of the rare times in my life, I call myself a grandson.

twelve

CALLOUS
HANDS

I ONCE MET AN OLDER NISEI AND HE ASKED WHERE MY GRANDPARENTS
came from. I answered, "Kumamoto and Hiroshima." He
grinned and shook my hand again, only harder. "Hiroshima
good, but *Kumamoto* the best. We country people know how to
work!" As his grip tightened, I could feel his dry, rough palms
scraping my skin.

I imagine the hands of my grandparents to be quite hard, their
thick calluses badges of honor earned only after years in the fields,
a carefully engraved character in the flesh of *inaka*—a term

Japanese "country folk" call themselves, quite conscious of the pejorative connotation of "peasant." The hands tell a story of worth, private statements like a *haiku* I would have written were I an immigrant—

Thick hands work
Under a harvest sun
Fortune with another callus!

But the calluses of Issei would have been hidden. The men bow and infrequently shake hands; the women smile and drop their heads, acts of humility that mask the coarseness folded in their laps. Their hands embrace a silence, their personal struggle to create a home in a new land.

I'm sure my grandparents also wore farmers' tans, dark arms and faces with a dividing line along the neck and the arms where collar and shirtsleeves stop. Both my grandmothers tried to hide their faces and arms from the sun by wearing bonnets and fore-arm coverings made from used rice sacks. The coarse cotton bags provided excellent protection. A Nisei farm wife described how a bonnet, with its bleached and faded white material, helped reflect the heat and the long sides and back panel blocked out sun-light. "For the brim, Chinese rice sacks worked better"—the material was stiff and made a better edge. Generations of Japan-ese farm women wore such bonnets, guarding against the intense rays, trying to maintain a delicate and pale face. Some succeeded, but most, like Baachan Masumoto, eventually gave up. The best and thickest bonnets could not prevent a dark tan and weathered complexion after hours and hours laboring in the sun.

When I first returned to the farm, I did not tan well. At first I worked without a shirt and my back stung from the exposure. I quickly learned to protect myself and wore T-shirts and work-shirts. Then on my hands the blisters began to appear. I tried to ignore the tingling patches of red skin until the bulbous pockets of flesh and fluid had swollen to near bursting. I jabbed at them, surprised by their sudden appearance, entranced as I poked them and felt the tickle of pain with my skin stretched and pulsating. I had no choice but to return to work. The blisters were quickly popped and shredded; the clear liquid trickled over the tingling surface, the tenderness stinging for days before new skin grew and I could peel away the dead tissue. Even after a week, I could only delicately pick up a shovel or gingerly grip the tractor steering wheel. My raw hands lacked time in the orchards and vineyards.

Gradually I grew tougher, yet I never established the same thick calluses as my dad or Baachan. Though I prune trees, tie vines, and dig out weeds, the physical work of my generation differs from the past. I have replaced a strong back with modern equipment and technology. Many times I find myself acting more like businessman than farmer, seeking bottom-line profits, accumulating capital, longing to expand my operation. Yet my hunger for success is not satisfied by money alone. I long to learn both how to farm and how to enjoy being a son, brother, husband, and father. I do not yet have answers and want to continue my journey. I realize my hands do not have the required history; only time and memory will bring me the success I am after.

I never touched the hands of my grandfathers. I only know the ragged fingertips and uneven palms of my grandmothers, especially Baachan Masumoto, who sometimes would *momo*/massage our backs.

She walks with old bony legs that shuffle through garden weeds. Her four-foot-eight-inch frame slouches forward as if walking against the wind. She still lugs buckets of fruit and vegetables from her garden, still possesses a strength earned by years of farmwork.

When we were children, she teased us kids by showing us her firm biceps. We asked if there was an egg underneath her skin. Mom translated and Baachan laughed out loud, one of the few times she did so. Then she clenched her fist tighter and the "egg" contracted, becoming rock-hard. We screamed and roared, then whispered to each other, "You touch it. You touch it." Eventually we bravely reached out and tapped her muscle, our eyes wide with amazement as we agreed that there was an egg in there. A chorus of more laughs and screams followed.

Baachan has worked in the fields for her entire life. The long years are manifested in her hands, gnarled with calluses, coarse with dry cracks in the hardened tips of her thumbs and index fingers. Her fingernails have yellowed, the flesh underneath long ago dried out, and appear brittle. Yet these are the same hands that become filled with a warmth as she massages our backs.

We kids called it "to *momo*," and one of the few Japanese phrases we knew was "Baachan, *momo, momo* us please!" We stood with our backs to her, our young, tanned bodies next to our gray-haired, wrinkled grandmother. She began slowly, moving in a circular motion on each shoulder blade, then randomly dancing across our skin, gently pressing with her hands. The calluses slid over our bones and muscles and generated heat. I closed my eyes, feeling her hand across my back, giggling when my sister or brother tried to push me out of the way to get their turn with Baachan. When her arm grew tired, she switched hands and renewed the warmth. I sometimes sighed out loud and she changed from rubbing to softly tapping. I would take a deeper breath and renew my sigh, listening to the pulsating sound created by air nudged from my lungs. We created a duet, a chant, a Japanese-American song of generations.

As we grew older, Baachan massaged the kids less and less, but every once in a while I feel her old farm hands. Since I have returned, I often think about her time as a worker. I have benefited much from each of the scars in her hands. As she begins to rub my skin, I can feel the coarseness of her memories. She has contributed to who and what I can become. I celebrate her life now that I too work the land. As her old hands playfully rub my young back, a soothing history passes between generations.

For my grandparents to succeed in America, they were forced to have callous hands. They believed that hard work would be rewarded and accepted their place, toiling on someone else's land, saving until they could buy their own.

Relocation Camp Food

In the winter of 1978, I drove out to the Arizona desert to search for Gila River Relocation Center, located an hour south of Phoenix. I spent hours wandering in the barren land, looking for remnants of the two camps that held over sixteen thousand from 1942 to 1946. My family lived in Canal Camp, which housed seventeen hundred families and almost seven thousand people. I found it hard to believe that in only thirty years, evidence of these miniature cities seemed to have been erased. The uneven, rocky landscape was broken only by scattered scrub brush and occasional dirt and gravel roads. A chilling breeze swept across the terrain, the thin fragile layer of topsoil threatened by each gust as a cold front passed through. Finally I stumbled upon a flat area with a southern dike and an outline of dirt roads scratched in the parched earth. I discovered scattered concrete foundation slabs, along with pieces of wood siding and cement-lined holes that were once fish ponds. I had found the desert home of the Masumoto and Sugimoto families.

Canal Camp had twenty-seven blocks. Sixteen were used as housing, and the rest were for administration offices, a hospital, the military police, and an elementary and high school. Each residential block held twelve to fourteen sets of identical barracks, twenty feet by one hundred feet, that contained four to six sections or "apartments" as the War Relocation Authority euphemistically named them. At the center of every block stood the men's and women's bathrooms and a shower facility. The Sugimoto family lived in Block 22, Building 2, Apartment D. "Block 22-2D—it's an address I will never forget," Mom says. "Six of us crowded into a tiny room. I don't think we ever called it home."

Dad's address was Block 23, but he does not recall the building number. "I never thought much about it," he explained. "I just knew where it was." He had completed high school in 1941 and was hungry for work, only to be then drafted into military service out of the relocation camps in 1943. I can't imagine him— the man who later would become a farmer, working almost every day of the year, wanting to go out in the fields "at least for exercise"—forced to remain idle, inactive, and lazy. "It felt like jail, sitting around, waiting for nothing."

Each block had its mess hall, used three times daily to feed hundreds of residents. It was the largest building in the block, a center for gathering. "And waiting—every day we stood in line for our meals," Mom recalled.

I discovered a few low cement pillars half sunken into the ground, bigger than the others and spaced more widely. They were the foundation for the mess hall of Block 22. A row of decorative small stones outlined the perimeter of the structure, and turned to where the main entrance must have stood, a cement landing marking where stairs led to the entry doors. Why would someone mark the outline of the building? A narrow strip of earth ran between the stones and the structure.

My aunt remembered the markings. "In Block 22 we were fortunate to have many gardeners. They knew we spent many hours alongside the mess hall. So they made some gardens, planting anything that would grow. It made the wait shorter."

Near Block 23, I found a pile of broken thick white dishes scattered across the open field. Their jagged edges had dulled with the years of exposure to the desert weather. They were covered with dirt and caked mud, partially buried in the coarse ground, hidden by chunks of small rock and uneven sand. Plain and heavy, they were designed for rough handling. I spent an hour digging, uncovering handles and chips, including a few larger pieces that were once part of a serving platter.

I brought them back to show my parents. Mom clutched the partial plate and, as if by memory, held the lip of it between her small hands. Dad grabbed the platter between a firm thumb and curled fingers and held it up as if to receive a helping of mash or a spoonful of beans. They exchanged a subtle grin that quickly disappeared when Dad shook his head and set down the fragment.

I asked about mealtimes. Did they serve food "family-style"?

Dad chuckled, "Haaa," ending with a sarcastic growl. He explained that in the beginning, families tried to stay together, waiting in long lines, huddling around the mess hall's wooden tables. Very soon, many of the teenagers stopped eating with their families, preferring to run off and talk with their friends, lost among the benches and cafeteria trays. Only the youngsters were forced to stay at the family table. Gradually, even many of the Issei segregated themselves, sitting off to one side, awkwardly holding forks and spoons or using their personal *hashi*/chopsticks brought from home or hand-carved while in camp, speaking in their native Japanese between bites of anonymous food. Everyone ate the same food as everyone else, on the same heavy white plates, and drank the desert water from faceless mugs, every day of the year for years. "Nothing was like family anymore," Dad told me. Very few celebrated with meals—no birthday parties or anniversary dinners. Camp broke up family.

I have a photograph that documents a meal at another relocation center at Jermone, Arkansas, during a holiday celebration in 1943. The table is covered with white linen and plates full of special food—turkey or chicken, potatoes, vegetables, a piece of pie with an orange, cups filled with a beverage, and even *hashi* neatly arranged next to the table setting. The picture was taken by the government authorities, who periodically wanted to demonstrate to the rest of America that these citizens were being cared for. A single photograph depicted a dinner better than most outsiders had during the wartime rationing and supply controls. I can imagine the caption—"Japanese served Holiday Meal!"—created resentment among other Americans. These images have stayed with many who continue to believe that Japanese Americans were fortunate to go to camps because they were taken care of during the war while the rest of America had to suffer and endure hardship.

Despite rationing of many foods, rice was not necessarily a staple that the rest of America demanded. Japanese diets happened to match the wartime food supply. And since meat was rationed, the camp menus often included large helpings of vegetables, not unlike the typical diet of Japanese Americans. Many of the relocation camps also grew their own version of "victory gardens." Just outside the fences, fields and fields of vegetables were grown and harvested in order both to feed the internees and reduce expenses. Dad says the thousands of farmers were anxious to work, just to get out from behind the guard towers. They were paid sixteen dollars a month by the government to become farmworkers once again ("professionals," such as medical staff and teachers, were paid nineteen dollars). "Better than doing nothing," Dad shrugged. He even signed up for a wartime emergency work program to harvest sugar beets in Montana. The pay was poor, the weather cold, but the air, Dad said, "felt free."

At Gila River, *daikon*, Japanese horseradish, was a popular crop, as it grew from seed into one-to-two-foot-long white roots in forty-five to fifty days. The interned Japanese Americans planted acres of it. Within weeks they had familiar food to go with their rice. "All too familiar," one Nisei man told me. "At Gila we must have grown enough *daikon* for the rest of the nation. We grew it, shipped it out to the other camps, and then had to eat it at every meal. Even for breakfast. Boiled *daikon*. Can you imagine that to start every day? That's what I remember about camp food."

Good Neighbors

In the summer of 1945, Jiichan Masumoto was seventy-three years old, Baachan fifty-three. Gila River Relocation Center was closing. Germany had surrendered, Japanese soldiers were retreating, and the authorities were allowing Japanese Americans to return home. Those who could find work had already left camp, traveling to the unrestricted zones in the East and Midwest. Often a son ventured out first, locating work and housing, then sent for the rest of his extended family. They were refugees, escaping political persecution and seeking sanctuary in their own country. As restrictions were lifted, many journeyed back to the West Coast. Those with farms were anxious to return to their homes and work their lands. Others who were too ill for travel, or the old and very young, were left behind the barbed wire.

Jiichan Masumoto's family was scattered. The eldest daughter had married and was living in Minnesota. Two sons had been drafted into the army; one was in Europe with the occupation forces. Another son worked in Michigan. The youngest child, a very young teenage daughter, was still with them and became their translator. Their number one son, who had been drafted before Pearl Harbor and fought with the 442nd Infantry Battalion, had been killed in Italy by German guns that didn't discriminate between Americans and Japanese Americans.

The Masumoto family had no land, owned no house, and had heard a variety of reports from those who had already gone to California—no parades would welcome the returning Americans. They trickled back from the war on trains and in cars, family by family coming home, anxiously trying to catch a glimpse of a farmhouse, a vineyard, or the barn where they had stored everything. The fortunate had good neighbors who had tended the land and guarded belongings. There usually wasn't a lease or formal document—the agreement was sealed with a handshake.

The Hiyama family owned land just outside of Fowler, California, before the war. As soon as possible they journeyed back to their farm and sent letters to Gila River, letting everyone else know what to expect. Their neighbor Kamm Oliver had taken care of their place. "I tried to farm their place just like it was mine," Kamm said.

During the war, the two families had written each other. "What do you folks need?" Kamm asked.

"Can you bring us some of our furniture? Our bed, a dresser, a small table?" responded the Hiyamas.

Oliver and another family, the Feavers, loaded up their pickup trucks and drove into the Arizona desert. Fifty miles south of Phoenix, in the middle of the parched desert, lay Gila River Relocation Center. Their journey became longer and longer as they plunged deeper into the barren landscape, bouncing down the dirt roads, past the scrub brush and rocks. Oliver recalled the "godforsaken countryside" and questioned, "How could anyone do this to a neighbor?"

The Kei Hiyama family were one of the first to return to the Fresno area. "On the day before Christmas, we got back," explained Kei. "The *Fresno Bee* even took a picture of us smiling while standing in a doorway of an old house." Kei recalled the bittersweet emotions of that day. "It really wasn't the doorway of our home. Someone was still living in our house, but they let us spend our first night in the shack in the back for field workers." He shook his head. "But the smiles were real," he added. "We were back home."

Not only farms but also personal belongings were often left behind. In the frantic weeks before evacuation, Japanese Americans tried to sell what they could or gave away clothes, pets, even children's toys and dolls. Yet some possessions were difficult to dispose of or part with. Sadako Tajima of Alameda, California, had just purchased a Baldwin piano. Her family was involved in the flower business, and she matched the natural beauty of her family's work with the harmony of her music—playing was her joy in life. Her family could not take the instrument with them; they had no choice except to leave it behind. However, a good neighbor and music teacher, Gladys Lotter, found a home for the instrument. Her son, Dick Lotter, kept it for the duration of the war.

Dick Lotter explained, "As soon as we learned the Japanese were going to be taken away, my mother called her friends and said they were going to do a 'help' project." A devoted musician and teacher of many Nisei, Gladys Lotter knew good homes would be needed. They acted quickly, held meetings, and matched pianos with families, entrusting instruments with guardians.

"We took care of those instruments," said Dick Lotter. "You know, a musical instrument has to be played often in order to keep tonal quality. The wood becomes dead without music. My family played it every day in order to keep it alive."

When Sadako Tajima returned, she was reunited with her piano. "I never worried about it for the years I was away. I knew one day I'd return and play once again."

Good neighbors took an interest; individuals took personal action to right the wrong. They rose to the challenge and did what was right. Few people talked about these acts of courage—it wasn't a popular stance either during or after the war. They were often labeled "Jap lovers," and their story has remained a secret between friends and neighbors. Japanese Americans were overjoyed to discover people who had kept their word and cared for property. Some, however, discovered that mysterious fires had destroyed their houses or property was missing or had been broken.

The Torii family returned to Selma, California, and, according to Dad, wrote to Jiichan Masumoto, still in camp with nowhere to go. The Toriis were also from Kumamoto province in Japan and would help take care of their fellow country folk. The

Masumotos were forced to leave Gila by that summer; the authorities wanted to end this chapter in American history quickly and perhaps quietly. "Later, when I got wind of it, I couldn't believe they kicked them out," said Dad, still stationed in Europe at that time. "Imagine, locking you up, then saying you have to get out."

Baachan wept, because she believed her oldest son would have taken care of things if he had still been alive. Jiichan turned to his Kumamoto-ken friends in Selma. I imagine their train ride from the Arizona desert to California and Fresno was very quiet. Jiichan would have to try to start over as an old man. Baachan carried the loss of her eldest son like a wound that would not heal. They would again have to accept their fate. They didn't have a choice.

Four families gratefully stayed in the Toriis' old grocery store, hanging blankets to divide the building into rooms, a bitter reminder of the internment camp barracks. These families faced similar circumstances—children departed from home, sons in the military, old couples and young children left behind. Baachan was still strong, and she knew they couldn't stay long with their friends, who wanted to reopen their store. She knew they needed work.

Dad tells the story of what happened after his discharge from the army in Philadelphia. He met with his brother, my uncle Jake, who was working in Detroit. They bought a used car and headed for California. They arrived and were shocked to see Jiichan and Baachan living in a tiny room, sharing the back storerooms with four other families. The first night back they slept on the floor. Uncle abruptly decided to head back to his job. He took the train and left the car. Dad began to relax on the second day, finally resting after getting out of the service. Baachan woke him up and asked in Japanese, "What are we going to do?"

"What do you mean, what are we going to do?" Dad answered. "I'm resting. First time in years. I'm resting."

Baachan spoke in short, rapid sentences. Her voice was low for a small woman, sharp and powerful. "We can't stay here. We need work."

Dad wanted to go back to his nap. Then Baachan muttered, at first not so loud, then gradually building into a crescendo. She talked about the number one son. "If only he were here. He'd take care of everything." She cried and blurted out more. "He'd be working." Then she quickly stopped. The next day Dad began to hunt for work.

Raisins were good to the Masumoto family. Harvests began in September, Dad found work for the family and a barn to live in. They shared it with one other family, cooking outdoors over a fire and rigging up a makeshift outhouse. After picking grapes all day they showered with a hose. Dad vowed that after harvest, he'd find a house to live in. Within months, he persuaded a farmer to let him run a forty-acre ranch with a tenant house. They moved in. Baachan joined a labor crew run by a family friend from Kumamoto. Every day Dad dropped her off at the Toriis' grocery store, where the workers gathered before being trucked off to the fields. After Dad completed his work on the rented property and Baachan finished another day as a farmworker, they met at the store and drove home.

Jiichan was too old to start over—no one wanted an elderly man in the fields. But Dad managed to persuade a farmer to prune some of the vines by piecework and hid Jiichan in the interior rows of the vineyard where he could snip and prune at his own pace. Jiichan was proud of his son and contented with the work. He understood and accepted the circumstances—his destiny would now be determined by his children.

Many Nisei men inherited the role of family head in their early twenties, when they returned home to care for their parents, sacrificing careers and the educational opportunities offered by the GI Bill. They had no choice but to return to the family and accept the work that had to be done.

Dad rented land for a year. "Got to thinking, why should I work so hard and have to share it with someone else?" he began the story. "So I started looking for a place of my own and finally found this farm. Not too bad—cheap, with a hill that was barren and not farmed, full of hardpan." He took a huge risk and bought the land.

Baachan was shocked and angered. "Why you take a gamble?" she badgered.

Dad said, "I told her that no one wants to keep living in run-down places. I had to try to make things better." She didn't respond.

According to Dad, Jiichan Masumoto helped make the move. He wanted to leave the old place and had no problem with Dad's trying to get a place of his own. He said, *"Ii ne"*—It's good. He helped gather their meager possessions. He realized that the family had a chance to have their own farm and their place in America. But when it came time to leave their tenant shack and move, Baachan refused to go. She sat at the kitchen table, blankly staring out the window. Dad packed up their belongings and threatened to leave without her. Jiichan shuffled to the car and waited inside.

Baachan grumbled about "gambling" and "they can take it away." She worried about losing everyone again and starting over. "We have a place to sleep and eat. We have food. Why take a chance?" she cried.

Dad delivered an ultimatum. "We'll wait fifteen minutes," he warned. "Then we'll go without you and I'll come back this evening to pick you up." He stormed out of the shack and joined Jiichan.

The minutes passed; the car grew warm in the spring sun. No one spoke. Finally, Baachan came out, some of her personal belongings wrapped in a *furoshiki*/cloth, the rest in a black suitcase with their family relocation number still stenciled in white, 40551. Dad opened the back door and helped her load her things. She sat and stared out the window, stroking her face with her rough, callused hands. They then drove to our farm in silence.

Honoring Memory

I take for granted my family's history. I never had to dream of a Masumoto farm; no land or property was ever taken away from me. I've never gone to sleep hungry. Yet my family's ghosts walk with me and whisper about a legacy. "Your work will become your mark," they seem to say in hushed voices behind a breeze as it stirs the drooping peach leaves or the sound of water tumbling into irrigation furrows. "And you will leave behind the things that matter, a healthy family, strong vines and vigorous trees." I will never be as bold as my grandfathers or grandmothers. I won't journey across an ocean to an unknown land, look for work without speaking the language, labor in strange fields with crops I have never seen before. I may never know the empty feeling of losing everything and growing old, then returning to a home and family that was taken away and forever altered. I am given different options.

But I think like an old farmer. I need to dirty my hands and taste my sweat. I enjoy hard physical work. I sustain old vineyards and wonderful-tasting peaches by using organic farming methods—applying natural fertilizers, nurturing cover crops, and maintaining a proper "eyes to acres" balance (farming on a small scale so there are enough eyes to monitor nature at work and respond with preventive treatments) in order to sustain a human presence on the land. My older varieties of fruit are susceptible to the whims of nature, and growing them makes me more of an artist than a businessman. I hope to integrate my family with the natural rhythms of a farm—together we pick and pack peaches for specialty markets and roll raisin trays to protect a harvest from September rains. I seek to honor the past by following these traditions and enjoy the unexpected flavor of each season. The farm now looks as it may have during Jiichan's workdays with weeds growing vigorously and keeping the fields alive and moist while a fresh set of work-boot footprints records recent farm walks. History matters as I farm; I value the old.

Yet modern farming points to a future often based on profits—the flavors of the past do not seem to matter. My older varieties are not suited to rapid picking, mechanical sorting, distant transporting, and long shelf life. Newer varieties have been bred to be grown with large dosages of technology and science, chemicals are a required input, fruits must tolerate mechanical storing, water and nutrients are applied via computers and electronic timers. A sage pair of hands is no longer required for a marketable piece of fruit. Costs and market prices drive decision-making. Even consumers reward this system by purchasing the cheapest produce no matter what the flavor or where it comes from, who owns the farm or how the fruit is grown. Memory of tastes from another generation are repressed as buyers save a few pennies per pound.

Sometimes I pass the time during a hot workday by imagining a science fiction film in which all memory has been prohibited, for it hinders progress. Old orchards and vineyards have been destroyed because they interfere with new marketing and promotional programs. Since this is my movie, I'm a heroic mad peasant and have kept hidden a sacred tree of knowledge. This tree holds the power to trigger memory and release the poet's soul alive deep within people's emotions. The power of nature's creative and chaotic forces can be liberated with a single taste, and the present can be reconnected to the past. Of course, my tree is always full of fruit.

I farm peaches with the taste for an older generation. Biting into one evokes recollections; people fondly recall flavors beyond the palate. But I must sweat and eat dust in order to keep this orchard. Old tastes are cursed with old farming methods—hand labor, walking the fields, trusting old shovels and shears. I must prune out dead wood and continually reshape my trees rather than digging out the old and replanting the new. I'll struggle with a less productive corner of a field for now because building the soil with compost, cover crops, and mulch requires years instead of a quick fix of synthetic fertilizer.

The taste of my fruits is enhanced with personal stories, moments when foods are remembered and enjoyed like a gift. I recall Baachan eating peaches without her teeth. She'd select a gushy one, missed by the pickers and hidden behind leaves and branches until overripe. She'd remove her dentures and gnaw the fruit, the juices squirting into her mouth and drooling down her chin, the meat rolling over her tongue and sliding down her throat. I wondered how it felt between her bare gums, soothing and soft. Sometimes she'd glance up with a toothless grin that looked like the smile of an infant. She'd then mumble, "*Mottainai!*"—Can't be wasteful!

Dad approached his peaches differently. He'd select a firm one, ripe but not so soft you could leave finger indentations. After nightfall, at the end of his workday and following his dinner and shower, he'd carefully spread a newspaper on a low table in front of his old easy chair. With a paring knife, he'd make an incision at the very tip of the peach. The curved steel blade, half worn away yet razor-sharp, sailed through the flesh, gliding just beneath the skin, a hint of juice dripping onto the handle, making the aged wood a dark brown. Dad's rough hands, with flattened fingernails and thick calluses, gently turned the peach, rotating it into the blade. While his right fingers held the knife, his thumb guided the fruit, subtly pushing it while feeling for spots where he'd dig deeper to slice out bruises or the pockmarks caused by a hungry bird's pecking.

Dangling beneath his hands, spiraling downward in an unbroken band, the peach skin curled onto the newspaper. On some evenings, the piece collected into an upright shape of a sculptured peach, hollow, with the precision of a fine craftsman's touch along the surface. The strips delicately balanced atop each other for a moment, then tumbled over, and the juices darkened the light newspaper. Dad then cut a slice from the naked fruit and slipped it into his mouth. He smacked his lips with the flavor and crunched the flesh with his teeth. He repeated the motion, the knife sliding through the meat, the metal blade becoming a serving utensil when he grabbed the slice with his teeth, his lips licking the steel. As he savored the dessert, he peered down at the newsprint and read the day's news. His eyes scanned the headlines and skimmed another story with each bite of his peach.

I serve myself the best peaches while walking my fields. I roam over the furrows and through the grass, searching for the golden amber shades of the ripest fruit. Often just the tip of a few fruit will have gone soft as I wait for the majority of the field to ripen for one of our rounds of picking. In the morning or evening, when the sun is at the horizon, the soft light enriches the color and the ripe fruit seem to glow, their juicy tips beckoning. I stop, pick one, and sink my teeth into the flesh. The juices burst out and the nectar explodes in my mouth. "This is ready," I say to myself as I make plans to start picking the field the next day.

Then I flip the peach to the side and hunt for another treat, assessing how "deep" we can harvest in the days to come, mentally scheduling the crew to cover half the field in a day, then delay a few days until the lower half matures. I reach for another fruit, take a single bite, and toss the rest. "Not as ripe," I note, relaxing as I realize the crop isn't getting away from me and won't become gushy and soft. Along the western edge of the orchard, I pick a dozen fruits, nibbling on each, then tossing them away. "We have to have a few too ripe so that the rest of the peaches are right," I rationalize.

I walk and snack for a few minutes more, decadently flicking aside the "single bite treats," grinning because I know my grandparents would probably be horrified at my waste. "We'd toss them out anyway and it doesn't pay to harvest just a few pieces at a time," I tell myself. "Besides, farmers should taste their own fruits. We don't allow ourselves to enjoy our harvests enough!"

No one hears except the trees laden with peaches, their branches hanging low from the weight of the crop. A few leaves stir and I can hear the plop of an overripe fruit falling from a limb and striking the damp earth.

Neither Jiichan Masumoto nor Jiichan Sugimoto planted my peach orchards, but they left behind the seeds of hard work that have sprouted and thrive today. I live in a world where you are often defined by what you do, yet hard work is devalued merely as a means to an end. Sweat garners little respect, callous hands are rarely valued. As men age, their experiences seem to carry little importance. Old men appear lost in an era of new technology; their histories are like fossils. I can't recall when a neighbor's son pointed to an elder and proclaimed, "I'm going to be like him." On a precious few farms, though, it's still okay to be old.

Now I know how and why many old farmers keep hanging on. In the early autumn, right after the first cold front passes through and the leaves begin to fall with a light shower or breeze, these aging men are the first ones out in the fields. They're anxious to begin their job, as if it's their responsibility to tend to the orchard or vineyard, their unspoken obligation to care for old trees and vines. Armed with their favorite shears, they prune and cut, shape and reshape old branches, and search for new canes. All the while, they fool nature. By pruning in the early autumn, they're telling the world that they intend to see the crop all the way through the next summer, to one more harvest.

Shikataganai

In a box of old photographs I find an envelope containing a fifty-dollar U.S. Savings Bond bought by Jiichan Masumoto in January 1942. During the weeks following the bombing of Pearl Harbor, numerous Japanese-American community organizations wanted to demonstrate the loyalty of a people who suddenly looked like the enemy. They urged everyone to buy a bond, support our country in its battle against Japan. Their efforts did little good—within months everyone of Japanese ancestry was rounded up and interned. Jiichan wanted to become more American at a time when America was taken away from him.

My family accepted their fate and packed belongings. Their hands must have grown calluses in the desert as they stuffed paper between floor planks to keep out the blowing sand, stretched ropes and blankets to divide barracks into compartments so that families could have some privacy, and dragged rocks and planted scraggly bushes to create gardens around new homes surrounded with barbed wire and guard towers. They discovered that Americans are not always treated like Americans.

I revisit the memorial service photograph of the Masumoto family at Gila River, Arizona. Jiichan Masumoto holds the flag given to him at his son's service. His fingers are interlocked and the flag is held between his body and his palms; his calluses rub against the white stars and blue field. He looks angry. Jiichan held his emotions in check, the pain, anguish, and confusion manifested a stark silence. Jiichan was learning to be American.

Baachan Masumoto holds up a photograph of her dead son. I imagine her nervously opening and closing her grip on the picture frame, rubbing her thumb and fingers together, kneading her thick calluses with her fingertips as she posed for the camera. She wears the blank look of a lost generation. She too is learning to become American.

Dad stands in the background of the photo, next to his brother and sisters. He wears a military uniform; he had been drafted out of the relocation camp and taken to boot camp in Florida in order to serve his country. While in basic training, he received news of his brother's death in Italy. The military questioned whether to give Dad the time to attend the memorial service and whether it was safe for him to travel across the country without escort. Perhaps the authorities could not deny the reality of the situation—a soldier killed in action, a brother drafted and trained to fight the enemy, a family at "home" in a compound under military guard needing their eldest living son at the memorial service. They granted him a pass, but he would lose his place with his training company and have to repeat boot camp. I cannot see Dad's hands but imagine his palms grew calluses from squeezing a rifle at a firing range with the enemy in his sights, just days before the family photograph was taken in the desert. He is learning to be American.

The people in these pictures no longer control their destiny. Perhaps they were biting their tongues and bleeding with pride as they accepted America with a bow of humility. Not weakness but silent strength. The photos mark a turning point for all Japanese Americans, a time that changed lives forever. Family histories became twisted. Some grandfathers died behind prison walls; the spirits of many others were broken. My grandmothers survived but carried the scars. They harbored a deep distrust for the rest of their lives, a fear of the unknown.

I recall Baachan Masumoto often saying, "Can't take a chance." As she grows more withdrawn, I find her staring out of a window, rubbing then holding her hands together, living with a speechless terror I can only begin to understand.

My family never talked about this. I grew up confusing their silence with a shameful quiet and an inability to speak out. I often heard the phrase *Shikataganai*. I was told this meant "It can't be helped."

In elementary school, I first heard about relocation from older friends and cousins. They were studying about it in college and returned home during vacation with questions. Once, during dinner, I asked my parents, "How did you feel? What did Jiichan and Baachan do? Why did it happen?"

Dad continued eating his rice and *okazu*/stir-fry vegetables. He shook his head with a tight-lipped frown. Mom softly smiled and asked if I'd like a second helping.

"Well," she finally said, "it was a bad time. I remember my mother explaining it to all us kids, *'Shikataganai.'* "

As I learned the story of the internment from the books of historians, I was angry and embarrassed. How would I react to evacuation? Once I thought I would protest, like the dissidents who were labeled "problems" and relocated to Tule Lake, California. They resisted, denounced the authorities, organized protests and violent demonstrations with bloodshed—publicly demonstrating their pain and humiliation. But out of 120,000 internees, only a small minority verbalized their discontent. Even fewer repatriated to Japan, leaving the America they could no longer call home.

Later, I asked Dad about the farm and why we hadn't owned land before the war. "There were laws," he answered. "They didn't let Ojiisan or Obaasan own a farm because they were Japanese." He sipped his tea.

"*Shikataganai?*" I commented for him.

But I did not know the real translation of the term, and only later, with the passage of time and experience, do I understand it. I can hear the voice of my grandfathers. They say, "*Shikataganai.* We have no choice." They made decisions early in life—to leave Japan, to build new homes, to live with certain contradictions all immigrants must endure. They learned to live with their memories. Once they settled in this land, they had few options and chose to stay.

Their memories live like ghosts. Jiichan does not wear a bitter or forsaken appearance. He owns a hardened face. As I begin my family and work these farmlands, I live with old snapshots and harvests from the past. I claim the baggage of history I must carry. I too am destined to possess hardened hands thickened with my own calluses.

What will I pass on to my children? When they look into a mirror, what will they see in their faces that carries a Japanese character? What spirits survive on the rich land I farm? How do they speak to me, and what can they say to my family? What stories will I find as I plow and plant the earth, the lands of my grandfathers? I too live with my memories. *Shikataganai*—I have no choice.

I never considered that thousands of mute voices could become more powerful than a rally or march. Stripped of their rights, guilty by their heritage, the stillness of individuals became a private solution to a personal pain. My family relinquished their Japanese character and replaced it with an American will—they claimed a home in this land through their silence, a willingness to accept conditions and the strength to move on. My grandfathers chose to remain in this adopted land. For the first time in my life, I stare at their photographs and see Americans.

thirteen

F A M I L Y
R E C I P E S

Cultural Delivery

I AM NOT PREPARED FOR THIS. I SHOULD HAVE BEEN FOREWARNED
when one of my wife's relatives became concerned about our
pregnancy and asked, "Gee, are you sure those kinds of babies
turn out okay?"

Marcy was furious. She bit her tongue and could not believe
her ears. This was not the 1800s in some sleepy backwoods town
of Hayseed, America. But this was family. Her tongue began to
bleed in her mouth.

245

"Those kinds of babies" meant a product of an interracial, intercultural marriage: a Japanese-American Buddhist with a Wisconsin German Lutheran. I say "intercultural" because our differences go beyond race—they necessarily involve a merger of two cultures, two worlds not always in harmony. The "melting pot theory" ignores the reality—diversity creates conflict. During the delivery of our firstborn these differences became clear.

We had been married for two years. I was struggling financially on the farm, and much of my writing remained unpublished. "My stories are like wine waiting for their right time," I joked. "And it makes for a complementary profession with my farming—neither is making much money, but both are full of life." Most mornings, Marcy gently smiled and left for her work as a health educator and trainer. Fortunately she accepted her dual career role, working in town as a professional woman, then returning home in the evening, the primary investor in and supporter of the family farm. We did not plan on the pregnancy, but concluded it was part of the "good chaos" of nature enveloping us.

I note the time of 5:00 a.m. as we leave home for the hospital. Labor contractions are five minutes apart. The rows and rows of grapes zip past our headlights; the peach trees have lost their leaves and stand naked in the transient moonlight. The highways are empty as night gives way to early dawn. Despite the slow pace of fall work, within a few hours these roads will be filled with laborers heading toward vineyards and orchards patiently awaiting to be pruned.

The attending nurse suggests that we walk around, because we still have a long way to go; the cervix is only at two centimeters. He reminds us that it has to dilate to ten centimeters in order for the baby's head to fit through. "And remember," he says to me, "delivery will be demanding. Be nice to the soon-to-be mother no matter what." I naively nod my head in agreement.

To pass the time we talk about names. We agree that one name will be a Japanese one. I hope my child will maintain a connection with his or her heritage and identity, a consciousness. If it's a boy, I think of Jiichan Masumoto's name, but a problem arises. The name listed on his official documents is misspelled—instead of Hikozo Masumoto it reads Hikazo. Which name is correct, which is authentic?

"But my family can't pronounce most of those names. We need to be selective," Marcy reminds me. "They still pronounce your name wrong half the time and can't seem to figure out why someone would use the name 'Moss.'"

I remind her that if we have a girl, one name will be Rose, after her grandmother and her mother and Marcy's own middle name. From the Ros-Lor dairy in Wisconsin to the Wesdamar goat dairy in Apple Valley, California, and now the Masumoto peach and grape farm in Del Rey, there would be another generation of Roses on a family farm. But whenever I hear Rose with a Japanese name like Yoko or Mariko, I keep thinking of Tokyo Rose from World War II.

At 8:00 a.m. the contractions become steady, three to five minutes apart. Dilation has progressed to four centimeters. Marcy's temper grows short.

"What do you think it'll be, a boy or girl?" I ask to distract her from the pain.

"There you go again with that boy-girl question," she snaps.

At first I wanted a boy, a combination of an image of Japanese culture—a little *samurai* son—coupled with the agrarian tradition of a son taking over the family farm, the passing on of the land and a legacy. But then with a series of financially disastrous years on the farm, I understand what a lot of Issei and Nisei farmers feel—no one would want a child to struggle like this. Children should go to college, get out of the fields, and escape. Suddenly a girl will do just fine.

"What about a woman in today's professional world?" Marcy says. "A lot of women are treated unfairly. Farming is still pretty much an old boy's game. And if she's part Asian, what about that quiet, passive stereotype she will have to contend with?" She pauses and takes some deep breaths, coping with another contraction, then continues, "Look at the Japanese community potlucks with all the men on one side, arms crossed, talking, nodding their heads, and all the women on the other side, aprons in place, busy with the food, cleaning up."

For the first few years, a lot of folks didn't expect Marcy to help out like the other women, because "after all, she is *hakujin*." Even worse, at the first potluck, a well-meaning and nice middle-aged Nisei woman politely whispered to her, "There's some buttered white bread on the serving table, on the other side of the *sushi* plates. And we have forks too."

I shrug my shoulders and suddenly am not sure which to hope for, a boy or a girl. Luckily a contraction keeps us from continuing our argument and we start our breathing exercises again. The subject is left unresolved.

From eleven in the morning to three in the afternoon, the contractions become monotonous, and we both grow weary. Dilation has advanced to six centimeters but is holding constant. We could go home, but our family doctor wants us to stay for observation. We tolerate the periodic contractions—easy for me to say—but the lack of progress troubles us. We are not used to things being out of our control. I still struggle with allowing nature to take over the farm. "How contradictory," I said to myself, "to work surrounded by nature yet fail to submit to nature." I keep hoping to find a win-win compromise—like the breathing exercises with delivery. The conflicts are natural; the process of coping with their pain is what we can manipulate.

We begin talking about the pain, whether to focus on it or to fight it and try to think about something else. I tell Marcy she would be very "Japanese" to focus on the pain, to accept it as part of the journey, much like suffering in Buddhism. She says this long labor must be part of the bargain, sort of like karma—an easy nine-month pregnancy and today she's paying her dues.

I think about an Eastern approach to spirituality and suffering while living within a Western world dominated by science and technology. Here in the hospital we are suspended in a world that seems to deny pain, as if drugs can overcome human nature. It reminds me of the modern factory farm, designed to manufacture peaches or grapes, depending on chemicals to overcome the pests of nature. But before coming to the hospital Marcy brewed and drank a special tea one of my aunts had given us. "To speed up the contractions," my aunt had explained as she handed me a brown paper bag filled with dark seeds, dried stalks, and yellowed leaves. "It may not stop the pain, but will help it along." At first we hesitated. We didn't understand what was meant by "helping the pain along." The brown liquid had a salty, tangy taste. Brewing and drinking it helped pass the time and enabled us to relax a little more at home. Now I wish we had the tea with us—a little bit of family tradition here at the hospital and a dosage of spiritual medicine.

By seven in the evening the contractions have surged to one right after the other. I vaguely recall this is termed the "transition stage" that begins at eight centimeters. Everything increases in intensity—the pain, the emotional swings—and yet the doctor fears we may still have a long wait. We struggle to maintain breathing patterns, trying to deal with the pain. Our emotions are drained, conversations become jagged and rambling, blunt statements are made out of context, often with piercing truths. "God, it hurts," Marcy cries.

God. My thoughts wander back to an earlier conversation about religion and this unborn child. Will we baptize the baby? Do we believe he or she must have a place in God's Kingdom through infant christening?

I was never baptized, and neither were my parents or grandparents. We never considered it. But I knew some Issei baptized their children; I don't know if they converted to Christianity or they thought it was part of becoming an American. Many Issei and Nisei used the Bible to select names for their children—it seemed the best source for American names.

Marcy's family never pressured us, yet I knew the issue remained. A surge of insecurity rises in me. Though I know our families have religious differences and we try to bridge the schism—we incorporated both Buddhist and Christian ministers in our wedding ceremony—a barrier remains: I am not Christian and Marcy is not Buddhist. Perhaps Marcy's family accepts that in me, but what about their own grandchild? Their belief will be absolute—salvation for this child must include baptism. But when? In her parents' church, one doesn't wait very long; you baptize infants so their souls can be saved. The infants don't choose—the family accepts such responsibility.

I stare at Marcy's face, contorted with pain. With every contraction a terror sweeps over her face and a sharp tightening surges within my chest. I feel challenged, responsible, and punished.

For two hours the ordeal continues, and after an examination the doctor informs us that Marcy has not progressed at all. We are still at eight centimeters. Marcy is ready to concede, and so am I.

"You gotta believe," I hear myself whispering to her. She nods, and a renewed look of determination grows on her face. I am still surprised by my comment. I sound like the old farmers who will joke and grin between deep sighs after September rain destroys a raisin crop, or the farm husband and wife who shake their heads at bad prices for peaches yet renew their spirits with the simple phrase "It will be better next year."

Gradually we slip into a rhythm, like a chant, breathing and believing with each contraction. "There are no absolute answers," I think to myself. "Just a belief that we will do the right thing." Our life as a couple and soon as a family will always be filled with differences. That is the spirit of our future, of our beliefs.

The baby is born at a quarter to midnight after over twenty

hours of labor and a difficult delivery. At one point we fought through each contraction with blind acceptance. Afterward we couldn't help but think of our grandmothers and mothers and the very different labor each experienced. One generation delivered inside a farmhouse, without a doctor, but attended by a warm country midwife who had delivered dozens of farm kids. Our mothers' generation lay alone in an operating room, under bright lights, surrounded by stainless steel and medical professionals. We began our family in a birthing room with soft lights and floral wallpaper with a "country pattern" that may have been like that used in old farmhouses. A team of nurses assisted us, with a family doctor helping with the actual delivery—the same doctor who sees my parents and sister.

Nikiko Rose Masumoto is born weighing eight pounds, ten ounces, a large baby with a huge head. We conclude that all of our conversations must have filled her head and no wonder she had trouble squeezing through. With her birth a new tradition begins for both of our families, an interracial child in an interracial family. Her first and perhaps only childhood home is located on a small rise in the middle of an eighty-acre farm, surrounded by neighbors and family friends we've inherited from my parents. The cultures Marcy and I were raised within may not always be in harmony. Yet despite a myriad of unsettled affairs, differences can be mediated. With the arrival of Nikiko Rose, a family is created.

Holiday Meals

My mother blames camp for her limited cooking skills. She was the youngest child of Japanese immigrants and entered Gila River Relocation Center as a young teenager. For four years she never washed rice, peeled a carrot, or cooked an egg. No one taught her how to plan a meal, shop for and purchase ingredients, or prepare a breakfast, lunch, or dinner. No one passed down family recipes during that time. The Sugimoto women never prepared a homemade feast for their clan. Mom does not recall even eating many meals with her mother. Baachan Sugimoto had become a widow while in camp and knew she'd have to work to support herself and the family, so she secured a job in the mess hall, mostly serving food and cleaning up, saving money for an uncertain future. Mom knew how to pick grapes and spread them on raisin trays better than how to make a sauce or soup base. Only later, along with many other Nisei women, did she take cooking classes at the Buddhist church, learning how to make *sushi* and properly set an American holiday table.

Mom tried her best to provide our family with traditional Thanksgiving and Christmas dinners. She'd lay out cookbooks and magazine menus on the kitchen counter in order to prepare the turkey or ham and the other customary dishes of mashed potatoes, stuffing, and pumpkin pie. In addition, she set out a bowl of cranberry sauce with the turkey or applesauce for the ham. By dinnertime, our table looked like a Norman Rockwell painting, except that the smiling faces with rosy cheeks were Japanese-American.

But there the similarity ended. Dad enjoyed white rice with his holiday meal and politely passed on the rolls and buns, shiny with glazed butter. We complimented Mom's picture-perfect feast with green tea instead of wine, toasting the occasion with Japanese ceramic teacups and loud slurps of the hot liquid. We *never* ate the cranberries or applesauce with our meats. We considered the fruits to be desserts and found it confusing to consume them as a sauce or condiment. We knew what a holiday table was supposed to look like, but no one told us how it was supposed to be eaten.

My grandparents never developed an appetite for American foods. Neither *baachan* cooked for the holidays. They both felt more comfortable in the fields than in the kitchen. I remember once Baachan Masumoto going out to work on Christmas Day. Mom made us delay opening our gifts until Baachan returned home for lunch. Then when we attacked the presents, tearing the paper and tossing the ribbon aside, Baachan sat by herself. She had no presents for any of her children or grandchildren. Instead she carefully folded the sheets of colorful paper and gently rolled the ribbon for future use. In the afternoon, while we were lost in our new toys and games, she slipped outside to work. Only now do I realize her subtle gift was her own labor as she'd prune one more vine and dig out one more weed. With the future harvests, I'd realize the fruits of her offerings.

While we were growing up, our holiday celebrations were very simple. Ordinary events were never overshadowed by gluttonous dinner tables. In elementary school, just before Christmas vacation, all of the kids would march into the auditorium, where boxes of oranges and some hard candy were stacked. We were given a paper bag and instructed to take one orange along with a handful of sweets. A nearby citrus grower had donated the produce to our school, a holiday gift to kids who had little money to spare, an act of kindness during a season of giving. Ironically, many of the farmworker parents of my classmates may well have harvested these oranges; their invisible fingerprints flavored each fruit with both pride and shame. It was a special event. My friends and I pondered whether to eat the orange at school or take it home to share with family. Today I still consider a simple orange as part of my holiday feast.

Marcy's family holidays come from Wisconsin—our two clans are separated by thousands of miles and two cultures from opposite sides of the world. We are Japanese and Buddhist, they are German and Lutheran or Catholic. We grow raisins and peaches in the heat of California, they work a small dairy through Wisconsin's demanding seasons. Yet we share a sense of tradition. Homegrown foods are an essential ingredient for holiday meals— they are part of being a close family. I realized my wife's family truly appreciated me when her Grandma Rose started asking for "Mas's raisins" for her Christmas baking. My farm and my produce had finally become part of their family holiday table.

My farm not only provides me with a livelihood, it also nourishes family and community traditions. Growing raisins and peaches becomes an asset during the holidays, especially when my mother-in-law discovers she now has an endless supply for her cooking. Raisins are part of her family's special recipe for turkey stuffing, and seeing those tiny black morsels mixed with the bread, celery, and seasoning makes me feel welcomed. In addition, my dried peaches go well with her Christmas tradition of fruit stollens served alongside their holiday oyster stew. Raised on seafood, I find an affinity with the oysters and please my in-laws by asking for seconds. I ask about the meaning of this ritual, as I don't normally associate seafood with the holidays.

"Why, it's the tradition!" is their answer, followed by another ladleful of stew into my bowl.

They sometimes take traditions to extremes. They often raise their own holiday turkeys—poor old tom can be seen walking around in their yard, his head bobbing up and down, back and forth, with his overconfident strut. The next day he joins us for dinner in a different form! Perhaps, though, I take this sense of family—and family pets—a bit too seriously.

On the other hand, holiday turkeys always created a problem for my own family. The men were given the "honor" of carving the grand bird, but none of us knew quite how to do it. We had no grandfathers to pass down their techniques and favorite knives, no role models to watch and imitate as we grew up. Dad sometimes started the task, studying the pictures in an old *Joy of Cooking*. But standing with family around, hungrily eyeing the meal we had anticipated all day, enticed by the aromas—this was not the time nor the place to learn a new ritual. Dad would give up and pass the bird to Mom. She then carried it back into the kitchen, where we heard her whacking and tearing the creature into tiny shreds, as if she were preparing strips for a *teriyaki* sauce or *okazu*/stir-fry.

At the age of thirty-five I reluctantly begin to learn how to carve, prompted by my frantic wife when she hosts the family holiday dinner. "Here," she says, thrusting the golden brown bird into my hands. I imagine her adding, "It's time you became a man." So I venture into new territory, my in-laws scrutinizing my rite of passage as I nervously stand before "their" bird. By now, though, I have learned a valuable lesson about family—how to defer gracefully to an older generation and let them show me how it's done. They quickly accept their familial roles. My father-in-law sharpens an old knife by whipping it up and down a sharpening steel. My mother-in-law tugs the drumstick up and down, testing to see if the turkey is properly done. She begins to grin as it works loose and looks up to a smiling husband as he leans over, knife glistening razor-sharp. Now all parties celebrate quite contentedly.

Japanese customs also find their way into our holidays. One annual celebration held at the end of the year is making *mochi*. *Mochi* is made from sticky steamed rice that is pounded and kneaded into a doughy cake. We eat it fried and seasoned with soy sauce or add it to traditional Japanese soups and stews. On cold winter nights, I boil the *mochi* and sweeten it by sprinkling on a mixture of sugar and soy powder.

We make *mochi* once a year, often hundreds of pounds at a time. This requires much help and many hands. A special sweet rice is first distributed to a dozen households, and for several days the grains are soaked, drained, and resoaked in water. Early on the *mochitsuki/mochi*-making day, the men rise early and build fires with old grape stumps and redwood stakes. The smoke hugs the earth, then wanders upward to blend with the winter fog. To keep warm, the men hug themselves and rock back and forth, shifting from one foot to the other. I can see their breath when they exhale.

They begin to cook batch after batch of rice. The steam seeps upward through a series of four flat wooden boxes, each with a thick portion of the white grains. The bottom box cooks the fastest, and is then refilled with uncooked rice and set atop the stack. The initial rice is often slightly overcooked, as some of the kernels may have browned because of the uneven temperature of the dancing flames before the fire settles into glowing embers. The men often treat themselves to a breakfast bowl of hot rice with tea and *umeboshi*/pickled plums, smacking their lips with the sharpness of the vinegary flavor.

With the next batch, the freshly cooked and steaming rice is dumped into a stone urn. A skilled team then pounds it with a wooden mallet, a team leader kneeling and quickly flipping the rice between whacks, blending the grains and gradually forming a huge ball of rice dough. A modern method has also been introduced, requiring less teamwork and timing: electric grinders mash the sticky grains together, creating a smooth paste while avoiding smashed fingers.

Finally, a line of hands must be ready to mold the hot dough into small two-or-three-inch flat cakes. An elder pulls a small lump from the ball and quickly passes it down a long table to a row of kneaders. Fingers pull at the dough, still steaming hot if the timing has been precise, stretching the outer skin until an even, smooth texture is created, pinching it together and creating an invisible seam on the bottom. As the rice cools, a glassy surface coats each cake.

In Japan, extended family gather for this holiday event. In America, only a few families were large enough to make *mochi* on their own. The required extra hands of aunts, uncles, and cousins remained in Japan. As a result, making *mochi* instead became a community function—neighbors, churches, and social clubs gathered as extended family. I often joined a church group to make *mochi* or our family partnered with a Japanese-American neighbor.

I wonder what new dishes will find their way onto my family's holiday tables of the future. Traditions must evolve—otherwise they become acts without meaning, fossils from dead civilizations, relics of a past that only remind us of where we were, not where we're going. Whether we like it or not, we're in continual pattern of updating family recipes. I toast the future, when my children will find ways to break through cultural barriers. My daughter wants to leave *manju*, a Japanese sweet cake, for Santa at Christmas. She says he must be getting tired of cookies all the time.

I smile when I see a new variation on a theme—like the time a young Yonsei (fourth-generation Japanese American) who grew up "very American" tried to follow tradition by bringing a rice dish to a Japanese community potluck. I still laugh to myself when I think of her placing "rice crispy treats" on the table alongside the *sushi*, fried rice, and *nigiri*/rice balls. Despite some of the whispers from the older women, the young woman saw nothing wrong with her effort; she fulfilled her commitment while working full-time and being a single parent. I admired her creativity.

One day I may see a near-vegetarian holiday feast, as some of my wife's cousins eat more lightly and have given up the heavy meat-and-potatoes meals of their childhood. Yet I can also see a plate of summer sausage on the table, especially if it's venison from the annual deer hunt in Wisconsin. A rite of passage—a son's or grandson's first deer—will continue to become part of the feast, just as it has been for generations.

Our foods will help place us. My children, who will have the opportunity to know their grandfathers from both sides of the family, will never have to apologize for the diversity of our holiday recipes. They will recall the simple *nigiri* my mom makes for them by rolling rice into a cylinder shape and wrapping it with a strip of *nori*/seaweed. They will laugh and retell the story of Marcy's first experience with *mochi*, eating a lump of it at a holiday meal of *ozoni*/soup. She chewed and chewed the sticky mass and finally attempted to swallow it in a single gulp. It became lodged in her throat, and for a moment she could not breathe, then it slipped down past her windpipe. I joke that she simply choked on Japanese culture. "And almost died," she retorts. "But I survived."

Marcy and I still plan to continue the Japanese tradition of celebrating New Year's Day with an open house. Plates of *teriyaki* chicken, *sushi*, and *somen* salad, along with symbolic dishes—long *soba*/buckwheat noodles for long life, *kuromame*/black beans for good luck, and herring for virility and the blessings of many children—fill the table as we host dozens of guests. My aunts and Mom are grateful for us continuing the tradition—they grew weary of all the cleaning and cooking that needed to be done. Initially the relatives made most of the Japanese food, not quite trusting my wife. But as with most customs, time has a way of overcoming prejudices, so that now they trust her skills. We are the new generation of Japanese Americans.

Throughout the day, guests will come by and visit as we welcome the new year with a toast of *sake*. I find myself repeating, "What better way to begin the year than with family and friends in celebration?" With our farmer relatives and neighbors, we are able to forget the disappointments of the past year and look forward to the new with our naive optimism. In keeping with Japanese traditions, we also serve everyone salmon. We tried precooking some one year, but found it awkward when served cold. Other years we used canned salmon, but that didn't seem right. I don't know how it's prepared in Japan, but for American palates, we found smoked salmon to work the best. Each year when I repeat the Japanese saying about why we serve salmon—"It's the one fish that always returns home"—I'm still greeted with warm smiles and comforting silence. We then know the new year has begun properly.

Jiichan's Sake

During his final years, Jiichan Masumoto shuffled through the fields, working when he could or wandering around the farm. Like many first-generation immigrants, he longed for a taste of his native land, and perhaps because of his age, his dream of ever sampling those flavors again must have seemed impossible. According to Mom, he overcame the distance when he made himself a still.

Jiichan brewed *sake*. Mom says he never drank too much, never became drunk. He would just disappear for a few hours and go visit one of the small buildings out near the barn, presumably to check his equipment and necessarily sample his latest brew. Jiichan was a quiet man, and the alcohol did not change his personality. Like him, his *sake* also had a private character. Dad doesn't recall ever tasting it, nor many Issei men dropping by for a visit and sharing a drink.

I ask if Dad knew Jiichan's recipe. "*Sake* is from rice, isn't it? Does it require a special rice?"

Dad pauses, then shrugs his shoulders. He doesn't remember much about the still. "Everyone was working so hard, we didn't ask a lot of questions," he explains. He imagines Jiichan likewise worked hard on the brewing operation.

The family of a friend of mine owned and operated one of the oldest Italian wineries in the area, a very, very small operation. His grandfather had bottled a table wine for Italian immigrants' tastes. He claims, "You had to be real Italian to enjoy that wine. It was pretty hearty, and if you kept it too long it'd turn into vinegar . . . but it was *good* vinegar!"

Over the years, better-quality wineries opened in Northern California and along the coast, leaving his family as one of the few remaining that produced an everyday Italian table wine. They had lots of offers to sell the facility—speculators wanted to turn it into a boutique winery. But his grandfather and father refused to sell and kept making the hearty wine until recently, when it became too much work for just the family.

"My dad kept it going as long as he could. For the old-timers," my friend explains, his voice trailing off. "Where else would they get *their* wine?"

I remember some of the old Italians, with rough, stubbled

complexions. They'd arrive in an old gray Dodge or Ford pickup, rolling to a stop in the gravel, stones popping beneath the tires as they coasted to a stop. In a wooden box in the bed of the dusty pickup sat a collection of dark green bottles filled with their wine. The bottles clattered as they drove into the yard. With their hands they'd wave a greeting while getting out to talk with Dad. Rusted doors often stuck and latches were often busted, so they'd have to bang their shoulder into the frame while reaching out through the open window to pop open the door. I could only overhear part of their conversations, discussing the weather and grapes, sharing an unsolicited opinion about farm politics, and ending with a request to glean some of our vineyards. Dad usually grinned and nodded, "Sure, go ahead," and the crusty men dipped their heads, a nod of appreciation. Were Jiichan Masumoto around, I picture these farmers excusing themselves to join a fellow old-timer out behind the shed or for a walk through the fields.

"Did Jiichan have that many Italian friends?" I ask.

Dad makes a frown. "Can't say that I knew for sure. They always asked for him, and I'd point them in the right direction. But Jiichan didn't speak any English," says Dad. "I don't know how in the hell he talked with those old Italians."

Perhaps in his final years, though, a Japanese immigrant befriended an Italian and took him back to the small shack near the barn. They came from opposite places on the globe and spoke few common words. They shared a lifetime in the fields as they tasted a special brew of Muscat-*sake*. I can hear lips smacking and sighs released from deep within as they gulped shots of home brew. One immigrant nodding his head with an occasional grunt. The other rattling off stories, waving his hands and arms, dramatically illustrating his point. I can picture two old farmers sitting in the shade of a tree near the end of summer, toasting the past and the future harvests.

fourteen

WHEN
THINGS BREAK

A Child Within

THE BRITTLE SNAP OF WOOD AND THE BLUNT WAIL OF TWISTING
metal. The grinding roar of a diesel engine as it jolts to a stop. A
blinding cloud of dust is whipped up as I crash the cane cutter into
one of my grape vines. The steel blade shreds the trunk and tears
into the metal stake. The cutter bends on impact, the crumpled
metal wrapping around the remains of a vine and stake. The
hydraulic motor squeals and I immediately jam the clutch. The
motor dies.

I back out of the vineyard and limp home. The twisted machine drags on the ground. Paint cracks off with each bump, making a trail of faded yellow chips along the dirt avenue. My thirty-year-old stomach tightens as I near the shed. I once again feel like a ten-year-old boy hanging his head after breaking something.

At the shed, Dad greets the broken implement and his farmer son. He doesn't need to ask what happened. He grabs a crescent wrench and begins to unbolt the tangled mess. He pauses, studying how best to remove the bent metal. I can see his old glassy eyes dart back and forth as he plans how to fix the cutter. I try to help, but instead slip into the role of the son watching his father fix things that break.

Later he will begin redesigning the machine's weakened joints. He uses backs of old envelopes as drafting paper, with pencil sketches of new support rods that can withstand a son driving too fast through a vineyard and having an accident.

When I returned to the farm, I hoped to escape the frantic pace of city life. I planned to take care of my aging parents. I did not expect to learn so much from my father. I did not anticipate slipping back into the role of a son. I was not prepared to be so fortunate.

Dad has slowed when shoveling weeds, and he no longer handles the spray program for worms or mildew. I worry about the long hours he spends in the hundred-degree heat of summer, his shirt stained dark with his sweat, his hair matted and wet. His strain manifests itself as leg cramps in the middle of the night from dehydration during the day. In the winter I fear he'll be struck by a virus, weakened by the bone-chilling wet cold of our fog; he insists on "heading out" to work early in the morning before the sun has burned off the mist. I've watched him trudge out into the vineyards, pruning shear under his arm, rubber boots slick with the morning dew, slipping into the white mist, disappearing until he returns later in the day for a meal. When mak-

ing my field rounds, I'll pass by the patch where he works and
sigh with relief to see him methodically suckering a peach tree or
pruning a grape vine. I wave or stop and ask a rhetorical question—"How's it going?"—in order to make small talk and mask
my true reason for driving by. I'm constantly haunted by a night-
marish image of finding him collapsed on the ground.

Dad planted most of the vines and trees on the farm and has
spent his entire lifetime getting to know each one. I have logged
numerous years on this land too, but consider myself a "young"
farmer. I'm still being introduced to these fields. Dad remains
my source of knowledge and information about how to farm this
land.

No matter how old I am, when something breaks, I feel like a
child. Dad has rarely yelled at me or scolded me when I've broken
something. Usually he has walked out to where the equipment lay
wounded and begun fixing it. Once when I ran over a stack of
metal picking buckets, he helped me pull them free of the tractor
tires and then methodically pounded them back into shape with
a hammer. Another time I bent the tongue of a vineyard wagon
by turning too sharply. I hoped he wouldn't notice and I parked it
behind our shed. The next morning he ate early and was absent
from the breakfast table. I found him working, heating the metal
with an acetylene torch and trying to straighten the contorted steel.

Sometimes I wish he had yelled at me. His silence was deafening.

A week later, the sprayer—heavy and filled with five hundred
gallons of water and twenty pounds of expensive "Bt" (*Bacillus
thuringiensus*, a naturally occurring bacteria that poisons
worms)—gets a flat in the fields. I manage to steer the tractor
and machine out of the field and onto the dirt avenue. The tire is
ripped in half, weakened from years in the sun and heat and
bouncing down dusty rows and furrows. I plan my repair strategy: I'll simply jack up the sprayer, pull off the old tire, and slap
on a spare. Tomorrow I'll get a new tire. As I pick up the jack

and spare from our barn, I mention my plan to Dad in passing. Within five minutes he joins me.

I've changed flats before. I've pulled them off trucks, cars, pickups, trailers, tractors, forklifts, disks. I've changed them along roadsides, in avenues, in the middle of fields. But I never changed one on a sprayer sitting in a dirt avenue with a tank full of water. I never pulled off an old shredded tire with lug nuts that had not been removed since we bought the sprayer twenty years ago.

Dad watches as I try to elevate the sprayer. My jack topples in the powdery dirt. I calculated the weight of the full sprayer. If a gallon of water weighs eight pounds, then the jack has to lift four thousand pounds plus the sprayer. I mumble out loud, "This is not going to be as easy as I thought."

I brace the jack with two pieces of wood and begin pumping. The wood sinks into the soft soil as if the jack works in reverse. I watch my wooden base descend into the powdery dirt, then snap in half under the weight of the sprayer. I stand back and survey the situation, desperately trying to think of options and trying not to hang my head.

Dad suggests, "Why not try putting the jack here, at the end of the frame?" He also points to a hard spot in the avenue, and somehow I sense he has done this before. "The jack will lift from the rear and work in tandem with the tractor drawbar in front. Raise the frame, not the tire. It ought to lift up."

He pulls the jack from beneath the axle and repositions it at his spot. He starts working the jack, and the sprayer shifts. I can hear the water sloshing back and forth inside. With each pump, the jack elevates the machine. Each stroke gets harder and harder. I take over and feel better. At least I can contribute my muscle and sweat to this repair job.

One day, when things break on the farm, I will have to try to fix them myself. I will practice for the day when Dad's not around—knowing I can never be fully ready for it. I'll miss my dad. The ten-year-old boy in me hangs his head not because he's ashamed of breaking something or worried about a scolding. He hangs his head because he's afraid. He fears the time when someone won't be around to help him. The fear is natural. The fear makes me appreciate what I have.

I believe Dad remembers this too, because every once in a while, he too wears a nervous smile when something doesn't work right. Perhaps his father's ghost is on this farm along with the shadow of another ten-year-old boy whenever something breaks.

Itchy Grass

The nippy mornings give way to bright sunshine. Though it's only in the sixties, in the sunlight I feel much warmer. I'm rushing to complete my winter work. Before the vine canes can be tied to the trellis, I must first fix the broken wire strands that are scattered throughout the vineyards. The vines are growing impatient; they are awakening from their winter slumber, water flowing from roots to the canes and dripping from pruning cuts.

As I drive past the peach orchards, I smile at the pale green blanket of mostly strawberry clover and vetches growing between the trees like a lush green oasis in the otherwise brown, dreary landscape. I'm reminded of spring colors only a few weeks away. But I make a huge error by not walking the orchards. An army of weeds is already launching its annual assault.

Baachan appropriately calls it "itchy grass." Also known as stinging nettle, this weed sprouts in the late autumn, and throughout the winter it hides, masquerading as a small, innocent plant camouflaged by the other low growth. In a few weeks, with the first hint of spring, it doubles in size to five or six inches high. The jagged leaves look like the serrated edge of a bread knife. Tiny fiber whiskers grow from the leaf surface and carry a natural skin irritant. If I brush the leaves, the stinging hairs will quickly create blisters on my skin.

As a toddler, I was rudely introduced to this poison while playing hide and seek with my brother and sister. I hid in a cluster of
stinging nettle, my fat tummy rolling against the pointed teeth,
and within seconds I felt a burning and itching. I pulled up my
T-shirt and shrieked at the welts already forming. They looked
like a column of swelling ant bites. As I scratched and rubbed
them, they grew pink and bulbous. I ran home crying. Mom tried
to calm me as she wiped my skin with a washcloth, poured
calamine lotion into her hands, and painted a pink band around
my gut.

"You Masumoto boys," she said, shaking her head. "You all
break out so badly with itchy grass." She then explained how my
older brother, Dad, and even Jiichan were extremely allergic to
the stinging nettle.

I tried to avoid the weed but still had terrible encounters. My
older brother was more careful, watching where he worked and
often wearing gloves. Dad dressed appropriately and seemed to
avoid contact, possibly because of his long-sleeved shirts and high
socks rising up his calf, well above his work boots. I don't know
how Jiichan protected himself. I asked Baachan about itchy grass.
She said, *"Dame, dame kusa"*—No good, no good grass. If she
found the weed in our fields, she furiously attacked it, stabbing
her shovel into the earth and flipping the severed plants. Her eyes
then roamed, searching out stray weeds that had escaped her
blade. She finished by swinging her shovel down with a hard
blow, thumping the small pile of itchy grass.

Over the years, Dad tried to purge the farm of stinging nettle
with frequent disking and an occasional shot of preemergent her-
bicide. When I came back to the farm after college, I rarely found
it and stopped worrying about it. But in one peach orchard, a
clump survived and quickly reseeded. The plants concealed their
seedpods under the serrated leaves, the tiny white flowers blooming in early spring. By the time I worked the fields in April, I was
too late, and the cultivator teeth only buried the seeds for the next

year and a larger threat to terrorize the hypersensitive skin of
Masumoto males. (For some reason, my mom and sister are not as
affected by this nettle.) I tried to control the weed, but it had multiplied geometrically and it would require years of diligent monitoring. I succeeded in restricting it to a single few acres of peaches
and planned to keep vigil over my land much as my father had.

MY KIDS RIDE with me into the fields. Nikiko, now ten years old,
balances against the tractor fender, thrilled by the roar of the
diesel engine. Korio, our four-year-old son, sits on my lap, playing
with the steering wheel, mimicking his father. He's a much more
playful child than Niki—while she loves to watch the birds and
wildlife and enjoys listening to the wind rustle the leaves, Kori
chases the crows, jumps into piles of leaves, and shakes tree
branches to see what will fall. As the tractor bounces down the
dirt avenue, they play a game with their voices, sighing as deeply
as they can and listening to the staccato vibrations as if someone
were pounding their chests. When we strike a pothole, they giggle
and scream and their small hands clutch my shirt.

I stop to fix a dozen vine wires, walking up and down the
rows, searching for and repairing a break with a new strand. The
children wander into the peach orchard and climb a tree until I
hear them snap a few small branches. They stop when I yell,
"Hey, what's going on there?" Nikiko then finds an old crow's
nest dangling from a treetop and studies the straggly collection
of sticks loosely woven together. Korio redirects his attention
downward, seeking the perfect stick to become a sword or walking cane. He tumbles in the uneven earth, brushes off the dirt on
his arms, wipes his hands on his pants and rubs his face.

Next I hear whining and imagine the kids are bickering. Kori
is upset, and Niki is not sure about what. I sense something is
wrong, though, when the complaint crescendos. I cut through
the fields, ducking under each vine row trellis, my head bobbing

up and down. By the time I arrive, thick welts have grown on Korio's fingers, palms, and arms. Fat red streaks swell on his cheek, as if someone had ripped fingernails across his soft flesh, gouging his face. Scratch marks are etched into his neck, and a row of tiny red dots bleed where he has torn his skin, seeking relief from the stinging. I look around and discover a dense cluster of itchy grass.

We scamper to the tractor. Kori is crying and doesn't understand what he did wrong. The itching grows worse by the minute. At home I wash him with water. He's shaking and tears stream down his face. He tries to be brave but can't stop rubbing his neck and face. As the water heats, I douse the welts. The water almost burns him, but then he realizes the itching has lessened. He sticks his hands into the stream of hot water and splashes his face. Gradually a soothing warmth replaces the biting sting.

While I dry him off, he asks what happened, and Niki wants to know why she wasn't bothered. I rub aloe lotion over his flushed skin and ponder how to describe stinging nettle and my memories of this noxious weed.

I begin, "Let me tell you a story. All the Masumoto boys have a curse. . . ." Their eyes widen and they lean closer.

Stuck

In late October we have a series of early rains. The parched ground drinks up the water until it's saturated, and puddles begin to form. The earth turns dark and damp.

Dad approaches with his slow stride, slouching slightly and almost dragging his boots. Rubbing his chin, he asks, "Say, you got a minute?" He runs his hand through his gray hair, sheepishly grins, shakes his head back and forth, and makes a soft clicking sound with his tongue—"Tsk, tsk, tsk." Finally he adds, "I need your help."

I straighten up from my shoveling. It's not often a son gets to help his father. It's not often a father asks his son for help. "Oh?" I answer, and I follow him to the shed.

He emerges with a heavy steel chain draped over his shoulder. The thick links rattle together and the end hooks drag on the cement. He coils it around the hydraulic lift arms behind a tractor. "Better grab your shovel," he says.

We drive out to the vineyards. I stand next to him on the tractor, leaning against the fender. Peering over the tops of the vines, I strain to see the piece of farm equipment that must be lodged in the mud. Why else would we be lugging the chain out to the fields? We do not speak to each other. He starts to back down a vine row in the area we call "the Hill." At the other end, over a hundred yards away, I can see the blue outline of our big Ford tractor leaning at an odd angle.

The tractor is stuck in a wet pocket of clay, a poorly drained area no larger than a twenty-foot-wide circle and with a layer of hardpan directly beneath. The surrounding soil of loam and sand quickly absorbs rain, but in that one strip, water pools to create a bog. Years ago that small spot was a shallow sinkhole. Dad scraped clay from another area of the farm and mounded it here to fill the depression. Ever since then, water here seeps into the ground at a much slower rate. While doing tractor work, I sometimes forget about that muddy stretch, and am abruptly reminded when my front tractor tires skid into the miniature slough and the rear tires spin in the slime. But as long as the tractor has momentum, I am usually able to slip and slide my way to the dry ground on the other side.

Dad and I stop a few feet away. The Ford tractor looks like a sad animal, trapped and beaten, awkwardly lying on its belly with its left rear leg helplessly lodged in the swamp. The rear differential is partially buried and the tandem disk that Dad has been using is equally stuck in the sludge, its sixteen metal blades half submerged in the quagmire. Dad has tried to dig his way out; slop is shoveled aside and piled under the adjacent vines. The ooze has stiffened into peaks of mud, like whipped cream.

We wrap the chain around the front axle and try to divert the mud away from the tires. Each shovelful has to be rocked, then pulled out. The mud and water create a suction against the metal blades, and a chorus of "schooops" accompany our efforts. Just about as much mud slides back into the hole to replace each shovel load taken out. My feet sink up to my ankles. I have to pull at my knees with my hands to free my boots from the sticky syrup.

I climb aboard the front tractor and rev the engine before slowly inching forward to take the slack out of the chain. Dad starts the Ford, cranks her up, and nods. With a lurch, the chain snaps tight and twists as the engines roar. Dad's tires begin to spin and gobs of goop shoot into the air and splash the fender and his back. A ridge of slop builds behind the tires. The earth refuses to release us. Dad shakes his head and waves his hand at me, a signal to quit. He sighs, and I see his shoulders drop. A silence suddenly descends on the fields.

"Damned mud," I say. "I never knew this spot got so bad."

Dad nods.

I continue, "Those old tractor tires—not enough traction from them. We should have gotten new ones a long time ago."

Dad climbs down from his tractor and picks up his shovel. I join him, and we again try to pull mud away from the tires. We have few choices. We can leave the tractor stuck for a few days, even weeks, and hope the earth cures—a risky option, because we're entering a season of rain, fog, and cold, with many overcast days in the thirties and forties. The ground may never adequately dry.

Another option is to unhook the tandem disk, then try to pull out the tractor. But the disk will lie stuck all winter, an embarrassing reminder of this incident. When I was a kid, a neighbor got his Ford 8N stuck in the middle of a young vineyard. It became a neighborhood tourist attraction. Folks stopped by to make suggestions about how to pull it free. Gradually his field became an informal meeting place for other farmers to gather and sling the bull. All winter the tractor was a landmark to orient out-of-town visitors. A photograph of it was published on the front page of our local weekly newspaper, a human-interest story for everyone except the poor farmer.

Dad and I work silently and do not discuss the options. I move behind the tractor to assess how difficult it will be to unhook the disk. But something is not right with the lift arms. Normally, the thick metal bars protrude from the rear of the tractor and are securely attached to the disk frame. Driven by the tractor's main hydraulics, these powerful arms can raise and lower implements; they are capable of lifting over a thousand pounds. I notice a pin is missing from the left arm; some of the holes don't match up and it swings freely instead of being bolted to the disk. This has resulted in the disk's dragging to the left, gouging the mud and digging itself into the bog. I study the ground a few vines behind us and can see that the pin must have slipped out when Dad started the row—the disk pattern is uneven, drifting to the left. When the disk encountered the muddy section, it plowed deeper, burrowing into the earth, burying itself.

I explain this to Dad and show him the tracks left behind. He frowns, then grins. I hop on the free tractor and return home to locate a replacement pin for the lift arm. Dad shovels with renewed vigor.

We struggle to reattach the lift arm to the tractor's hydraulics, trying to insert a steel pin into two holes for a snug fit. Finally it slips in, and we look up at each other with a grin. I step out of the way and Dad pulls a lever to lift the disk. At first the tractor sinks a few inches, then the disk begins to rise. The blades strain to free themselves of the mud and manage to shake loose. Atop the tractors, we resume positions and signal each other with a wave. Both tractors begin to pull. The chain twists and the tires spin, but we inch forward. I sense either something will soon break or we'll break free.

With a pop we lurch forward. The rear tires grab and regain traction. The Ford slides out from the bog; the disk still drags but is freed from the mud. We drive down to the avenue. Dad signals for me to stop; the chain hangs limp between us. With a childlike leap, he jumps off the Ford, unhooks the links, and wraps them behind my tractor. He delivers a thumbs-up sign and turns to drive home. As I head to my nearby farmhouse, I turn around and see his back stained with splashes of mud. Chunks of earth flake off the tractor tires, spotting the avenue with a dark brown clay.

Vine Runners

Baachan trudges behind me, slouching forward, her eighty-year-old feet shuffling through the damp fields after an autumn shower. She carries her shovel over both shoulders like a peasant lugging water or produce down a country trail. Her pant legs grow dark, stained with the morning dew from the chickweed growing wild between the vine rows.

Earlier that morning, Baachan stood next to the dining-room window, blankly staring out at the orchards and vineyards. She stroked strands of her gray hair, mumbling to herself. I asked if she'd like to help me, and within minutes she was standing outside in her work shoes, old faded shirt, and dusty black pants. As we walk into the fields, I can hear her humming a Japanese children's folk song.

During the prior summer, I flagged thirty weak vines that need replacing, not a large number for an eighty-acre farm, considering my continual experiments with organic fertility programs. I believed the vines enjoyed the flavor of compost and the lushness of clovers and vetches tickling their surface roots. But I noticed a few vines had scrawny canes and stringy bunches. Throughout the year, their leaves remained yellow instead of a healthy deep green. Gradually their production declined. These old vines seemed to beg for euthanasia.

I search for my orange flags marking the weak vines that need to be removed. We will plant "vine runners" in their place— pulling a long, thick cane from a neighboring vine, burying it, and tying it to a grape stake, replacing the old with the new. Within a few months, new roots will begin to flourish. After another year or two, we'll cut the cord from the mother vine and a new generation will stand alone.

As I select a healthy cane to plant, Baachan begins digging out the old vine. She leans over the shovel, her feet firmly planted in the earth. Legs bent, she shifts her weight and pushes the cutting blade through a carpet of weeds. With a grunt and shove, she slides the shovel into the moist soil. Her biceps flex under her flannel shirt. Deftly, she flips the dirt to the side and repeats the process. Her face is taut, wrinkles tightening with each shovelful of earth. Her hands are callused from years in the fields. I soon join her, and together we dig and toss, exposing roots. Our blades tap against each other only once.

I hear the thud first, then see her arms shaking. Her arm muscles twitch, her hands stiffen. She then releases and regrips the wooden handle, raising and dropping the blade. Again she strikes something solid. She has uncovered a thick taproot a few feet beneath the surface. Baachan tries again, and this time her blade wedges in the wood. She tries to wiggle it free, but the wood holds tightly. Blood vessels in her forehead bulge as she attempts to yank and pull the shovel free. The root will not let go. Finally I use my shovel to knock hers free. Then I ram my shovel into the fiber, snapping it apart, only to uncover an even thicker one below.

I say, *"Dame ne!"* —It's no good. "Too much roots, Baachan!" She nods and picks at the shredded wood with her shovel, reluctantly accepting that the old vine will have to stay. But we only need room for the young runner to go alongside the old. The two can live side by side.

She says, "*Shoganai*"—It can't be helped. She straightens, swinging the shovel over her shoulder, searching for the next runner to plant.

fifteen

G I F T
O F   H O M E

The Hailstorm

By mid-June, fleshy peaches hang from weary branches. The old crusty wood strains under the weight of the fruit, the limbs bending toward the ground like the hunched back of an elderly worker who has seen too many harvests. I tie ropes around the tops of the trees, hoping to keep the limbs from breaking. A few still snap under the pressure, the crack echoing through the fields, followed by a muffled pounding of wood and fruit crashing

275

against the grassy earth. A small cloud of dust explodes into the air and the remaining branches of the tree bounce and shake as if rocked by an earthquake. The surviving fruit sways back and forth before gently coming to rest while the dirt settles.

With each summer day, the peaches swell and grow fat. The immature fruit gradually changes from a yellow-green to an amber gold as the juices build inside. On the high branches and along the outside edge rows where more sunlight strikes, I can detect the faint aroma of peach. Harvest approaches.

Nature teases me in these few weeks prior to harvest. I begin to believe that the hours of my labor will result in wonderful and luscious peaches. I start listening to market reports—the price quotations begin to acquire meaning. I covertly calculate my expenses relative to a potential sales price, growing excited when the numbers are in my favor. Recently a special demand has been created because of my writing a book about my peaches, and I may realize rewards I have till now only dreamed of. A dangerous optimism creeps into my conversations. I talk about harvests still two weeks away, return calls about inquiries, and start thinking like a salesman.

Occupied with my dreams of harvest, I do not pay attention to weather reports. An odd Arctic air mass has moved much farther south than usual and hovers off the northwest coast. Then it breaks toward the southeast as a cold northern storm sweeps into California, tangling with the warm tropical jet stream from the south. Unusually powerful storms are forecast for the Sierras; campers and backpackers are cautioned about sudden shifts in weather and advised to plan accordingly. I too should have been forewarned.

At worst, I anticipate rain, which fragile peaches do not like. Their delicate skin, if broken and exposed to excessive moisture, becomes a breeding ground for brown rot. Too much rain and cold days confuse the trees—the fruit may stop growing and ripen in an odd way, the tips of peaches becoming soft while the rest remains green, or the flesh may refuse to redden, remaining an off-yellow color. I had hoped for dry weather, but a few tenths of an inch of rain should not hurt too much.

I have never seen clouds shoot across the sky so fast. They whirl overhead, catapulted by winds that fling them from one horizon to the other. I watch them race from the west toward the east, imagining the black clouds splashing against the Sierra Nevadas. Another series of gray billows across beneath, blown by a more northerly current. They do not crash but pass above and below one another, driven by different rivers of air. The sky becomes a swirling cauldron, churning with energy and motion. Massive forces flex their strength above my farm. I look around for a cold front of dark clouds marching across the valley but see none. I realize I'm directly underneath the rolling band of thunderheads. My stomach tightens.

On the radio a high shrill electronic pitch sounds. Growing up, I heard "emergency warning" broadcasts, the piercing tone, followed by a dead-air pause before the calming voice of announcer advised listeners, "This is a test. . . ." We were told these broadcasts could warn us of pending nuclear attack. I imagined Russian jets winging their way to America, ready to drop their atomic bombs, as I practiced my "duck and cover" drill. But this announcement forewarns us of a series of violent thunderstorms about to strike an area south of Fresno. Accompanying lightning and heavy hail have been reported, and all are advised to take shelter. I think of hiding beneath a schoolroom desk. I stop my farmwork and run inside. I've been through this before—rain on raisins, spring showers blasting delicate peach blossoms, windstorms ripping grapevine shoots. I sit on the porch and watch.

The winds whip across the yard and fields. The individual grape leaves pop inside out like thousands of miniature umbrellas whipping wildly in the gale. Entire trees bounce up and down as gusts strike the branches heavy with ripening fruit. The wind tosses the peaches, battering them against the branches and limbs, leaving bruises and scars.

The rains begin. Damned rains. The water will quickly seep into any scratch or nick, pathogens will multiply and thrive in the lush cocktail of juices, moisture, and summer heat. Brown rot spores will drip from fruit to fruit, anchoring themselves in niches and feeding on the sugars of ripening peaches. I only hope the storm remains fast-moving and the sun comes out quickly to dry fresh wounds.

The breezes suddenly churn into gusts that hurl the falling drops in different directions. The sheets of rain whirl and twist like a swarm of birds or insects, blowing from the north, then west, swirling as the storm tries to make up its mind. shifting in some mysterious and powerful pattern. The drops grow huge and pound my porch roof. I watch them strike the ground and splash up mud on the side of the barn. With each wind change, the sheets of rain seemingly reenergize. My vines are whipped with each shift of direction; the battered leaves are shredded, the drenched foliage too weary to resist. The green BB-size grape berries are exposed and vulnerable to damage. I hear the crack of a distant peach limb and the thump as it tumbles to the earth.

Distant thunder rolls across the valley. I try and watch for the light and count the seconds to determine the distance. Then lightning strikes nearby, and though it is the middle of the afternoon, the entire sky is illuminated in a giant flash. The thunder cracks immediately and shakes the wood-framed farmhouse. My head spins from the raw power surging around me. Another flash, a pause; I'm enveloped by a moment of complete silence before the thunder pummels my ears.

Then the hail falls. It begins with an occasional pellet that bounces on the porch. Then larger and larger hailstones tumble to the ground and soon pile into small mounds. I beg for it to keep raining—hail will be much worse, slashing peaches and slicing

grape bunches. The air is thick with rain, hail, and wind. The
sky grows dark; nightfall comes in the afternoon. I sense the
power of the gods, the terror of a biblical plague, the wrath of
nature.

The storm strikes hard and intensely. I cannot tell if it's passing over me nor which direction it's heading. I do not know if
the worst is over or about to come. The air turns green with rain
and savage winds. I believe I see a funnel cloud but cannot see
anything clearly. The hail increases in tempo, beating the earth
faster and faster; the cadence increases until the sounds blur
together into an uneven beat of wave after wave of ice balls, res-
onating like *taiko* drums. A few hailstones bounce onto the porch
and roll and ricochet off my work boots. They must be over half
an inch in diameter, but I am afraid to measure them—I do not
want to know. Their edges are sharp, not smooth and round. The
wind turns and the hail is blown nearly parallel to the ground. I
imagine each stone slicing into my harvest, razor-sharp edges
slitting the delicate flesh and nicking the vulnerable peaches and
grapes, leaving behind the wounded and bleeding. This hail lasts
for only ten minutes. I fear my harvest is over.

Almost as quickly as it began, the storm passes. The hail grows
smaller, the pounding suddenly reduces to a tapping, then, following a final flurry of drops, the showers abruptly cease. Rain
continues to run off my eaves and drip from the vines and trees.
The ground is white with ice. The wind piles drifts of hail against
end posts and vine trunks. A patch of sunlight peaks through the
clouds, then the sky clears. I look to the east and watch the black-
ness continue its march toward my neighbors' fields. The horizon
is darkened from heaven to earth: the rain and hail is repeating
the same drama over and over at another and another farm.

Within an hour, all the dark clouds swagger toward the Sierras. They leave behind a trail of terror, vineyards and orchards
beaten and broken. Sunshine taunts me as I wander out to inspect
the damage. Shredded leaves blanket the ground beneath my

vines and trees. Some of the grapes are already turning brown, bruised by the hailstones. The berries on the outside edge of each bunch, the ones exposed to the elements, are slit open, their guts oozing out. I walk to my peach orchard, dodging the puddles drying in the sunlight. I examine a peach and rub my fingers over the cracked skin. Pockmarks are visible and will quickly become infected, turning gray as mold settles in.

Numbed by the speed of the storm, I have questions that I know cannot be answered. I attempt to quantify what I see and feel. The rain gauge shows that close to an inch fell in a few minutes; the hail floating in the glass tube will melt and add more. I estimate that twenty percent of every grape bunch has been damaged, verified by my visual inspection. The peaches are a different matter. Easily a third of the crop has been sliced and diced by the hail; all of the fruit on the west and north sides of the trees have been damaged. Another third will soon show their wounds, and the rot will follow. Yet I may not know the extent of damage until I climb into the treetops and start harvesting.

I roughly calculate the losses. During those twenty minutes, forty or fifty thousand of dollars in the peaches, ten or twenty thousand in the grapes was lost. No matter how hard I labor, I can never make up that income. It is gone. I ask how much longer I can keep going. Then I cry out loud, "Why should I keep going?"

I visit with Dad. As I drive in, he's sweeping hail out of his shed, trying to dry the floor. I jump out of my pickup and walk up to him. "Can you believe that storm?" I blurt.

He stops sweeping and looks up at me. "It's never hailed like this in June." His eyes scan the fields, a glare reflecting from a large puddle catches in his eyes. He blinks once, twice, and shakes his head. His eyes drop to the earth. "Never," he repeats.

This hailstorm is not a story Dad has passed down to me, not like the many rains on raisins he has seen or the late-spring frosts before I was born. For the first time in my life, a disaster becomes a story we share together. We both stop and look out to the fields.

I take a deep breath, sharing the moment with my father. A breeze sends ripples over one of the larger puddles that has collected in a low spot.

Unlike a freeze or windstorm that devastates an entire area, hail leaves behind a distinct trail. I can watch the path of a black storm and map the path of destruction. During the next few days I make phone calls or stop and talk with neighbors. Our conversations are mixed. At times I shake my head when I hear of another farmer's loss. Other times I weakly smile when a neighbor is relieved the storm missed his farm just a few miles to the south of me. I can't help but shrink into a moment of self-pity when an energized friend tells me an amazing story: the thunder seemed to part the clouds and the storm bypassed his orchard. He can't hide his relief, and I don't blame him. Quickly, though, I contact friends along the storm's track, finding comfort in shared grief.

One friend lost most of his grape crop. He's passed through depression before, surviving a bout with cancer. It still doesn't lessen his emotional reaction. He tells me about walking into his still-damp vineyard of fat table grapes that would have been harvested in a few weeks. Instead, the hail has slit berries, the bunches drip with juice, and fruit flies already hover around each one. "I threw my shovel I was so damned mad," he says. I can picture him flinging the tool in a moment of rage: the brown wooden handle sails through the air, the metal blade catches the sunlight with a brilliant glare, bouncing off a vine, gouging the wood and ripping out a piece of the trunk, then crashing against the earth. The vine will bleed water, trickling down the pale gray bark, staining it with tears.

Another friend jokes about setting up a telephone hot line. "For suicide watches," he says. "No farmer should be left alone." I realize he wants to talk a bit, and we exchange stories, slipping into a game of "who-suffered-the-worse-damage" that makes us both chuckle. He ends with a warning: "Watch out for farmers climbing up ladders near their big trees. And make sure they aren't carrying a rope with a noose." He hangs up, and I pause for a moment, holding the now silent phone. I redial immediately, and when he answers I ask, "You don't have some rope I can borrow, do you?"

I talk with the wife of another neighbor. They too were hit hard. He was out surveying the damage. She's a schoolteacher and repeats how thankful she is that she has work to help support the farm. She says their pastor was by, dropping in on the farmers in the area, assessing both the physical and spiritual damage. She ends our conversation by adding, "It's that bad."

I see my aunt at a practice for the Obon folk dance. She comes scurrying up to me and whispers, "How bad was it?" Before I can answer, she describes to me their farm and how angry she got when the hail fell. "I was so mad!" She stamps her feet. I nod in agreement. She leans toward me and says, "*Doo ni ka ni naru!*"

I do not understand her Japanese, though I have heard the phrase before, in conversations grown-ups had with each other when I was a child. "*Doo ni ka?*" I asked.

"*Doo ni ka ni naru!* That means—somehow we will get out of it!" she explains. "Ohhh, that son-of-a-bitch hailstorm!" She seems embarrassed by her swearing and quickly turns away, dashing to her next encounter.

A week after the storm, a newspaper reporter calls and wants to talk with me about the damage to my peaches. I warn him, "Farmers aren't very good talking about disasters. There will be lots of silence when we walk through the fields."

He doesn't mind, and we walk without talking before the interview. During one intense moment, I blurt out, "Most of your readers won't understand this."

He asks me to explain.

"When was the last time city people were affected by rain? A canceled picnic? A delayed tee-off time? People are insulated from nature. They will have a tough time understanding this." I walk away and say no more. He's a good reporter and stops writing notes.

Later, we walk and I have a wooden stick with me to knock off fruit that's damaged and rotting. The falling fruit sounds like hail striking the earth. "An optimistic part of me wants to see the cup half full—maybe there's just a fifty percent loss." We both know I'm lying; the damage is even more pervasive.

There are a few good peaches. With daily phone calls from buyers wanting to try my fruit, we pick a small harvest. My folks help me select and ship some of the very best fruit for an exclusive market. During our home packing operation, Mom keeps shaking her head. She hates to see wonderful fruit being tossed away just because there's a cut mark on one side. "Can't people just slice out those defects with their knives?" she asks.

I snatch the scarred fruit from her hands and cut into it. Beneath the seemingly innocuous cut, the rot is beginning to fester, the brown decay of the flesh is spreading into the pit area. I hold it open to her. She looks away and starts to sort the fruit again. I'm frustrated and mean. All of us work quietly for the next few days.

I feel bad for my workers. We try to harvest, but I calculate my losses and conclude that with such a high cull rate, it's better to leave the crop on the trees. When I explain there's no more work, they paw the ground with their feet, eyes down. Other farmers are having the same conversation, laying off hundreds of workers.

I estimate the storm cost my farm fifty thousand dollars' worth of peach sales, and twenty to thirty thousand more in grapes. Then I imagine that multiplied by a hundred other orchards in the valley. The majority of that money was to go for wages, for the farmworkers picking and packing my peaches, for the local box company that made the shipping cartons, for my broker and trucker, who won't have product. We farmers will tighten our belts and spend less this coming year for fertilizer, compost, equipment, extra help. Our farms will be shut down for months, and no money will flow through our local economy. The entire community will suffer. A trucker will quietly move to another state in search for a job; unemployed workers will sit and squat in front of their homes. Tension and emotions will flare during long, hot nights. In the future, the hurt may be nearly invisible, but the stories of a June hail will last for generations.

A month later I'm talking with some people about my writing. They ask if I've kept those wonderful-tasting peaches.

I shrug, nod yes, and say, "I'm destined to keep that peach orchard."

Then they ask, "But then isn't the title of your book, *Epitaph for a Peach*, not quite correct?"

I take a deep breath and say, "Let me tell you about a hailstorm in June. . . ."

Following the disaster, a joke starts circulating in the community, farm to farm, farmer to farmer. Like good humor, it makes all of us smile, even just a little, as we grapple with the grief from the hail.

"They did an autopsy on an old farmer, and when they opened him up, they found he was full of 'next years.' "

I now feel like an old farmer.

Wild Flowers

After an hour of shoveling, my pile of severed johnsongrass stalks and roots has grown into a small mound. I remember Baachan calling this weed *abunai kusa*, dangerous grass, because it's a voracious grower, densely and tightly rooted. It can murder a farmer. I straighten my back and wipe the sweat from my eyes. They burn from the salt and I squeeze them shut, forcing tears to dilute the sting.

I look up and watch a car drive down my roadway, followed by a cloud of dust. Woody, my neighbor's father, waves his hand through an open window and slowly pulls himself out of the car. We shake hands and talk about johnsongrass. He's an old farmer, has more history with weeds than I will ever hope to have, and his body is failing him. Then he leans against the door and reaches inside for his cane and a small bag. With a grin he opens the bag and nods his head, beckoning me to look inside.

Inside the crumpled brown paper sack, light filters through the creases and illuminates a collection of very tiny black round seeds scattered on the bottom with yellowed stalks and specks of withering leaves. A thin layer of dry tan dirt collects in the corners. "Poppies," he informs me. "Goool-den poppies."

I nod. I know these seeds. Every fall I plant thousands of wild-flower seeds—"to make the farm look prettier," as Marcy says. I started growing wildflowers the year I began farming organically. They seem to fit my approach to the land, working with nature, appreciating the life she grants us, giving up on my feeble attempts to control the natural chaos in these fields. Besides, Marcy loves seeing something green throughout the winter and the blooming colors of early spring. I need to make her happy. Her stable income helps the farm, allowing me the luxury of taking risks.

Wildflowers seem fragile, spindly, and delicate, and yet they fool you. The hardy plants will grow with little care; they're tough enough to find niches in which to germinate and reseed. No year is ever the same—they bloom and flourish differently with each season.

Woody hands me the bag and whispers, "They're wild. From my place."

I recall a conversation I had with another neighbor. He could not believe I planted wildflowers. "I mean, how can you plant wildflowers?" he asked, leaning out of his pickup window. "Wildflowers must be wild, right?"

Before I could answer, he drove off down our shared drive-way. I've thought about that many times and concluded that ever since the first farmer planted a seed and nurtured a harvest, we've manipulated nature. Yet as long as we work with nature and do not try to control her, we still have something "wild" in our lives. Yes, I can plant wildflowers.

Autumn chill arrives and I misplace Woody's seeds. I plant a mix of cover crops, red, strawberry, and crimson clovers along with common vetch and a blend of medics. I toss in handfuls of my wildflower seeds and anticipate clusters of baby blue-eyes, five-spots, and mountain garlands with their bright colors. Months from now, I hope to discover early-blooming Cape daisies, their showy orange petals contrasting with the late-winter gray horizon, anticipating the arrival of spring.

During a Thanksgiving rainstorm, I find Woody's brown paper bag still filled with his seeds. To honor the old farmer, I trudge out in the drizzle and hand-sow the seeds, scattering them at end posts by the roadside. If they grow, I hope Woody will see them as he drives in to visit.

In the early spring, Woody's poppies are the first to germinate. They push up lush, dark green stalks and grow in thick clumps. Only a few bloom. Later, when I spy Woody's car sitting in his driveway, I think to myself, "I can show him the poppies some other time, perhaps in a good, flashy year for wildflowers." Because I don't disk the earth around the end posts, a few of the plants keep growing throughout the spring and most of the summer before withering. The few flowers are large, with big seedpods that cure in the hundred-degree heat. I reach to pick a few and they pop open, reaffirming their name as they scatter a new generation of seeds.

Another year passes, and the next spring stronger plants grow and their bright hues attract my eyes toward their color. With the slightest breeze they sway back and forth. The greens of my vineyards become background hues and tones for the dance of the poppies. These flowers have deep roots and live for months, tapping into the moisture when I irrigate my vineyards, strengthening their claim to my farm. Throughout the summer they continue blooming, producing another season of flowers and seeds, protected by the shade of my grapevines.

But I no longer see Woody. A series of physical setbacks prevents him from driving. He stops dropping by. Later I find out he is confined to a wheelchair; on good days he may get outside to feel the sun on his face. His eyesight is also failing. I doubt if he will ever come out to visit me again.

Yet his poppies keep flowering. They haven't spread much beyond the original area, but seem intent on establishing a foothold for themselves instead of trying to dominate my fields like a weed. Some years their colors are brilliant; other years the petals are small and as the seasons change, you have to search for them quietly tucked beneath a vine canopy.

"Goool-den poppies."

Baachan rarely planted flowers in her garden. I recall her productive patch of cucumbers and tomatoes along with healthy plots of *napa*/Japanese cabbage, *nasubi*/Japanese eggplant, and *daikon*/horseradish. She grew food for our dinner table, saving money as we gorged ourselves on her summer harvests. Other Japanese families raised lots of flowers—gladiolas, snapdragons, chrysanthemums, and sweet peas. We sometimes found a bundle of flowers wrapped in newspaper sitting by our back door, a gift from a neighbor. We'd return the favor later in the year with our peaches or grapes. Jiichan and Baachan let the experts grow flowers while they concentrated on what they did best—hard and long work in the orchards and vineyards. But the resilience of wildflowers reminds me of them.

Mom does remember Baachan growing a few irises, which were usually gone by the first summer heat. Mom explains that many of the Issei widows meticulously cared for beds of early-season flowers dedicated for a late-May picking. Bouquets were harvested for Memorial Day visits to the cemetery and the graves of Issei husbands.

Fertilizing

Every spring the orchards must be fertilized. The prior year's harvest has exhausted the soil; my peaches have taken much from the earth, and I must return the favor. Roots are awakening from winter sleep, hungry and temperamental. I've learned that with inadequate nutrients at this time of the year, the rousing trees can quickly turn grumpy and it may take weeks for them to catch up in growth. Peaches do not grow well when grouchy.

In the past, we used synthetic fertilizers. They were easy to apply, tested formulations of "triple 15" or "calcium nitrate" that guaranteed rapid tree vigor. They worked sometimes too well, and our vines and trees responded with rank growth, heavy foliage, and irregular fruit sets. Insect pests seemed to enjoy the flavor of these overfed plants; the new shoots flourished with tasty and delicate leaves and buds. Yet these peaches seemed to lack taste. They were fuzzy balls of pulp and water with only a hint of peach flavor.

Now we've switched to an organic program, augmenting my composting and cover-cropping with a spoon-fed dose of natural fertilizer made from bonemeal and feathers. The dry granules slowly dissolve to be absorbed by roots. The nutrients combine with the dense organic matter in my soil and the magic of nature is allowed to work—the combination of many individual parts creates something new, a synergy pulsates through my fields. The trees respond with strong crops of leaves, branches, and peaches. A sustained, gentle pace replaces the race to harvest. I have fewer insect pest problems and the fruit seems to have a fuller flavor, as if it wasn't in a rush to get fat and round. I get rich slowly.

My efforts carry meaning beyond the immediate. It will take months, even years, to see results. A healthy farm is built only by gradual accrual. Fertilizing is like planting seeds—it's done for the future.

Most farms use large machines to spread fertilizer. For my older trees with their outstretched root systems, I utilize a rusting "EZEE Flow" broadcaster that rattles down each row, wheel-driven gears and chains pushing the fertilizer pellets out of a row of slots. This method is not precise but is good enough, although the control lever is broken and I must hold it upward during turns. At the end of each row I twist backward, contort my torso, and, with one hand, thrust up the control bar that interrupts the fertilizer stream. Then with the other hand I pull the steering wheel, maneuver the tractor around a tree, and coax it into the next row. As I drop my exhausted arm the metal plates shift and the fertilizer once again drains from the EZEE Flow to hungry trees.

But the old contraption wastes the expensive fertilizer in young orchards a year or two old and only a few feet high. These root systems have yet to mature and spread and instead remain huddled around trunks. Instead of the peach trees, my weeds have a grand spring picnic with the fertilizer. So I revert to an old system of spreading by hand and using family labor. I cannot do this work alone unless I carry a bucket to each tree. That would take hours—my muscles would quickly ache and my shoulders grow weary. But a family working together reduces the total hours needed.

Ten-year-old Nikiko drives the tractor. Her feet can barely reach the pedals, yet she feels confident enough to start the motor and agrees to try to drive straight down each row. Standing and jumping down on the clutch with both feet, she shifts into gear, then engages the engine with a very slow and cautious release of the clutch. On her first efforts, she releases too quickly, sending us flying over the bags of fertilizer on the wagon behind the tractor.

I yelled, "Niii-kii!" and she responds with "Sor-ry!" From then on, whenever we stop, it takes seemingly forever to get going again. Niki painstakingly raises the clutch inch by inch, vowing never to jerk the tractor and wagon again.

Marcy and I sit on either side of an old vineyard wagon, a flatbed trailer four and a half feet wide, built to be pulled between the rows of grapes. The ingenuity of the design lies in the turntable axles that pivot with each other. While making a turn, the front set of wheels rotates on a turntable and follow in the tractor tire tracks, while the back set does the same. We make tight turns without risk of hooking a vine or tree with the back end of the trailer. Niki can focus forward and not worry about having to look behind her.

I grew up working on these wagons, playing and jumping on and off them, sleeping beneath them in the shade. We used them to pick up raisin rolls from the vineyards and take them into the barnyard to box them. Other times we mounted side boards and Dad and I hauled load after load of hardpan from the uneven "Hill" block and tossed the stones onto the ditch bank. In the winter, I've carried piles of dead vine stumps and peach tree limbs to a burn pile. We still use the wagons for odd jobs, carrying new metal grape stakes or fertilizer for young peach trees.

Some of the wooden planks in the wagon bed are badly abraded and split. In the large gaps I can see the ground pass beneath. A few of the boards came from our old barn, the faded red paint barely visible, still adhering deep within the weathered grain. Of our four wagons only two are working. Atop one of the abandoned wagons in the barnyard corner now sits a collection of brown metal pipes and bars along with random pieces of steel that Dad uses for welding and repair jobs. Like a portable junk pile, he'll move it around whenever he decides to "clean up" his work area.

We sit on the bed, and tiny slivers hook our pants and easily break off. As we lean to one side, a dozen tiny pins jab our rears. Marcy shifts and grabs an empty bag of fertilizer to sit on. Two galvanized troughs sit along each side of the wagon. I've dumped a hundred pounds of fertilizer into each. We'll scoop from these containers and toss the granules at the base of each small tree.

We don't wear gloves. We clutch small containers about the size of a two-pound coffee can. These cans have always been part of our farm. They stored bolts and nuts, held mysterious powders and concoctions, and served as dispensers and scoops. I remember dipping old coffee cans in fertilizer, measuring the dosage, and tossing it next to a young tree. In rougher financial years, in order to dole out reduced rations, we'd use smaller tuna fish cans. A farm's economic health could be judged during fertilizing season by the size of the cans used.

Korio sits on an open bag and sifts his hands through the fine material. He insists on helping us, and we give him a small can. Immediately he scoops some of the fertilizer and randomly tosses it into the air. We try to teach him the correct method and end up confusing him with our different techniques. I like to create patterns on the ground with my applications, trying to flick my wrist and make a crescent shape hugging each tree. Marcy seems to use two rhythmic shakes of the can so that the pellets fly out and land in a zigzag shape above root zones. We have a contest to develop the perfect pattern and the precise technique. Kori maintains his random, uncontrollable rhythm and has great fun.

Our wagon begins to smell like a moving chicken ranch. The odor envelops us, a dry, sharp smell unlike cow manure. "Chicken parts," Marcy concludes, reading from the bag ingredients.

I offer my opinion. "The trees will like it. Maybe they'll say, 'Mmmm . . . tastes like chicken.'"

Marcy tosses a can of fertilizer at me. I lift my arms to protect myself but some of the pellets land inside my shirt collar. As I brush them away, a few slip under my T-shirt and I can feel them against my skin. I stand to shake them out. Marcy and Korio laugh; Nikiko glances back from her tractor perch and wonders if she's supposed to stop. While I'm preoccupied, a few trees slip by, and I stubbornly refuse to ask for help. I frantically try to hurl my fertilizer allotment twenty feet behind me in order to catch the ones I missed. They sprinkle to the earth in a random pattern.

"Ah! That's not a crescent shape!" Marcy scolds.

After we complete a few more passes, Marcy and I establish a cadence in our work, and a rhythm settles into our conversations. Away from the interruptions of phone calls and distractions like the television, we can enjoy each other's company, surrounded by family. I've felt this before, while hiking in the Sierras or playing on the beach, when our family is engaged with its environment, allowing the landscape to affect our emotions.

We also play games—competing over the best fertilizer toss, teasing Niki about her cautious clutching and restarting, using Kori as a human paperweight for the growing stack of empty bags and watching him delight in the noise of crumpling paper beneath him. Niki asks for a short break and I take over driving. Marcy and Niki complete one row while I tease them by accelerating and watching them frantically scooping and flinging faster and faster. Neither will give in and yell for me to slow down; both women are too proud. Then I drive farther and farther from Marcy's side of the trees and she has to toss the granules farther and farther. I howl and she accepts my challenge.

Overhead the pale blue sky of spring stretches from horizon to horizon. A large pile of clouds collects against the Sierras, and I can see another frontal system appearing in the western sky. We're in between the storms, basking in the bright sunshine. As we work, we peel off layers of clothes. Gradually, the pile grows and marks our time in the fields. Back and forth we travel down each row. Instead of journeying in a single direction, every few minutes we turn to fully enjoy a panoramic view of the sky above us. The bank of clouds streams from west to east; one minute we're covered by a shadow that sends a cooling chill down our sweat-dampened shirts, the next minute sunshine warms our backs.

By late afternoon, the work becomes tedious. My thoughts wander. "Isn't there something else better I can be doing? Spreading chicken parts isn't my goal in life. . . ." The trees pass slower and the dirt, dust, and odor begin to bother us. Marcy's throwing arm tires; she changes her technique and uses the other arm. Kori begins to grow bored and restless. I wonder what other place Niki is visiting in her mind.

For the first few hours, at the end of each row, Niki stops the tractor and I jump off the wagon to help her complete the turn down into the next row. Later she tries to pull the steering wheel herself as I ride next to her, passing instructions and lending a hand when her young muscles strain against the manual column. Eventually she asks me not to ride up on the tractor with her, and Marcy and I watch as she downshifts and gamely pulls at the wheel, guiding the machine at the slowest possible speed, making a turn that requires an excruciatingly long time to negotiate. Marcy tells me to have patience. Niki is proud of her effort and will later want to announce her accomplishment to her grandmother and grandfather.

Kori, though, becomes bored and anxious to move on to something else. As we near my folks' house, he asks to be let off. He sees them in the yard and squirms, begging to get out of the fields. I yell to Niki, "Whoooa," and as the wagon rolls to a stop, Kori jumps and plods through the soft earth toward them. I yell to him to be careful. He runs and is proud to go by himself. We continue down our row, losing sight of him behind trees, but catch glimpses of him greeting my folks and pointing to us, explaining where we are. Mom looks up and waves, points to herself and then at Dad, who's shoveling weeds nearby, signaling that they'll help watch Kori.

As we turn for our final pass down a row, Niki accelerates, hoping we won't notice. She's hot and anxious to go home. Marcy and I are quiet now. We know this is the last row, and we've talked enough to be lost in thought.

Kori is playing with Dad. They both have shovels, Kori precariously trying to work the oversized tool, clutching it with his tiny hands. He struggles for balance, and the metal drags while the long wooden handle swings freely in the air. Dad weeds around a vine end post as Kori tosses small heaps of dry earth into the air and watches them crash down like dirt bombs.

As we drive closer, we can see that a trail of dust accompanies Kori as he wanders around Dad. The fine particles hug the earth like a low cloud. One minute my son stands in front of Dad, the next he disappears, hidden in my father's shadow. As we move, I see Dad's silhouette. He's hunched over, his shovel slicing the earth over and over. I imagine his back must be bent over in pain, the years of farmwork aging his joints, his body broken from the thousands of weeds he has cleared from the land. But he crouches with knees bent and dances with the shovel, a graceful movement of arms, shoulders, and legs. Man and tool labor in unison, meticulous motions, a subtle sway of the torso, a cadence that hesitates when encountering a deep root. Then with a forceful lift from his legs and back the old farmer flicks his wrists and flings a severed plant through the air to land gently in a growing pile of weeds. The rhythm is slow and embodies a patience learned from decades of work.

We pass them and Kori returns into view, pretending to clear the land one shovelful at a time. Dad tosses a clump of johnsongrass next to Kori, who smiles and pounces on it. He too scoops up the withering green mass of roots and stalks and tries to toss it to the side like his grandfather. They're both playing.

I don't recall a lesson about shoveling weeds from Dad. I can only remember working with him in silence, first as a young boy trying to please him, then as a teenager who sought only to complete a chore and escape from the fields. We rarely discussed farming. I received no lectures about the work ethic and Japanese traditions or the importance of keeping the land clear. When I returned to the farm as an adult with innovative ideas about organic farming, I discovered the weeds still growing and joined with Dad in shoveling them. The sound of our steel blades striking the earth was then punctuated with new conversation. I thought out loud about our work. I talked about the decisions I had to make. I learned about farming from his stories.

"Weeds will always be here," I announced. "I will forever have work." Looking up to Dad, I add, "And so will you."

Dad listened. He became my best listener.

From the wagon, I turn back and see Dad leaning on his shovel, watching Kori. He seems to grin as the child mimics his grandfather. Dad points, says something, and the boy responds by flinging a big weed with lots of dirt into the wind. They both cheer as a cloud of dust dances in the breeze and coats their skin with a fine, delicate layer. My son wants to repeat the effort and scoops another shovelful of the earth, then catapults it upward. For a moment it hangs in the air, suspended in time. Marcy, Niki, and I continue down the row, and between scoops of fertilizer for our young peach trees, I watch the grandson and the *jiichan* playing.

Planting A Vineyard

When I visit with my folks for morning coffee, news from the daily obituaries works its way into our conversations. I listen to them talk about the death of a Japanese-American neighbor—who's related to whom, stories about failing health and the last time they saw him or her well. Then they debate about whether or not to go to the funeral and how much money they should *koden*/contribute as a funeral offering. In complex situations of protocol, I'll watch them pull a list of guests and donations from a relative's funeral. The chart will help them weave their way through the intricate maze of Japanese obligations and traditions. But the obituaries leave out information about the circumstances surrounding a death. It then occurs to me that I never knew how Jiichan Masumoto died.

"It happened about springtime—in March?" Dad wonders aloud. "Just about now." Dad remembers the season because he and his brother, Uncle Alan, were planting cuttings for a new vineyard. Five acres of gnarled old Muscat vines—the ones we annually sold to an Italian winery—were declining in production. So Dad decided to replace them with Thompson grapes for future raisin harvests.

Vine cuttings saved us money. Poor farmers who couldn't afford to buy nursery grafts or rootings grew their own young vines a year in advance. Two winters before, Dad had taken some of his healthiest vine canes and cut them into segments about a foot long. He then planted them near the house so they'd get water and care. He needed about 2,500 vines, so in addition to his other work, he operated this miniature nursery with rows and rows of cuttings. A year later they'd have roots and could be trans-planted—a new vineyard regenerated from the old.

Dad explained the planting process. The old Muscats were pulled, stacked, and burned months earlier. Dad worked the block with a spring tooth cultivator, combing the ground, gath-ering and disposing of the old roots. At every row, he stretched a wire that had little pieces of white adhesive tape every seven feet. Next to each mark he jammed a stick into the soft earth. Then he and Uncle Alan lugged buckets of vine cuttings to the open land, and they dug a hole at each stick with a narrow shovel, inserted a new vine, filled in the soil, and packed the earth with their boots. Later in the day, they'd irrigate and give the new plantings a drink of water.

Jiichan was eighty years old. He wanted to work hard but had slowed down. He could only perform a few simple jobs such as watching the kids and trimming the vine cuttings. He sat in the shade of a yard tree, a series of wide metal tubs surrounding him. One was filled with cuttings just dug from Dad's nursery, with dirt still clinging to the plants. Jiichan filled another tub with water and rinsed each young vine. Then he carefully clipped the roots, snipping off the small, delicate hairs, saving a strong tap-root. Rootbound vines would not grow well in the new land; he wanted to stimulate growth and encourage the new, deep roots. Jiichan also hoped to make the cuttings compact enough for his sons to slip them into their holes easily without breaking a main artery. Finally he soaked them in a tub with water until Dad and Uncle Alan returned for more vines.

In the spring morning air, Jiichan washed, snipped, clipped, and soaked. He'd only trim what they needed for that day, keeping the cuttings moist and ready for planting. By the end of the afternoon he was surrounded by a mound of sheared root fibers engulfing his legs and piled against the wooden raisin sweat box he used as a bench. I wonder what he thought as he worked— "Another new vineyard, one of many in life as a farmworker"?

This vineyard was different, though. By 1953, memories of the war must have been fading with each passing year. Dad had bought his own place, full of hardpan, with old Ribier and Muscat grapes. Each year our family would try to make improvements, sweat equity planted in the soil, building up the land one acre at a time. We had bought the land cheap. If we added labor and planted hope, with luck, in a few years when the new vines grew fat bunches, the land would pay for itself.

Dad and Uncle Alan worked in an odd block of vines—half weak Muscats ready to be pulled out, the other half Thompson grapes established in rows eleven feet apart, an old spacing used when equipment was pulled by horses and mules. (Most vineyard rows are now twelve feet apart to accommodate tractors and larger equipment.) But the original Thompsons in the field were strong and healthy, and Dad didn't want to uproot what was already working. When he bought the ranch, those eleven-foot vines were decades old, just reaching their prime production years. They were planted the year Baachan had immigrated to America, 1918.

While Jiichan snipped and Dad and Uncle Alan planted, Mom was out tying vines, lashing the canes to the wire trellis. She enjoyed her work but missed socializing with friends. Children helped fill the void. Maintaining a household with a mother- and father-in-law kept her busy. Baachan was at home with Jiichan and their grandkids. I was not yet born. My sister was only a year old but already a toddler, walking and scraping her knees on the wooden floor of the farmhouse. My brother, Rodney, was three and Grandpa's pal. He spoke Japanese with Jiichan, and they spent hours together.

Rod sat with Jiichan, playing with the pile of trimmed roots. No one knows exactly what happened. They say Jiichan slumped over and slowly rolled onto the earth. He lay next to the new vine rootings, probably suffering from a stroke. Rod bolted into the house, yelling, "*Taoreta! Jiichan taoreta!*"—Grandpa fell down! He added, "*Jiichan mizu!*"—needs water! Baachan darted outside, then ran out into the fields to fetch her sons.

The two brothers looked up from their work. Baachan had a shrill voice that carried in the still air of the farm. A piercing shriek, a voice of terror and fear, the wail of death. She shouted in short bursts, crying for them to come home. Jiichan needed them. The sons dropped their shovels and unconsciously jammed the unplanted cuttings back into the bucket with water. They raced home.

Rod had pushed a chair up against the kitchen sink. The wooden legs bumped against the counter as he pulled himself up to the top. Grabbing a glass, he turned the faucet handle and filled the cup with water. Then he carefully climbed back down, trying not to spill the contents but rushing as fast as he could. I don't know if Jiichan was awake; I don't know if he was able to respond. Rod tried to help his fallen grandfather with one of the few things he could offer. The three-year-old grandson tried to give his dying grandfather a drink of water.

Dad called the family doctor, and "Doc Binkley" came within an hour. The same country doctor that had delivered all of the grandkids would have bad news. When they took him to the hospital, Jiichan was still breathing, but the odds were slim that he'd recover from the stroke. He passed away before the end of the day.

Dad says at least Jiichan died on his own place.

After Jiichan's death, Rod stopped speaking Japanese. Today he doesn't recall ever knowing a foreign language.

I remember taking Baachan to the cemetery to lay flowers on Jiichan's grave. An open area lies next to him—Baachan knows where she will be buried. Down the row of headstones is Uncle George's grave, and Mom and Dad have purchased a plot too. This is where the Masumoto family belongs, a final claim to a place.

I still farm those eleven-foot vines. Following Jiichan's funeral, Dad finished the planting. Now the healthy, lush vines are rooted deeply in the ground and produce heavy crops of juicy grapes under a harvest sun. Every year, as I work that vineyard, a grandson has stories to remember.

A C K N O W L E D G M E N T S

I HAVE BEEN FORTUNATE TO HARVEST A WEALTH OF STORIES — GROWN by my family, especially my parents, and nurtured by my wife, Marcy, and children, Nikiko and Korio. Without them, the warmth and strength of a family farm would be lost.

Many thanks to Elizabeth Wales and Alane Mason for their support and for believing in a voice from someone who works the land and calls a farm home.

I especially hope to honor my grandparents and the spirit of immigrants who understood the meaning of family and community, the rewards of work and home, and the value of culture and traditions. I dedicate my stories to their passion and the legacy of generations.